CANON PYON

Canon Pyon

A Herefordshire manor and parish in the 17th century

Sonja Smith

Copyright © Sonja Smith 2022

The right of Sonja Smith to be identified as the author of this work has been asserted by her in accordance with the Copyright, Designs and Patents Act 1988.

First published in 2022 by Custodian Books
Greenacre, Canon Pyon, Hereford, HR4 8PE
www.custodianbooks.co.uk

The publisher has no responsibility for the continuation or accuracy of URLs for websites referred to in this book and does not guarantee that content on such websites remains accurate.

British Library Cataloguing-in-Publication Data
A catalogue record for this book is available from the British Library

ISBN 978 1 3999 2094 0

Typeset in Garamond, 11.5 on 15

Printed by Lightning Source

Cover illustrations:

Front: manor house from Isaac Taylor's map of *c.* 1755, believed to be The Court (HARC BN81.) Image digitally restored by Phil Smith.
Back: (left to right) border from Inspeximus of Award 1624 (HCA 4257), wall of the pound November 2019 (photograph by S Smith), cartouche for Anthony Sawyer and a drawing of the church (both from Isaac Taylor's map, *c.* 1755 HARC BN81).

Dedicated to

Rosemarie Leetham
1936-2020

Your perseverance was my inspiration

Contents

Acknowledgements	viii
Abbreviations	ix
Canon Pyon map	x
Introduction	1
1 'Corn for the Canons': the manor of Canon Pyon	4
2 Lost townships and changing names	34
3 Canon Pyon church and the 'rectory impropriated'	58
4 The clergy of Canon Pyon 1600-1707	79
5 'Our watch and ward have been duly kept': maintaining law and order	118
6 'Labourer, husbandman, yeoman, gent': more inhabitants of Canon Pyon	148
Afterword	178
Appendix 1: The customs of the manor of Canon Pyon	181
Appendix 2: The tenures of Edward Broughton and George Vaughan	183
Appendix 3: Canon Pyon churchwardens 1662 – 1699	188
Select chronology	190
Select bibliography	194
Index	198

Acknowledgements

My thanks to all the staff at Hereford Cathedral Archives (HCA) and at Hereford Archives and Record Centre (HARC) for their patience and legwork in retrieving documents for me (and also for their encouragement). I am indebted to Dr. Wendy Brogden and Dr. Bethany Hamblen for their expert opinion and suggestions on some of my work; any errors or misjudgements in the content of this book are mine alone. Also, thanks to David Lovelace for his introduction to the contents of the Cathedral archives and hints and tips on camera usage which enabled study of documents at length in my own time; any shortcomings in the quality of photographs in the book are my own. Particular thanks go to John Chandler for a great British Association for Local History 'Zoom' meeting on self-publishing, a process that I had not anticipated following but was pleased that I did (in the end!). Last but not least, I gratefully acknowledge the patience of my family who have put up with my obsession and tales of Canon Pyon history.

Abbreviations

HARC	Herefordshire Archive and Record Centre
HCA	Hereford Cathedral Archives
HPL	Hereford Public Library
PCC	Prerogative Court of Canterbury
TNA	The National Archives

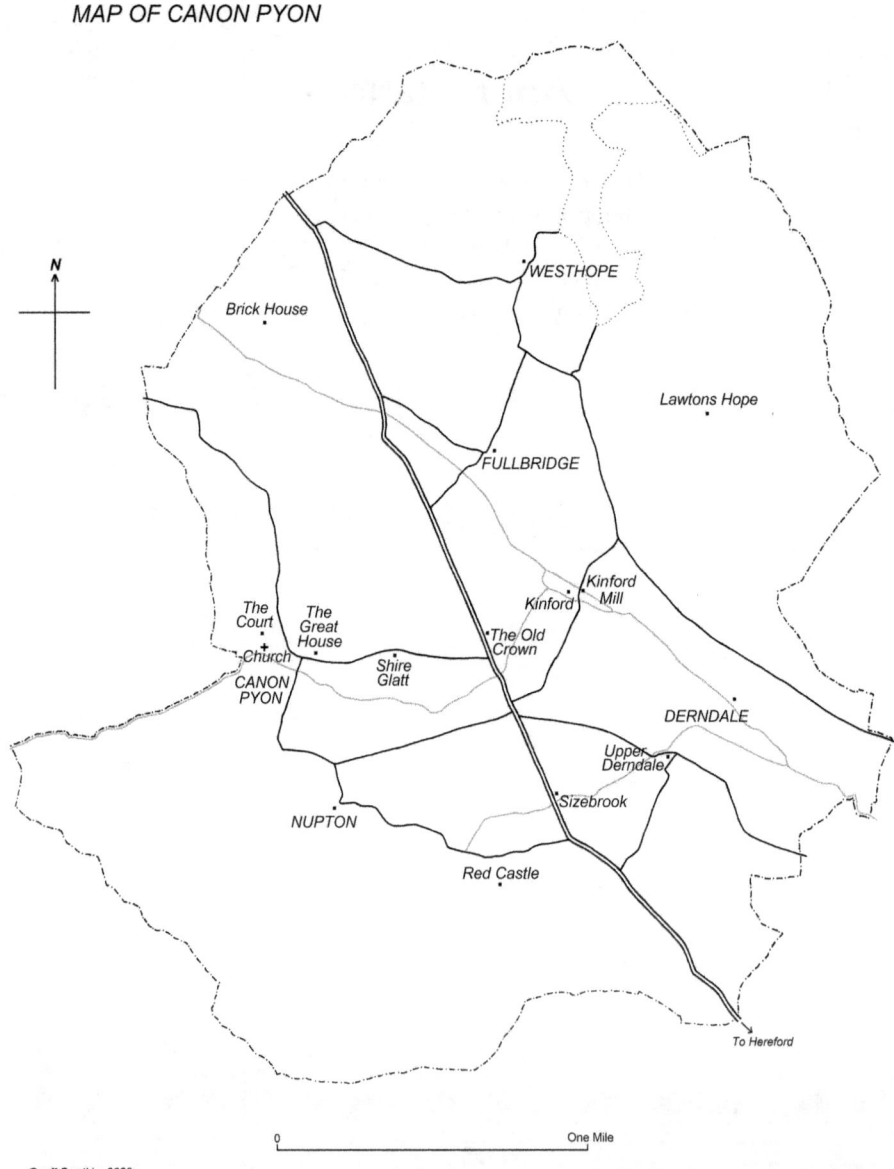

Introduction

One might ask, 'Why choose the 17th century'? A number of reasons make this a fascinating period to study. The earlier Tudor religious reformation was certainly not a clear cut switch from one set of ideals to another. Protestantism evolved painfully throughout the following century amid Catholic persistence, the blossoming of puritan zeal and the emergence of new groups such as the Quakers, Independents and Baptists. It was a time in British history when a parliament was able to wage war against (and ultimately execute) a king, changing the relationship between the British monarchy, parliament and the people forever. But for all these momentous events, ordinary people continued with their lives as best as they could. This book is essentially about the lives of some of these people in Canon Pyon, mainly in the 17th century but sometimes in the years either side for reasons of clarity and closure. As well as the parishioners themselves, the book considers the built environment, landscape and regulations which impacted their lives on a daily basis.

There are limitations with respect to some important records. Although the church in Canon Pyon is ancient, the early parish registers are missing, surviving only from 1704. A run of bishop's transcripts from 1664 survives (albeit with gaps) and many of these are signed by the vicar and churchwardens. The loss of the earlier registers is keenly felt when attempting to reconstruct the families of the parish, many of whom had lived in the parish for a number of generations. By using manorial records, wills and deeds it has been possible to piece together numerous family groups of two or three generations but frustratingly difficult to link the groups together into larger family trees.

As well as missing parish registers, there are no accounts of the churchwardens or overseers of the poor from the 17th century which would have given information about expenditure on the church and the parish needy at this time. There are some existing churchwardens' presentments which were the means by which bishops and archdeacons monitored and 'corrected' the behaviour of parishioners and clergy as well as managing the state of the fabric and 'ornaments' of the church. All these are dated post-1660 and some are in a poor condition but ecclesiastical court books have provided some pre-Civil War material to work with. As well as the manorial records, wills and deeds, material has been used from court papers (locally and nationally), records of the Dean and Chapter of Hereford Cathedral and a host of secondary sources. As is usually the case, those who led a more controversial life usually left the most documentary evidence to discover.

Two maps have been most useful; the 1840 tithe map (and Geoff Gwatkin's research map based on the same, being invaluable for home use) and a map of Anthony Sawyer's estate, made by Isaac Taylor *c.* 1755. Although closer to the time period researched for this work, the latter only covers the parts of Canon Pyon in which Sawyer held land so there are areas which have little or no information - parts of Westhope and Derndale in particular. Nevertheless, there would be far less to say about the parish without the detail given on the rest of the map.

This work is descriptive rather than analytical in nature, partly due to the lack of certain records but also because of the relatively small region of study. Very brief accounts of the national political and religious situation are included where appropriate, particularly within the biographies of the incumbents whose lives were often deeply affected by these events. I would encourage the reader to seek out scholarly works on the many political and religious upheavals of the 1600s for a broader understanding of the time than I have conveyed.

The manor had a huge influence on parish life and in the case of Canon Pyon, the manor and the parish were synonymous. The first chapter considers the manor boundaries, customs and the people who held the lease of the manor, along with a discussion of the open fields which still existed. This is followed in Chapter 2 by a look at the 'townships' and places which existed in the parish in the 17th century but have since disappeared as well as some which have changed their names.

In Chapter 3, we look at the parish church in terms of its links between the Dean and Chapter, the lessee of the manor, the vicar and the parishioners; relationships which did not always prove agreeable. We also look at the evidence for Quakers and Roman Catholics in the parish, the former belonging to a relatively new way of thinking and the latter of ancient tradition but both suffering persecution of varying degrees in this period.

Chapter 4 considers the lives of the six incumbents who had the cure of souls of the parishioners between *c.* 1600 and 1707 and in many ways this was the most satisfying but surprising research. Apart from the years of the Civil War and Interregnum, for

Introduction

which there are uncertainties due to lack of documentary evidence, the parish seems to have been spritually well covered with no long absenteeism of incumbents.

Life in the manor was regulated by the manorial court and this is the subject of Chapter 5 which also includes examples of Canon Pyon residents in cases with the church, civil and equity courts. What it meant to be a churchwarden or parish constable at that time is also discussed. In the last chapter, the social hierarchy of the parishioners is considered along with some of their occupations, the evidence existing for poor relief and finally, an example of a long-standing surname in the parish and how it may have evolved.

Most of the primary sources used for this work have been accessed locally at the Hereford Cathedral Library Archives and Herefordshire Archive and Record Centre, in addition to some from the National Archives. Occasional use has also been made of online sources, many of which were discovered and explored whilst writing up research during the pandemic lockdowns of 2020, and these are included in the Bibliography. Whilst the enforced confinement offered motivation to begin work on writing, the lack of access to archives to 'fill in the gaps' was frustrating and certainly increased my appreciation of our nation's archival heritage.

The original spelling and phrase structure from the documents have been maintained in the quotations throughout the book; I feel they help convey the nature of the language and thought processes of the time. Square brackets in the quotations indicate where abbreviated words have been extended or implied words have been added, for readability's sake.

I once read somewhere that researching history only serves to educate the researcher unless the results are shared with others (or words to that effect) so this work is my attempt to share some of Canon Pyon's past with anyone who is interested.

Sonja Smith
Canon Pyon, March 2022

1

'Corn for the Canons': the manor of Canon Pyon

Canon Pyon manor is believed to have been gifted to the Cathedral Church of Hereford by Wulviva, sister to Godiva, long before the Norman Conquest.[1] In the 13th century, it was impropriated by Bishop Aquablanca (Peter of Aigueblanche) to the Dean & Chapter to use the profits for maintaining the canons resident at the cathedral.[2] Remarkably, the manor remained in church hands for at least 1000 years, excepting only the time of the Interregnum years of 1649-1660 when the Dean and Chapter was abolished and administration was carried out by Parliamentarians. Apart from that relatively short period, the manor paid rent in wheat and oats for the Canons Residentiary of the Cathedral Church of Hereford.[3]

The clearest descriptions of the boundaries, customs, copyholders and other aspects of the manor in the 17th century can be found in a 1649 survey taken a few months after the execution of Charles I and after the establishment of republican rule.[4] Surveys of lands and prebendal properties of the Cathedral were undertaken to assess their value in order to either sell them or raise funds for the 'deserving parochial clergy and school teachers'.[5] Whilst bearing in mind the reason for their compilation, and that the surveyors indicate that the rental value of the lands was far greater than the actual rents, they nevertheless provide a valuable insight into the manor in the mid-17th century.

The surveyors of Canon Pyon manor - Miles Hill, Richard Nicholetts, Francis Eedes and James Cook - viewed and perambulated the manor and questioned a jury of sworn tenants, the names of whom appear regularly as manorial court jurors and were of yeoman or gentleman status. These jurors were John Monno (possibly Munne) esquire, gentleman, Oliver Gardner, Edward Monnington, Richard Gayley, Walter Nash, Thomas Jay, George Bayneham, junior, Richard Bayneham, Thomas Stephens, Edward Yeomans, Philip Ceelye and George Scarlett.[6] They were all from families with a long history in the parish and were most likely well-respected.

THE BOUNDARY OF THE MANOR

Taken from the survey, the following extract describes the manor's boundaries and for those who know the parish, it is clear that the manor boundary was very close to today's parish boundary:

> The said mannor beginning in the roadway to Hereford at a place called the Parke at a gutter near the further end of cawsey and soe goeth south wards a long coppice called Badnedge in Burghfields p[ar]ish until it cometh to a place called Wormesley Grange in the p[ar]ish of Wormesley and continueth then Westwards against Kings Pyon parish until it cometh to a place called the upper end of the Strowde and then including the Strowde goeth northwards and including Little Pyon continueth against the p[ar]ish of Kings Pyon until it cometh to a gate in the highway leading from Hereford to Stretfords bridge and soe against the p[ar]ish of Bearly northwards untill it cometh to a tree on the top of West hopes Hill called oakes and from thence eastwards against the parish of hope under Dinmer until it cometh by Dinmer ground onto a place called Coleys Yate and thence southwards against the parish of Wellington to a Great Moore in the Thatchie Land in Derndall field and soe southwards to a gate called Adsers Gate and from then to a place called the Parkes and soe to Hereford highway to the place called the Parkes at the same gutter in the cawsey where it began being in compasse about 5 miles.

THE CUSTOMS OF THE MANOR

The same survey describes the customs in some detail. English manors varied widely in their customs so this is helpful to our understanding of those that governed the tenants at Canon Pyon.

Many of the customs deal with the regulation of tenancies. Tenants were given a copy of the court roll (hence the term 'copyhold') and had 'estate of inheritance'. This meant that the tenant could not be evicted and the land could be bequeathed to heirs, usually the eldest son but in the absence of a male heir, the eldest daughter or sister. Widows of deceased tenants could not claim 'freebench' (the income of one-third of the late husband's land). In most of the surrenders seen, widows were usually named in the copyhold so did not need the freebench.[7] In the case of an heir being an infant, the nearest kin who was 'furthest from the land' (presumably to prevent neighbouring kin obtaining very large holdings) was normally appointed guardian during the child's minority unless the father had named another.

Deceased tenants and his or her heir were named and recorded at the next appointed manor court and soon after the heir would be officially admitted to the tenement or land, provided they 'made fealty' to the lord. The rents and fines in this type of copyhold were generally fixed and did not alter much over time.[8]

When a copyhold was sold or passed to the next heir, a heriot was due to be paid to the lord. This was either the best beast (or goods if no beast) or the sum of 26s. 8d. at the choice of the lord. Fines for entering a property were also paid and were stated as 'arbitrary' although they did not usually exceed the value of three years rent. Fines and rents were only to be paid to the bailiff, a person chosen by the homage at the end of the Michaelmas court session.[9] In total, rents of 24 pounds and 4 ½ pence, as well as fourteen hens and 'threescore and ten eggs' were to be paid to the lord by the bailiff each year, although the survey does not explain who was to provide the hens and eggs. If the bailiff defaulted on his obligation to present the annual rents to the lord, the latter may 'enter upon his land or distreyne him or imprison him for it'.

There were a number of other rules that tenants had to abide by. They were not to lease out their property for more than a year and a day without a licence. Nor could they demolish any building or sell any timber from the property without the obligatory licence to do so. It was permitted, however, for a tenant to use wood from their own copyhold to build or repair the property or for mending hedges, fences, carts and ploughs and for firewood. Conversely, the lords could not take any of the wood on tenants' premises without compensating the copyholder.

Manorial courts were to be held regularly and all the manor's inhabitants were expected to attend, both freeholders and copyholders. The courts dealt with waifs and strays (any apparently ownerless property), the setting of rules for the maintenance of fields, gates and hedges and the ancient assizes of bread and beer (ensuring no short measures or weights).[10] There is more on the manorial courts in the chapter on maintaining law in the parish.

The waste land of the manor was important enough to be identified in the customs. By 1649, the only 'waste' left in the parish seems to have been Westhope Hill, an area of 60 acres on which some tenants had rights of common. This term means they had a 'right of use rather than of property' and may involve six different types where appropriate; that of common of pasture, common of mast, common of estovers, common of turbary, common of soil and common of piscary.[11] Only two of these are mentioned in the Canon Pyon customs; the right to 'fell underwoods and vallett woods without Licence' (common of estovers) and the right to 'digg stones for their uses without Licence' (common of soil which includes sand, gravel, stone and coal). It is possible that common of pasture and common of mast (allowing pigs to forage, usually in woodland) also took place but this was probably in the common fields, rather than on the waste or in the woodlands. Two examples from manorial court records illustrate this possibility:

> In 1642: It is commanded to all those that have any lande in Westhopes field [to] not tye or keepe any cattle in the said field untill Lamas day next [--- on pain of] vij s[12]

> In 1673: Wee lay a paine of 10s on everie on[e] of the inhabitantes within the parish that they yoake and ringe theire swine by the fifte of October and for to keepe them at all times till wee [comand][13]

Faced with increasing enclosure of common land, any remnants of waste became ever more important to the poorer parishioners. Indeed, it was in the same year of the 1649 survey that Gerrard Winstanley began his campaign to protect commons and waste land for the use of the 'common people'. His Digger communities, so called because they dug, manured, and sowed grain and vegetables on common land, lasted little more than a year in various parts of the country. Winstanley, however, continued to promote his cause by publishing pamphlets and broadsheets, railing against lords of manors in particular, believing that everyone had equal rights to cultivate the land.

The final part of the customs in the survey relates to the lord of the manor (the Dean and Chapter of Hereford Cathedral). They were to have the tithes of Canon Pyon, the fishing of Derndall brook (trout and eels) and the advowson of the church (the privilege of presenting a vicar). In return, they were to maintain the chancel of the church, pay the vicar in wheat and oats, repair the pound and 'find the jury a dinner at every court'. Some of these requirements were passed to the tenant of the manor's demesne lands and this will be considered further in the sections on the manor leases.

The full text of the customs of Canon Pyon manor from the 1649 survey is given in Appendix 1.

PLOUGHING THE LORD'S LAND

Some of the copyhold lands in the manor had ploughing services attached to them and the 1649 survey informs us that:

> There is a custome for the owners of the land now of Mr Thomas Berrington, Mr John Munn, Katherine Ceely widow, Thomas Stephens, Mr Richard Weaver, Edward Yeomans, John Mason, Phillipp Ceely, William Knapp, Elizabeth Price widow, and Thomas Jay are in respect of the tenure of their coppieholds to plough for the ffarmer [the lessee] of the said manor about eight acres to an odd marke (vizt) for the first ploughing to doe it and to plough a harow for sowing at mich[aelm]as and to plough the like porc[i]on for lent sowing and they are to have for their paines a peece of beefe and a goose.

Occasionally, a manorial court record reports when this service was not done, as in October 1679 when the estate at Kinard (Kinford) was presented 'wherin William Venmore inhabits ... for not plowing the custom land and we order him to do it from hence forward according [to] custom under the paine of 39s' and also in October 1685 when Charles Somerset, esquire, returned Hugh Jay 'for not ploughing the customary ground'.[14]

LEASES OF THE 'SITE OF THE MANOR'

The manor farm was leased to a tenant by the Dean and Chapter during the 17th century but the lease situation was a little complicated at the beginning of this period so it is necessary to look at earlier documents to throw some light on the sequence of events.

EDWARD BROUGHTON AND GEORGE VAUGHAN

On 30 January 1560/1, Edward Broughton signed a lease with the Dean and Chapter for the 'farm and site of the manor of Cannon Pewne' including the 'demesne lands, grange, meadows, leasows and pastures, moors, water, stanks and fish pools' and also the 'tithe corn and hay of the parish of Cannon Pewne ... and other tithes with the custom fines work silver with all other commodities and profits.[15] Along with the manor, the lease also included a 'messuage lying in Dernedall .... with all lands, meadows, leasows and pastures ... with all manner of tithe corn and hay... now in the tenure of one Thomas Apenam'. The lease also included the rents of the tenants 'both free and custom', the 'perquisites of the courts, ward of marriage, heriott, escheats, fines of lands, mills, hunting and hawking, and the portion of the vicarage ... [with] the nomination of the vicar of Cannon Pewne' when the position was free.

The term of the lease was for 40 years, to begin immediately after the next 'feast of saint michaell tharchangell' following the 'surrender or forfeiture of a lease or demise made and granted by the Dean and Chapter foresaid unto the said Edward Braughton and to his assignes of the premises for xviij^{ten} years yet to come'. So the lease was a renewal of an earlier one, which had still 18 years to run.

In the conditions of his lease, Broughton had a long list of responsibilities. The first was to provide the following yearly corn rent, all between the 'ffeast of all saints and thannunciacon of our lady the virgin' (between 1 November to 25 March):

- To every canon resident at Hereford one quarter of wheat and ten bushels of oats, to be delivered to the house of every canon resident at Broughton's own cost

- Sixteen quarters of wheat (sweet and well winnowed) to be delivered to the Canon Bakehouse at Hereford
- To every canon not resident (being personally sworn) one quarter of wheat and ten bushels of oats to be delivered at Canon Pewne (the corn due being termed their petty commons)
- To every canon not sworn personally and for 'every prebend that is void', the said one quarter of wheat and ten bushels of oats and an extra six bushels of oats to be delivered to the Canon Bakehouse
- To the vicar of Canon Pewne church thirty-two bushels of oats

Non-resident canons were those who did not live at the Cathedral premises but in other parts of the diocese. If any non-resident canon did not collect his petty commons, Broughton was to deliver such corn to the Canon Bakehouse and receive 1d. a bushel from the Dean and Chapter for his troubles.

Broughton's other responsibilities were to repair and maintain the buildings, houses, water courses, ditches, ways and hedges at his own cost and leave them in a sufficient state of repair at the end of the term. He was allowed to take timber from the lord's woods to make necessary repairs and also allowed 'heybott, housebott, ffyrebott and ploughebott' as long as he made no waste.[16]

Certain fields were to be tilled and sown with wheat and those being made ready for winter wheat he should leave 'well dunged'. On this subject, he was not allowed to sell any dung produced on the manor or move it to anywhere else. It could only be used within the manor and any of this valuable asset that was unused by the end of the term was to be left on the manor.

Twice yearly, a manor court was to be held and Broughton must pay for a dinner for the clavinger and steward 'thether to keep court' and to find hay and oats for their horses at both times.[17] Most leases also have a re-entry clause and in this case the Dean and Chapter could re-enter the property if the rents were 'unpaid in the space of two months next after any time or times that it aught to be paid'.

An interesting aspect of this lease, in terms of woodland management and the enclosure of land, is that the Dean and Chapter appointed Broughton the woodwardship of the manor. He was granted an annuity of 14d. for the execution of the office, which was to begin at the same time and for the same term as the manor lease. Broughton had to covenant that he would not make any waste or destruction in any of the woods. Vittoria Di Palma describes waste of forest as 'any mismanagement of land within the jurisdiction of the forest' and specifies that wood should be cut in the right season and then enclosed to allow for herbage and trees to regrow without damage from grazing animals.[18] This is echoed in the manor customs which states that woodland was to be hedged and enclosed and enough 'tylthe and stuff for tynding and enclosinge of the said woodde' could be taken from the wood to do so, although the enclosing itself should be undertaken at the tenant's own cost.

Broughton was also granted the Vallett woods in the lordship of Cannon Pewne, with their 'profits and commodities', during the same 40-year term.[19] He was allowed to cut down and take away wood and 'to convert the said valett ground to his best advantage and profit' and for this he was to pay the Dean and Chapter 13s. 4d. per annum at the Feast of St Michael the Archangel (29 September).

In a terrier dated 1568/9, the Canon Vallet is described as '20 acres lying betwixt Byrleis Common on the west and Esthops Hill on the east and the Lye Vallet north and ov[er] Woodfield south'. This is possibly the Vallets shown on Isaac Taylor's map of *c.* 1755. Although the key of the woodlands A-D on the map is damaged and those names are missing, the above description places the vallets very close to, if not the same as, the area on the map.

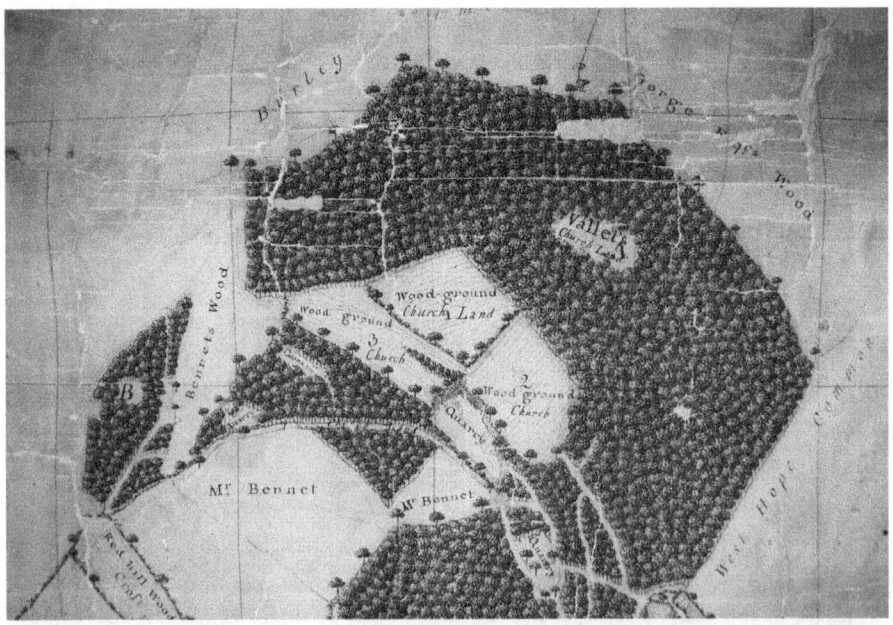

Detail from Isaac Taylor's map *c.* 1755 showing the Vallets, lying between the Birley's boundary and Westhope common. Upper Woodfield is to the south of this image (off the map) (HARC BN81).

The shape of the woodland shows some similarities with modern-day topography and the cultivated ground within the area stills exists today. In the same terrier, Pewne (Pyon) Hill is described as:

> ....lying between Haftecomer on the south and e[a]st p[ar]te, Old Fi[e]ld north and a p[ar]cel of glebe land belonging to the vicarage north which the said Edward now by consent hath in severalt[y] but hath alwaies before that agre[e]m[en]t lay as wast and common to the tenants of Pewne.[21]

This does suggest that Pyon Hill was not wooded in 1568/9 (as it is today) but was beginning to be enclosed and no longer available as common land.

Edward Broughton's lease in January 1560/1 was for 40 years but on 18 June 1569, another lease was drawn up between the Dean and Chapter and George Vaughan.[22] This lease recites that of 1560/1 with Broughton in all details of the property except that the tenant of Derndall is given as John A Beynham, not Thomas Apenam. To Vaughan, the Dean and Chapter 'by their [w]hole assent and consent for div[er]se good causes and consideracons' granted the farm and site of the manor of Canon Pewne for the term of three score and one years to begin at the Feast of St Michael next, following the surrender or forfeiture of the lease granted to Broughton for 40 years.

On first impression, this would appear to be a straightforward change of tenant from Broughton to Vaughan but there is evidence that Broughton and his family remained at the manor for a long time after this. The manorial court roll for this date is marked as unfit to produce so it is not possible to check if any other information exists.[23]

George Vaughan's lease was almost identical to Broughton's; the various amounts of corn for the canons, the repair and maintenance of the property, leaving the fields ready seeded or manured at the end of the lease, not removing dung from the manor, paying for two dinners for the court officers and hay and oats for their horses. The corn for the vicar, however, had been increased from thirty-two bushels of oats to two bushels of wheat and forty-two bushels of oats.

The Canon Vallets was also part of Vaughan's lease, along with the right to take wood as required for the same 13s. 4d. fee and the right to haybote, firebote and ploughbote, but there is no mention of the woodwardship. Two items were new to Vaughan's lease; the first was a covenant to provide a survey 'of all the demesne lands, woods, waste, grounds and copyhold of the said Dean and Chapter w[i]thin their lordships of Preston, Woolhope, Canon Pewne and Norton of the number of acres and the place where the same doe lie' and to provide a terrier of the same and deliver

Canon Pyon

it at his own cost. That would have been quite some task; work enough to compile a terrier for one manor but all four was a substantial requirement. The second new item was that Vaughan was to maintain and repair the chancel of the parish church, notable because this is a custom already part of the manor and is not mentioned in Broughton's lease.

When Edward Broughton made his will in 1570 (proved in 1573), he left all his goods and 'living leases and farms' to his son William with the proviso that he 'keeps and maintains' his mother for her life.[24] Unfortunately, the will does not give any details of the leases and farms. Several years later another lease was signed, this time between the Dean and Chapter and Ellynor Broughton, widow of Canon Pewne, on 25 Jun 1589.[25] This lease recited the original 1560/1 agreed with Edward Broughton but made no mention of the Vaughan lease. The main purpose of Ellynor's lease appears to have been to grant her 'and her assignes to have and take necessary heybote, firebote and ploughbote and tynneth upon the premises before letted and woods and vallet before mentioned when and as often as need shall require during the time in the said lease' (the original 40 years) and to also use the timber for repairing houses and buildings when required. A later document (1625) informs us that Broughton's son William had died intestate in about 1580 and the administration of his goods was granted to Ellynor who then held the lease for 20 years after which the lease was assigned to her son Edward Broughton.[26] Ellynor, or Elianor, was William's widow and the daughter of Edward Wolrich of Dinmore.[27]

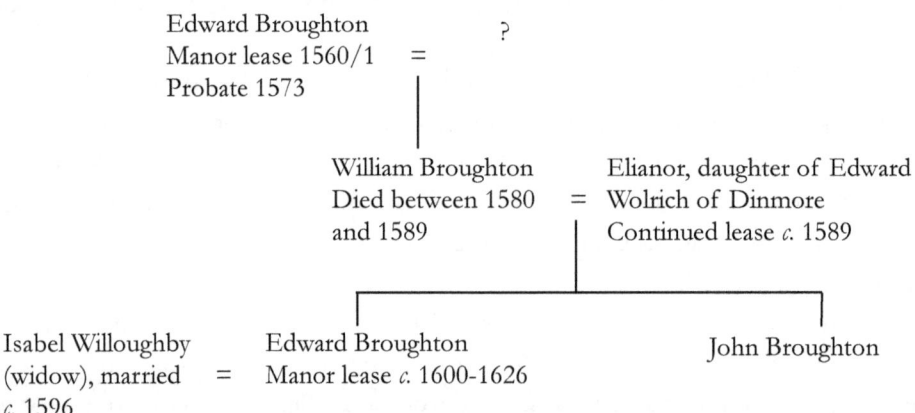

In the meantime, George Vaughan also made his will, proved on 19 January 1584/5. He left to his son Oliver Vaughan 'my lease for years which I have in Canon Pewne aforesaid ... of the farm and parsonage of Canon Pewne of the demise and grant of the Dean and Chapter of the Cathedral Church of Hereford...' The 'farm and parsonage'

is notable as his lease only mentioned the farm and site of the manor. Oliver himself left a will, proved in 1601, in which he leaves 'the lease granted to George Vaughan my father and his assigns, from the Dean and Chapter of the Cathedral Church of Hereford, which my father gave me by his will' first to his four daughters and then to his son George within 6 months of his reaching 21 years, for the 'five years it contains'.[28]

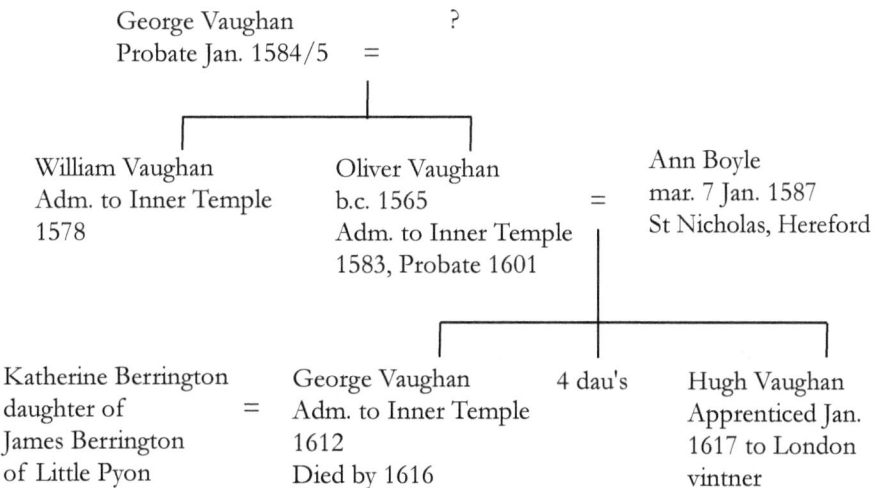

Therefore, around 1601, the two leases were held by Edward Broughton, grandson of Edward Broughton and George Vaughan, grandson of George Vaughan! For some time the lease puzzle remained unsolved until the discovery of an 18th century copy of a terrier (without an original date) entitled 'demesnes, woods, waste and copyhold of the Lordship of Canon Pewne, belonging to the Dean and Chapter of the Cathedral church made by the survey of George Vaughan'.[29] The terrier lists 'The demaynes in the tenure of Edward Boughton by indenture' and also a list of 'George Vaughan's copyhold land in Pewne'. This document does in fact appear to be a partial copy of the terrier held at the Cathedral Archives (listed as 1568 but is probably the one that George Vaughan was required to compile in 1569) and which also lists the lands of other copyhold tenants.[30]

The terrier names the land holdings of the two men and confirms that both held demesne land at the same time (see Part A of Appendix 1). For those interested in the manor's field names it is well worth studying, being significantly earlier than the *c.* 1755 map by Isaac Taylor. We also see that Broughton held 'the manor house with two barns and Gatt [Gate] house', whereas Vaughan's list mentions no buildings at all. In fact Vaughan was also the tenant of a considerable amount of other copyhold land in the manor, including a mease house at Fulbridge.³¹ Both held demesne lands throughout the manor with no obvious division, though not all field names can be directly identified with those on the *c.* 1755 map. Thus the terrier does not give any clue as to why their leases were virtually identical.

THE LAST YEARS OF BROUGHTON'S LEASE

The 1620s signalled a change for the Broughtons. We will meet Edward Broughton (junior) again in the chapter on maintaining law and order but on this occasion he was in trouble with regards to his lease. In 1623 the Dean and Chapter brought a case against him for non-payment of rents and in 1624 Broughton made a counter claim in the Court of Chancery in the same regard.³² The counter-claim and the judgement is recorded in a summary of the case, which is helpful in explaining the sequence of events.³³ This document begins by reciting the terms of the original lease in 1560/1 and the various corn rents due to the canons and that after a bond of £40 was agreed, Edward Broughton (senior) 'did afterwards quietly enjoy the said mannor and premises for many yeares according to his lease and paid his rents and performed all the covenants of the said lease'. He then made his will 'about fifty years past' and devised the lease to his son William who, when he entered the manor, 'quietly enjoyed the same according to the said lease and during his life paid the rents and performed the said covenants'. Then 'about forty four years past' William died intestate, his widow Elianor was granted administration of his estate and for more than twenty years held the lease. Following this 'about twenty four years past' Elianor assigned the lease to her son Edward who also 'entered and enjoyed the premises, all rents and convenants being paid and performed during his and his mother's time'.

However, a prebendary of the Cathedral church - one John Best - had 'lately endeavoured to frustrate the complainant's [Edward Broughton, junior] interest in the said lease and to make the same void' and incited the Dean to take up a case against him for:

> ... a breache of covenant upon the not delivering of eight bushells of wheat and tenne bushells of oates unto the defendant Robert Burghill one of the cannons of the said church sworn and not resident at the cannon backhowse.

Broughton pleaded against this, urging that he did deliver the corn to the bakehouse but that Robert Burghill nor any other would take it, nor would John Best take the corn or any 'money value' for it. He was still willing to deliver the corn (or money) and make amends for any breach of covenant but the defendant (Best) 'did utterley refuse to accept thereof'. The defendants (Best and Burghill) were unrelenting and most uncomplimentary about Broughton's character; that he had:

> ... demeaned himself very unworthily toward them for many years; and had offered them many abuses in their said answer particularly expressed both to their great loss and hinderance and also to the encouragement of other their tenants in the like nature, and that the compleynant had been both deficient and remiss in performance of his covenant and violent and intemperate in his speeches against the Dean and Chapter and has made default from time to time in payment of his said rent.

This behaviour caused the Dean, who had 'for a long time patiently endured', to request Dr Best to prosecute 'for the good of the church' and he proposed that Broughton had breached six covenants, that the Dean and Chapter might have re-entered the manor but that they did not want to take advantage, instead 'hoping to reform his perverse dealings'. They were aware that he was 'a man full of troubles and suits [of law]'.

In time, the case was referred to Justice Whitlock, whose report stated that Broughton had broken the covenants:

> ... for reparation of houses, for not committing waste in woods, for giving entertainment to their offices at their courts, and for paying several measures of corn or petty commons to several prebendaries in the church.

As the breaking of these covenants had cost the Dean and Chapter more than the value of the original bond, Whitlock declared that Broughton should pay damages of £30 but when he declined to do so, suggested that a new bond of £40 should be agreed.

It is doubtful that Broughton complied. The case had persisted until 1629 but in 1627/8 a taxation certificate of residence gives Broughton's residence as Hereford, not Grimsworth (Canon Pyon's hundred), and after this date there is no evidence of Broughton in the parish or manor.[34] It is difficult to assess the ratio of truth to fabrication in the allegations made by Best and Burghill regarding Broughton's character but he evidently attracted trouble for he was involved in several other court cases.[35]

What happened to Broughton in the immediate aftermath of this case is unknown but an Edward Broughton later became involved in the Parliamentary activity of the Civil War. An associate of Sir Robert Harley, he was appointed a J.P. around 1642 (to the distaste of some) and by 1646 was an active member of the Parliamentary Committee of Hereford.[36] John Aubrey, in his *'Brief Lives...'* written in the late 17th century, did make the connection between this Edward Broughton and the one at Canon Pyon, stating that he lived at 'the manor house at Canon Peon' and wrote of him with some admiration when discussing Broughton's daughter Elizabeth:

> I doe remember her father [1646], neer 80, the handsomest shaped man that ever my eies beheld, a very wise man and of an admirable elocution. He was a Committee-man in Herefordshire and Glocestershire. He was commissary to colonel Massey. He was of the Puritan party heretofore; had a great guift in praying, etc. His wife (I have heard my grandmother say, who was her neighbour) had as great parts as he. He was the first that used the improvement of lands by soape-ashes when he lived at Bridstow, where they then threw it away.[37]

This description does not fit too well with the Broughton we have encountered but it was written many years later. Aubrey refers to the Heralds' records which links this family with the Broughtons of Kington and before this, Bitterley in Shropshire. This is probably correct; in 1626, during the last few months of his time in Canon Pyon, Broughton was presented to the church court for not attending the communion at Easter and in his defence he brought a certificate from the minister at Kington confirming that he had attended communion there.[38]

THE CUSTOM OF 'WARDSHIP AND MARRIAGE'

Returning again to the Vaughans, by August 1616 George Vaughan had died leaving his widow Katherine to continue with the lease. In a covenant dated 1 August, Katherine agreed to continue paying forty-two quarters of wheat and twenty somes of oats to the Chapter and also thirty-two bushels of wheat and forty-two of oats to the vicar.[39] George and Katherine had only one child, Judith, who was to be heir to the Vaughan property but by around 1620 Katherine had remarried to Robert Lochard of the Byletts, Pembridge.

Soon after, there was yet another dispute, this time relating to the heriots due to the lord of the manor at George Vaughan's death. The first indication is in a View of Frankpledge of 16 October 1619 when a date was given by which the jury should enquire into the death of George Vaughan. They were to present to the court a report of the messuages and land he held of the lords at the time of his death and 'what mortis [fine on death] was due to the lords'.[40] The enquiry has not survived in the manorial records but by 1621 the Dean and Chapter had taken up a case against Robert Lochard and Katharine his wife (formerly Vaughan), Hughe Yeomans, Daniell Taylor and Phillip Clotworthie.[41]

At first sight this dispute seemed to be purely about money matters but in fact involved an ancient custom of the manor; that of 'wardship and marriage'. This custom gave the lords of the manor guardianship of the lands and the person of any infant who was heir to a tenancy if the father died during the child's minority and this included the right to arrange their marriage. An inspeximus, or royal grant, of an award in the Court of Chancery relating to this case survives at the Cathedral archives.[42] A beautiful document with the Great Seal of James I appended, the inspeximus details the process and along the way provides more detail about the Vaughans and the manor.

The inspeximus explains that when George Vaughan died in 1616, he had been seised of certain copyhold property, much of it in Fulbridge, and also freehold property held of the Dean & Chapter by knight service (see the list of lands in part B of Appendix 2). George had only one infant daughter, Judith, who would be entitled to be admitted as tenant. However, the Dean and Chapter claimed that the custom of the manor was that they, as lords of the manor, had the 'wardship of the body and land and marriage of all heirs of tenants within the age of 21 years' whether the tenant held copyhold land or freehold and if freehold, both by socage or knight service (by rental payment/fixed services, or by military service). They also claimed that they were due a heriot of the best beast after the death of every freeholder for every freehold messuage or toft or part thereof, and after the death of every copyholder for every messuage or toft. Therefore, after the death of George they should have had the wardship, marriage and custody of Judith and her lands and several fines for admittance to customary land as well as heriots for the freehold and customary land.

George's father Oliver Vaughan and grandfather George Vaughan had held the post of steward or deputy steward of the manor for over 30 years and had the custody of all the court rolls and evidences. George (junior) himself had been left in custody of these after his father's death. The Dean & Chapter claimed that they therefore did not know the tenures, whether copyhold or freehold, the rents, boundaries, customs, services, wardships or heriots. Furthermore, they also accused Robert Lochard and Katherine his wife (Judith's mother) of embezzling the documents with the intent to defraud the Dean & Chapter of the wardship of Judith and her lands & profits. To that aim, Robert & Katherine had 'possessed themselves' of the ward (she then being under 8 years of age) and were moving her 'to places unknown' so that she could not be seized, nor did they allow her to attend court to be admitted tenant or pay the complainant any fine.

Without knowledge of the boundaries of the copyhold and freehold land, the Dean & Chapter were unable to use the common law to make any claim, hence the appeal to the Court of Chancery, a Court of Equity which dealt with cases on a more ethical basis rather than purely the letter of the law. The Dean at this time was Silvanus Griffiths, a Herefordshire man who is likely to have known the Vaughan family through his various postings at the Cathedral (treasurer 1604, archdeacon 1606, commissary 1617)[43] but who did not take up the post of Dean until after the death of George Vaughan in 1616. As the first indication of investigations did not occur until 1619, it is possible that the Dean's 'quarrel' was with Robert Lochard.

On Friday 8 November 1622, the 'learned counsel' debated the matter. In their answers to the Bill, the defendants (the Lochards) confessed that they held several copyhold and freehold properties (even more than was set in the Bill) but denied knowledge of the custom of wardship and marriage. They believed that this was a matter of common law and confirmed that their fines for customary land were 'arbitrable at the will of the lords'. On this matter, it was decided by the court that the fines should be arbitrable but that a commission be arranged to produce evidence (from both sides) to ascertain the free and copyhold lands, rents and services. In the meantime, Master Justice Chamberlain was requested to investigate the custom of wardship.

On Saturday 10 May 1623, a new hearing was held and here we find some enlightenment on the custom of wardship and marriage. It was decided that the manor of Canon Pyon and the manors of Preston (on Wye), Woolhope and Norton (Canon) were the ancient possessions of the Church, long before the time of the reign of Henry III (from 1216). In Henry III's eight years of reign, the Dean & Chapter did claim by custom that time out of mind they had wardship of their freehold tenants (whether by socage or knight service) and had seised an infant who had held land in socage by the custom. The court saw many court rolls and other records showing, from time to time, examples of their wardship and marriage of their (under-age) tenants dating from the times of 'King Edward I, Edward II, Edward III, Richard II, Henrie IV, Henrie VI, Henrie VII, Henrie VIII, Edward VI and Queene Elizabeth'. As this custom had been in place for so long and 'constantly continued' it was decreed that the lords of the manor did have wardship of tenants 'within age' for freehold land held in socage or knight service. As for wardship of copyhold tenants, this was to be left to be tried by common law as it was not proven to extend to copyhold lands. The court also did not 'conceive it equitable' that copyholders paying heriots and 'arbitrable fines' should also be subject to 'wardship and marriage'.

The many court rolls also showed that with regard to heriots for freehold land, one heriot was due for every messuage and toft (or part messuage and toft). As far as the heriots for copyhold land, the complainants had already been paid six and the court referred them to take this up within common law if they thought that they had a right. Because the complainants were churchmen, they were persuaded by the court to 'deal kindly and favourably with the defendant for the wardship and marriage' of Judith and with other tenants if this shall reoccur. Furthermore, should any future disagreement occur, the complainants should bring their cause to the Bishop of the Diocese and thus avoid 'suits and controversies' with their tenants.

That the court went through so many ancient manorial court rolls to prove the consistent use of the custom of wardship and marriage is testament to their diligence but also highlights the important consideration given to maintaining custom. Quite a number of these court rolls, the earliest from the end of the 13th century, are still held at Hereford Cathedral Archives. As for Judith, we will continue her story presently but she later married Walter Baskervile, son of Walter and Frances of nearby Wormsley. It is unlikely that the Dean & Chapter had any involvement with this arrangement as Walter Baskervile was presented at the church court in 1636 'for being maryed to Judith his wife without banes or licence'.[44]

The later manorial survey (1649) does not mention the custom of wardship and marriage but that for customary tenants an infant's guardian was to be the closest relative who lived most distant unless the father had appointed another before he had died. 'Ward and marriage' is noted in the manor leases though it is not specified whether it relates to copyhold or freehold tenants.

DESCENT OF THE MANOR LEASE CONTINUES

Canon Pyon manor in the 1620s therefore seems to have been in a period of stasis but the Lochards were not in disfavour for too long. With Edward Broughton no longer in Canon Pyon, his part of the manorial lease was now available. On 8 November 1631, Robert Lochard signed a 1 year lease and entered into a bond for £100.[45] This lease was identical to that of Broughton's grandfather in 1560/1 in terms of the amount of wheat and oats to be paid to the Canons of the Cathedral church and the vicar of Canon Pyon (70 years without a rent rise!) and in the general terms of maintaining the property, not selling the manor's dung, paying for two dinners for the court and providing hay and oats for the officers' horses, as before. There is however, a new clause in this lease, no doubt in response to the troubles encountered with the previous tenant who evidently left the Dean and Chapter out of pocket. This lease stipulates that if the grain rent was unpaid for two months, the Dean and Chapter could distrain any goods and chattels of Lochard 'and the same to sell away to satisfie themselves the true value of the aforesaide rente wheate and oates that shalbe unsatisfied… (without any 'contradiction' or 'interruption' by Lochard)'.

This 1631 document is the last of the 17th century leases in the bundle, the next in the sequence being agreed on 25 June 1776 with Anthony Sawyer. Sawyer was a descendant of George and Katherine Vaughan through their daughter Judith and so the manorial lease stayed in the family for quite some time. The two generations following George and Katherine Vaughan saw an inordinate number of marriages in the family, many of which have not been found and may well be in the missing parish registers but can be surmised from other sources. Katherine's marriage to Robert Lochard produced eight known children but it was Katherine's first daughter, Judith, who had the 'right of inheritance' according to the custom of the manor.[46]

Judith Vaughan first married Walter Baskervile, gentleman, the son of Walter and Frances of The Grange at Wormesley.[47] They had a daughter Katherine Baskervile, possibly born at the Byletts home of the Lochards and quite probably where Judith's mother was living.[48] Walter (junior) was presented at the church court in 1636 for 'having a child borne and baptised in the howse of Robert Lochard, gent ... and not brought to the church at all'.[49]

Sadly, Walter died relatively young and by 1649, Judith had remarried to William Lochard, the nephew of Robert her step-father.[50] The 1649 survey of the manor sets out the copyhold lands held by William Lochard in the right of his wife Judith and her heirs. Smaller holdings, with indentures dating from between 1634 and 1641, include two acres in Housemore, one cottage and ten acres of land (formerly William Pritchard's), one acre of land at Round Hawthorn, one messuage, orchard and croft (formerly Margaret Jefferies'), two acres in One Acre Field, four acres in the Stroode (formerly Partridge's), and a close called Pope Close (probably the one involved in the dispute in the 1620s).

THE 1649 MANORIAL SURVEY OFFERS MORE INFORMATION
Two other records of leases in the 1649 survey are of great interest. The first gives us some information about the house where George Vaughan (senior) had lived. It recites that William Lochard and Judith his wife (in the right of Judith and her heirs) 'freely hold one messuage built in which George Vaughan did heretofore inhabit with one close of land containing one acre to the said messuage belonging'. The rent was 20d., the heriot 10s. and relief 20d. (fines on the death of a tenant) and suit of court was owed according to an indenture date 20 September 1565. This is the only known record of this document, which is four years earlier than the lease Vaughan took out for the farm and site of the manor, and probably indicates that he did not live at the manor house.

The second informs us that James Tompkins of Monnington on Wye, esquire, and Thomas Berrington of Little Pyon, gentleman, were the assigns of George Vaughan of Canon Pyon, gent, deceased (no will has been found) and they held in trust for Judith, wife of William Lochard and for Katherine Baskerville her daughter, the farm and site of the manor of Canon Pyon 'by indenture of lease 18 June 1569'. The details of the lease are as before but included this time is a description of the premises (presumably as of 1649):

> One anncient farmehouse conteyning nyne bayes of buildings, two barnes and a gatehouse conteyning eight bayes and a halfe of building, one hundred acres of arable land in several places within the said parish. And thirtie and two acres of pasture in several places there, twentie acres and a halfe of vallett wood ground there, ffifteen acres of barren pasture ground called Pyon Hill [so still unwooded] and sixteen acres of meadow ground inclosed in several parcells there, and one little croft there called Dovers Croft conteyning about halfe an acre.[51]

This is unlikely to be the same house that George Vaughan had previously occupied with the one acre close attached and evidently smaller than the one above.

The hearth tax list for Canon Pyon in 1665 shows the biggest house was charged for nine hearths which might fit the 'nyne bayes' description of the above house.[52] Home Farm on the *c.* 1755 map by Isaac Taylor is in the same location as the house now known as The Great House although it now looks quite different to the image also shown on Taylor's map. There is documentary evidence that Anthony Sawyer was assigned a new lease in 1783, 'having engaged and undertaken to rebuild the said dwellinghouse' which may be, at least in part, the house that we see today.[53]

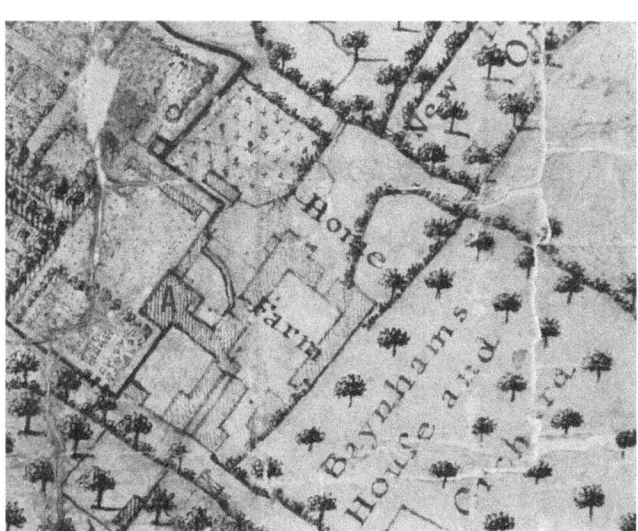

Detail from Isaac Taylor's map *c.* 1755, showing Home Farm and buildings. The lane to the church is across the bottom left corner of the image. 'A' marks the location of the main house today.
(HARC BN81)

Canon Pyon

When Oliver Vaughan left the 'farm and parsonage' to his son George in 1601, this probably referred to the The Court (site of Court Farm). Home Farm (the Great House) was not built in 1601 and was unlikely to have been there for the 1665 hearth tax. There may have been an earlier house on or near the site and a possibility for this is the house marked 'Baynhams House' on Isaac Taylor's map (see Lost Houses in Chapter 2).

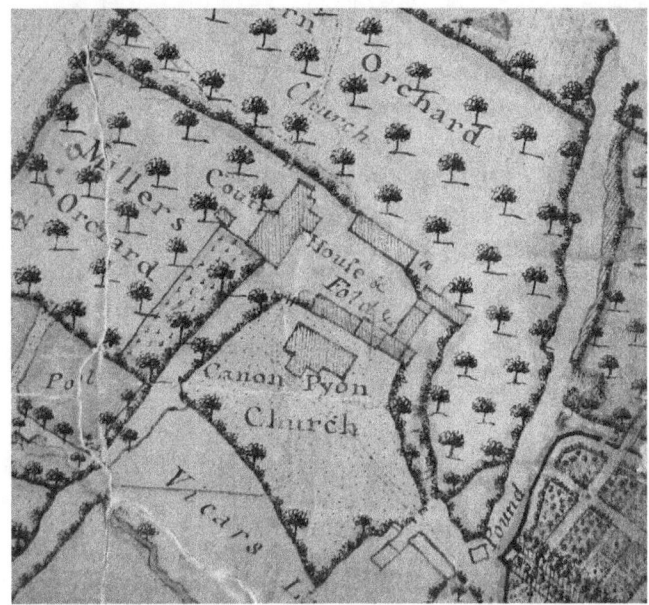

The Court with house and fold (centre), *c.* 1755, which could fit the description 'with two barns and a gatehouse'. The corner of the gardens belonging to Home Farm can be seen in the bottom right of the image.
(HARC BN81)

William Lochard made his will in December of 1649 and it was proved in July 1650.[54] He left property in Pembridge to various relatives and the residue of his personal goods to Judith (after debts, legacies and funeral expenses). He did not forget the poor of Pembridge or Canon Pyon, leaving £5 to each 'towards a stocke for them'.[55]

Judith's third husband was John Barneby and they married around 1654.[56] Barneby was involved in local politics and a Member of Parliament, sitting for Weobley 1661-1678 but when Judith died he never stood for election again.[57] She was buried at Canon Pyon on 2 May 1678.

THE SAWYERS
The manorial lease now descended to Judith's daughter Katherine Baskerville. Katherine had married George Sawyer, esquire (of the Inner Temple, London) at St Andrew's, Holborn, London on 2 November 1654.[58] The entry in the register is a marvellous example of an Interregnum marriage, the intent rather than banns being published in the market place and the marriage being undertaken by a Justice of the Peace:

'Corn for the Canons': the manor of Canon Pyon

> An agreement and intent of Marriage Betweene George Sawyer Esqr. sonne of Sir Edmon Sawyer knight And Katherine Barrowe widdowe and daughter of Walter Baskervile Esqr both of this parish was published in Newgate Markett on three Markett dayes & in three severall weekes Vidlt [videlicet – that is to say] On the 9th On the 16th and on the 23th dayes of October 1654. They were married by Robert Tichborne Alderman one of the Justic[e]s of the peace for the City of London & Countie of Midd: the second day of November 1654.

A big surprise was that Katherine was already a widow. Her first marriage has not been found but further investigation has brought to light two cases in the Court of Chancery brought by George and Katherine Sawyer against members of the Barrow/e family (in 1659 and 1660), the latter regarding the personal estate of the deceased Richard Barrow of Herefordshire.[59] Katherine is mentioned in a lease of property at Lower Bullingham dated 20 April 1653 when she was noted as being the wife of James Barrowe. When George Sawyer himself died in 1665, his will stated that he was from Nether Bullingham, not Canon Pyon, though he did not mention Bullingham in his bequests. The Hearth Tax returns for 1665 also reveal that Katherine Sawyer was still living at Bullingham.[60]

James Barrowe left a will (proved in October 1654) and although he did not name his 'dearly beloved' wife in the main body of the will or in the appointment of her as executor, Katherine 'the relict' was named as having proved the will. James requested that most of his assets were to go to his younger brothers and sister 'according to the true intent of the last will and testament of my deceased father Richard Barrowe', with any surplus to go to his wife. Quite possibly this is the reason for the Chancery court case. James' father, Richard Barrowe, had died 1649/50 and left quite large money legacies to his six children and James was the sole executor.[61]

George and Katherine Sawyer had four children - George, Edmund and Herbert and one who died young - but only Herbert Sawyer's baptism is recorded at Canon Pyon, on 6 May 1663.[62] It is likely that the couple spent a lot of time in London; George had been admitted to the Inner Temple in 1646 and called to the Bar in 1653, just a year before their marriage.[63]

The Sawyer family had lived at Heywood Manor in Berkshire since 1623 and his father Sir Edmund Sawyer still lived there.[64] When George died at Bullingham, Herefordshire in 1665, he requested to be buried at White Waltham church in Berkshire, near to his mother and son and this happened on 7 September. However, the couple must also have spent time at Canon Pyon as Ralph Darnall, who leased Lawton's Hope and who was also of the Inner Temple, was named as a trustee in George's will.

Canon Pyon

Local men John Barneby (Katherine's step-father) and Thomas Berington (her uncle) were also named as overseers.

In April 1666, a marriage licence was taken out for a marriage at St Clement Danes in London between Katherine Sawyer of Bullingham and Peter Dauncer of Moreton on Lugg.[65] There is no evidence that the marriage took place and Cooke thinks not, but it interesting to note that Katherine still kept a house at Bullingham, the home of the Barrowe family.[66]

Between 1666 and 1668, Katherine married again, to Charles Somersett.[67] They had several children and Charles eventually outlived his wife (no marriage record, baptisms of the children, or burial records have been found). Charles Somersett continued with the manor lease, even though George Sawyer was the eldest son of Katherine and, by custom of the manor, was entitled to entry of the lease.

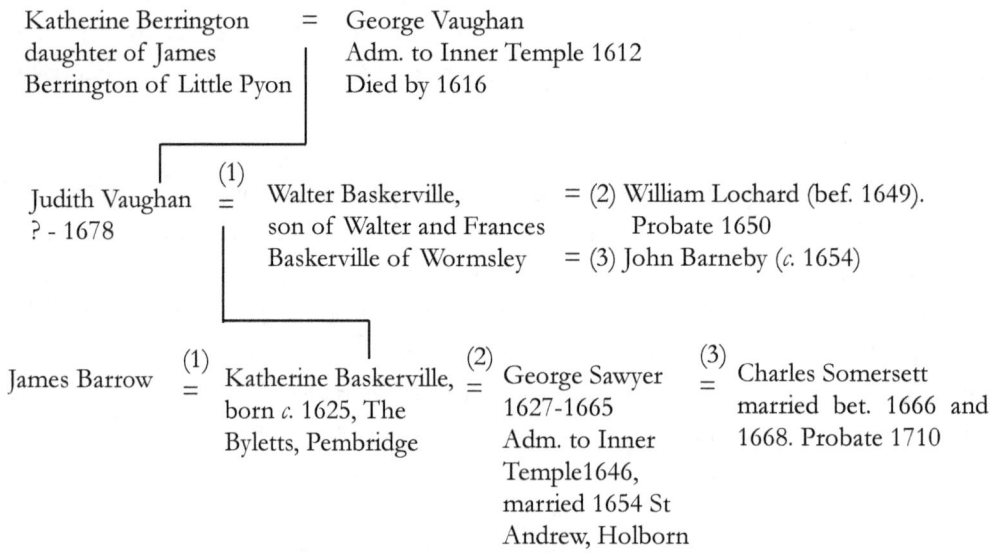

After Somerset's death in 1710 and that of his son Charles Somersett, junior, in 1712, there was another disagreement with the Dean and Chapter, this time over the rights to the entry of the manor lease and various other lands that Charles Somersett had purchased.[68] To his credit, George Sawyer does not seem to have held a grudge. Sawyer's will of 1724 refers to a deed of Bargain and Sale dated 1 February 1716 which specifies that his freehold and copyhold estate in the parish of Canon Pyon is to be held for the lives of his (half) brothers Charles and Henry Somerset.[69] He also gave personal security to Charles of three-score pounds per annum and twenty pounds per annum to Henry, to be charged from the freehold and copyhold estate, for the term that he held the estate. Sawyer stated in his will that the copyhold lands and tenements were granted to himself and his heirs according to the custom of the manor but he generously assigned the Somersett brothers their usage during his lifetime.

The manor lease descended through three more generations of Sawyers before being sold at the beginning of the 19th century. It would be remiss to leave the Sawyer family without paying tribute to Anthony Sawyer, great-grandson of George and Katherine Sawyer. He was responsible for commissioning Isaac Taylor to draw up the map of his estate in around 1755, without which our knowledge of the parish of Canon Pyon and its fields would be all the poorer.

THE MANOR'S OPEN FIELDS

Although considerable enclosure of land in the manor had already taken place by the 17th century there were still a number of larger open fields divided into sections or strips, usually consisting of one to three acres. Sometimes ridges, butts and selions are found as descriptive units in the manorial surrenders and admissions to the land and these could be of variable size.[70]

Each field would contain many of these strips and tenants might hold several parcels of land in the same field, not necessarily adjacent to each other. Every year the whole field would be sown with the same crop or left fallow as part of a rotation system. Tenants with strips in these fields were also allowed to graze sheep and cattle in them at certain times of the year. Owning parcels in different fields thus had the benefit of a variety of harvestable crops and grazing area.

These fields were the remnants of a larger open field system where only the outer boundary of the field was fenced. The presentments at the manorial court (twice a year, spring and autumn) set down the rules agreed by the homage as to when the boundary hedges, fences and gates were to be 'made sufficient' to prevent animals encroaching on the crops and to specify the fines due for any default. Gates were not permanent fixtures and would be moved to where they were required and tied in place; some fences may also have been of the hurdle type, requiring regular checking and maintenance.

In the 25 years between 1664 and 1689 (with a consistent run of records), only corn and pulse fields were mentioned in the Canon Pyon presentments.[71] Wheat was sown in late autumn and peas, beans and some rye and oats sown in spring. In the earlier of these years, the autumn presentment (usually October) required that all inhabitants of the parish make good their hedges and fences and hang sufficient gates in the corn fields, sometimes by a specific date but always to be kept in place until the end of harvest.

The spring presentment (usually March or April) stipulated the same for the pulse fields, sometimes referred to as the Lent fields. By the later years, both the corn and pulse fields were covered by the autumn presentment.

Occasionally, instead of the 'end of harvest', the rule would be in place until the fields were 'rid' or 'ridd' and on one occasion 'until harvest is in and all fields be rid'. This may be an earlier version of the term 'riddering' meaning 'cleaning wheat by means of a large sieve or wheat-ridder' and the implement used was a 'ridder or rudder' to separate the corn from the chaff'.[72] But it may simply refer to ensuring the field was clear of any remaining wheat; as two of the examples in the presentments involved not allowing horses or cattle on the fields until they had been 'ridd', either would make sense.

The fine or 'pain laid' for breaking these rules (between 1664 and 1689) varied widely from 10s. to a massive 39s. 11d. (in 1680) and it was not a gradual increase but seemingly random from year to year. Further research may uncover a correlation of high fines with dearth years or other more local issues. Over the course of this quarter century, only one record of rule-breaking has been found when in October 1682 'Francis Loachard retorneth Thomas Burton gent for breakinge the paine laid at the court against the keeping of cattle in the corne and pulse fields the paine being 20s'.

Few of the open fields are named as such in the presentments but admissions of tenants to land often mention common fields. As the fields contained many parcels of land, some of which changed hands regularly, they are recognisable by their many entries and their generic pattern of 'one acre in a field called Upper Wood Field' followed by 'two other acres in Upper Wood Field' for the same admission. Fields which have been identified as open fields with a fair degree of confidence are shown in Table 1 (overleaf) and a guide to their location in the parish is shown on the map (opposite).

This list is not exhaustive; there were others which were probably open fields but were not mentioned in the presentments as frequently and thus not as clearly defined. Park Field, near present day The Parks, still showed evidence of strips farmed by different tenants on the 1840 tithe map, but the area is not represented on the earlier *c.* 1755 map.[73] There was also Hassell Field, Claylands and one possible example of 'a common field called Seven Ridges' (so far unidentified). The lists of Edward Broughton's and George Vaughan's leased land, given in Appendix 1, shows the parcels of land they held in some of the open fields at the earlier date of 1568 and also offers more possibilities for open fields.

Parcels of land in open fields were governed by the same rules of ownership as any other customary land of the manor and they could be passed to the next generation. In October 1666, Katherine Wiles surrendered a cottage in New Inn with 'two acres in

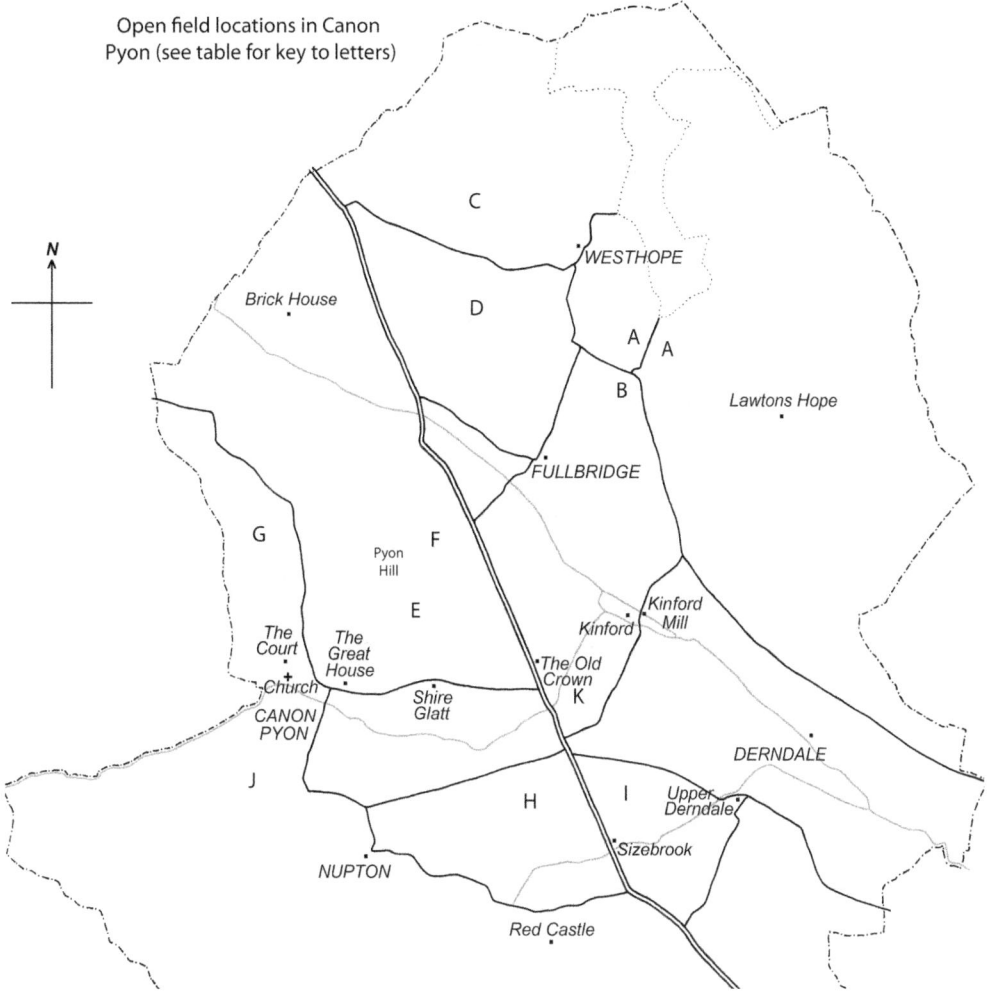

Location of 16th century open fields in Canon Pyon (A-K: see Table 1 for field names and details.)

a field called Old Field and two half acres in a field called Rie field' to her own use for her 'natural life' and then to the use of her son Oliver Prise and his wife Mary and the heirs of Oliver 'according to the custom of the manor'. Or the parcels could be sold; in the same year, Thomas Stephens bought from Richard Cox five acres of land 'more or less' in One Acre field in parcels of thirteen ridges, three butts, four butts and eight ridges and all were meticulously described in terms of where they lay in relation to other tenants' lands.

Westhope	Approximate Location	Map Ref
Cinders/Sinders	On the north side of the lane, on each side of Cinders Cottage	A
One Acre Field	On the south side of the lane opposite Cinders Cottage	B
Upper Wood Field	Land below Westhope Wood	C
Lower Wood Field	Between Upper Wood Field and Fulbridge	D

Canon Pyon	Approximate Location	Map Ref
Half Comer Field	On the South side of Pyon Hill	E
Old Field	On the north-west side of Pyon Hill	F
Stroud	To the east of Pyon Hill, stretching roughly from The Shrewd at King Pyon's border almost as far as Canon Pyon church	G
Ashill Field	Probably a large area between the Nupton Lane and Sizebrook and adjoining the road through the Canon Pyon. It is marked as Lower Pyons Field on Taylors c. 1755 map but by the 1840 tithe map, part of it was called Ashell Bush Field	H
Rye Field	On the opposite side of the road from Ashill Field	I
West Field	To the south-west of the church with the lane to the Buttas as its boundary	J
Upper and Lower Mill Fields	Only Mill Field is marked as a common field in the c. 1755 map, on the east side of the road near to where the brook flows beneath. By 1840 it is called Lower Mill Field but the location of Upper Mill Field is not known	K

Table 1. Open fields in the late 17th century (from manorial surrenders and admissions and presentments in HCA 4735, with reference to HARC BN81, Isaac Taylor's map of c. 1755)

By *c.* 1755, all of the open fields showed partial enclosure and they were extensively enclosed by 1840.[74] Not only was there a gradual change in the agricultural landscape but so too in the built environment and this is the subject of the next chapter.

NOTES

1. Bannister, Arthur Thomas, *The Cathedral Church of Hereford, its history and constitution*, Society for Promoting Christian Knowledge, Macmillan, 1924, p.126n.

2. Impropriation is the act of putting a benefice in the hands of a layman, who had to provide a cleric for the cure of souls whereas appropriation is the act of putting a benefice in the hands of a monastery or other spiritual organisation, who also had to provide a cleric for the cure of souls.

3. Aylmer Gerald and Tiller, John (eds.), *Hereford Cathedral – A History*, Hambledon Continuum, 2000, pp. 104-5, see also HCA 7001/2, manorial survey 1649.

4. HCA 7001/2, a contemporary or near contemporary copy, the original being held at Lambeth Palace.

5. Aylmer Gerald and Tiller, John (eds.), *Hereford Cathedral*, pp. 104-5.

6. HCA 7001/2.

7. Surrenders: at the end of a tenancy term or when a tenant died, or simply when a tenant gives up copyhold property, it is returned or 'surrendered' to the lord of the manor. A surrender is very often accompanied by an admission whereby the tenant is either re-admitted for a new term or his next named heir (or a completely new tenant) is admitted to the property for a new term.

8. For a useful explanation of the different rental systems, see Mildred Campbell's *The English Yeoman in the Tudor and Early Stuart Age*, Merlin Press Ltd, 1983, reproduced and printed in Great Britain by Whitstable Litho Ltd, Whitstable, Kent. (First published 1942 by Yale University Press), pp. 121-2.

9. Homage: in this example, the collective name for the assembled body of tenants at the manor court. It may also refer to the loyalty or obligation of the tenant to the lord of the manor.

10. Waifs: any property but usually animals, apparently ownerless, strays: wandering livestock. If not claimed by a customary time, often a year and a day, they became the lord's property.

11. Di Palma, Vittoria, *Wasteland – a History*, Yale University Press, 2014, p. 30. Two common rights not mentioned further: common of turbary – the right to cut turf or peat for fuel and common of piscary – the right to take fish from ponds, pools or streams.

Canon Pyon

12 HCA R1042.

13 HCA 4735. Pig yokes were wooden frames hung around the neck of the animal to stop them from breaking through fences; the rings through the nose allowed strays to be lead away to the pound or other enclosure.

14 HCA 4735, 20 October 1679 and 15 October 1685.

15 HCA 4720/1.

16 "… bote" was the right to take timber from the waste, or inferior common land, of the manor, for the repair of fences and hedges (heybote), houses (housebote), firewood (firebote), and tools of husbandry (ploughbote).

17 Clavinger: originally keeper of the keys or treasurer. Probably the person who gathered the fines and other monies and conveyed them to the Cathedral coffers.

18 Di Palma, *Wasteland...*, p.183.

19 Vallets were woodlands which were yearly felled, or sometimes land cleared of trees – see Cavill, Paul, *A New English Dictionary of English Field-Names*, English Place Name Society, 2018.

20 HCA 7001/1, 1568/9.

21 *Ibid.*, see also a copy of the tenures of Edward Broughton and George Vaughan in HARC R28/11599. Severalty: owning several parcels of land.

22 HCA 4720/2 and counterpart 4720/3.

23 HCA R1040 Court Roll, 1559 - 1595, with gaps.

24 TNA PROB 11/55/350, proved 21 August 1573.

25 HCA 4720/4, lease dated 31 Elizabeth.

26 HCA 3338, 22 July 1625, Broughton v. Dean & Chapter.

27 Siddons, Michael Powell (transcribed and edited by), *Visitation of Herefordshire 1634*, Harleian Society, London, 2002, p. 118.

28 George Vaughan: TNA PROB 11/68/20, 19 January 1584/5, Oliver Vaughan: TNA PROB 11/116/428, 17 November 1601.

29 HARC R28/11599.

30 HCA 7001/1 (with Woolhope in the second half of the volume).

31 *Ibid.*, see ffulbridge.

32 HCA 5237 and TNA C 3/337/16, 1624, Broughton v. Price.

33 HCA 3338, Inspeximus of award, Dean & Chapter v. Broughton.

34 TNA E 115/65/72.

35 See for example, STAC 8/61/32, STAC 8/68/23, STAC 8/76/4.

36 Ross, David, *Royalist, But ... Herefordshire in the English Civil War, 1640-51*, Logaston Press, 2012, pp. 35 & 128.

37 Clark, Andrew, *Brief Lives, chiefly of Contemporaries, set down by John Aubrey between the years 1669 & 1696*, edited from the Author's manuscript, Clarendon Press, 1898, p. 128, accessed June 2020 from https://archive.org/details/brieflives01clargoog
also ...soap ashes - similar to wood ash, processed into the more purified form of potash used in the making of soap. Once the lye had been extracted, the residue could be used as a manure; at this stage, the residue may have been called soap or soapers ashes. Extracted from: - https://www.british-history.ac.uk/no-series/traded-goods-dictionary/1550-1820/soap-ashes-soy (accessed June 2020).

38 HCA 7002/1/3, Acts of Office 1619-1630, f. 187 & 191.

39 HCA 3501.

40 HCA R1041.

41 HCA 4734.

42 HCA 4257.

43 Clergy of the Church of England Database: https://theclergydatabase.org.uk/.

44 HARC HD4/1/184, 16 May 1636.

45 HCA 4720/5 and 5a.

46 Siddons, Michael Powell (transcribed and edited by), *Visitation of Herefordshire 1634*, Harleian Society, London, 2002 (Lochard.)

47 *Ibid.* (Baskervile).

48 Cooke, Henry William, *Collections towards the History and Antiquities of the County of Hereford, in continuation of Duncumb's History*, London, 1886 (Hundred of Grimsworth), p.71.

49 HARC HD4/1/184, 16 May 1636.

50 HCA 7001/2, p. 5.

51 HCA 7001/2, p. 45.

52 *Hearth Tax Assessment for Michaelmas 1665 for Herefordshire and Comparison with the Hereford Militia Assessments of 1663*, transcribed by J. Hamden, accessed from The Woolhope Club web site, July 2020, for discussion on the 'bays' of a house and the variety within clergy houses, see also O'Day, Rosemary, *The English Clergy; the Emergence and Consolidation of a Profession, 1558-1642*, Leicester University Press, 1979, p. 179.

53 HCA 4720/8-9, leases.

54 TNA PROB 11/212/886, proved July 1650.

55 Money lent out on bond by the churchwardens to suitable parishioners to use for profit.

56 Confirmation of marriage settlement 30 Nov; U92/A/9/1, Canterbury Cathedral Archives.

57 http://www.historyofparliamentonline.org/volume/1660-1690/member/barneby-john-1621-1701, accessed March 2020.

58 London Metropolitan Archives; London, England; Reference Number: P69/AND2/A/002/MS06668/005, viewed on www.ancestry.co.uk, November 2020.

59 TNA C6/152/193 and C5/431/66.

60 HARC W70/3/1, lease, 20 April 1653.

61 TNA PROB 11/237/458, James Barrowe, 14 Oct 1654 & TNA PROB 11/211/349, Richard Barrowe, 14 February 1650.

62 Children named in George's will, 31 October 1665, TNA PROB 11/318/346.

63 www.innertemplearchives.org.uk, accessed May 2020.

64 D/EX1625, Berkshire Record Office. George's father was an auditor for the Exchequer and his brother Robert became Attorney General: - www.historyofparliamentonline.org.

65 Listed on www.findmypast.co.uk, Licences of the Vicar General of Archbishop of Canterbury, accessed May 2020.

66 Cooke, *Collections...*, p. 72.

67 TNA PROB 4/14997, will of Thomas Berrington who left his 'cozon' Katherine Somersett some of the money she owed him. Also HCA 5261/1-14 (dispute with Dean & Chapter 1711-13), particularly 13, recites a deed of 16 May 1666, intending marriage and outlining Katherines land holdings in Canon Pyon and Berkshire.

68 TNA PROB 11/515/292, 1710 (will of Charles Somersett, senior), TNA PROB 11/527/42, 1712 (will Charles Somersett, junior) and case papers in HCA 5261 (1-14), 1711-1713.

69 TNA PROB 11/598/41, 1724.

70 The strips were also called selions and were not uniform in size, butts were strips abutting roughly at right-angles to selions and were often shorter and part of an irregular shape.

71 All the examples in this section are from HCA 4735.

72 Britten, James, *Old Country and Farming Words: gleaned from agricultural books*, Trübner & Co., London, 1880. 'Riddering' is taken from William Ellis's *The Modern Husbandman*, London 1750. The 'ridder or rudder' is taken from *Dictionarium Rusticum* by J. Worlridge, 1681.

73 1840 tithe map: HARC BR39.

74 *Ibid.*, and HARC BN81 (Isaac Taylor's map).

2

Lost townships and changing names

The manor contained a number of small settlements, or townships, whose names are no longer in use but existed in the 17th century. It is likely that these lost places consisted of just one large farmstead or a cluster of cottages. Pre-1645 court rolls recorded the dealings of each township in turn and named the townships as 'Canon Pewne', 'Eston ffolyatt', 'Dernedall and Brocketown [or Brockton]', 'Esthope and ffulbridge', 'Westhope' and 'Nupton and Colwall'.[1] Of these, the place names which have fallen by the wayside are Eston ffolyatt, Brocketown, Esthope and Colwall; most are partnered with a place that still exists which offers a clue to their locations.

BROCKTON AND ESTON FOLYATT

Both of these are associated with Derndale in 17th century documents which usually named the place as either Derndall, Derndall and Brockton, or Derndall alias Eston Folyatt (with various spellings of Derndall and Brockton).

Isaac Taylor's map of *c.* 1755 is not particularly detailed in the Derndale area, showing Upper Derndale 'floating' in an empty space, though there is a little more for Lower Derndale. The map does indicate that the 'Upper' and 'Lower' nomenclature were in use by this date but that the big house currently at 'Lower' Derndale was not yet built.

In 1624/5 John Gardner paid William and Ann Cooke £70 for a messuage with a barn, stable, garden, orchard, forty-two acres of land, ten acres of meadow and ten acres of pasture in 'Derndall alias Easton Falyatt'.[2] By 1649, Oliver Gardner held 'one messuage in Derndall called Eston ffoliatt'.[3]

The property was still in the occupation of the Gardners in 1673, when William Gardner married Elizabeth Fletcher. It was common practice to settle property on a couple and any future heirs; William and Elizabeth's marriage settlement included:

Lost townships and changing names

> ... the messuage or tenement with appurtenances situate in Derndall als Easton Falyatt within the parish of Canon Pyon, which Oliver Gardner [William's father] has purchased from William Cook, gent, with 42 acres of arable land, 7 acres of meadow and pasture, and the third part of one parcel of ground called Hewing Grove in Derndall als Easton Falyatt', for the life of William Gardner, Elizabeth his wife and their children.[4]

However, the first reference which specifically links Eston Foliott with Upper Derndale is contained in a manorial surrender of land by Charles and Catherine Somerset, to the use of Catherine's mother and stepfather, the Barnebys. Some of their land was excepted from the surrender and this included customary lands and tenements 'situate in Upp[er] Dearndall als Eston ffoliott' on 15 January 1666/7.[5] Currently, this is the earliest reference to the use of 'Upper' Derndale.

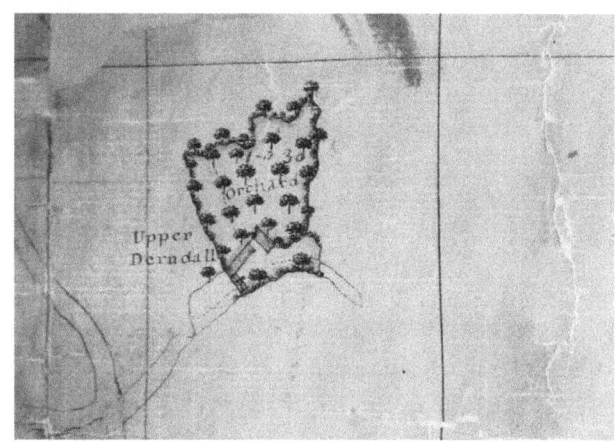

Upper Derndall *c.* 1755, from Isaac Taylor's map. The junction at the bottom left of the image represents the small lane which leads to Upper Derndale from the main road (HARC BN81).

Brocketown (variably spelt Brockton, Bockton, Brockedon) also appears in deeds with Derndale. In 1605, the messuage and lands called Dearndall and B[r]ockton in Cannon Pewne was then or late in the tenure of Rowland Gardyner, yeoman; clearly this family had strong connections with Derndale during the 17th century. The exact location of Brockton is not clear but if Eston Folyatt is associated with Upper Derndale, then it would be logical to surmise that Brockton would be closer to Lower Derndale near the brook. Brockton's name most probably originates from the Old English *brōc* + *tūn*, meaning 'farmstead by a brook' which complements this theory.[7]

That Derndale as a whole was an ancient settlement cannot be doubted; Richard Baily of Derndale leased the site of the 'manor of Derndale with all buildings and lands pertaining' for the annual rent of seven marks from the Dean and Chapter in around 1398.[8] Whether or not Derndale was actually ever a manor in its own right is unknown as no manorial records appear to have survived but it was certainly a Dean and Chapter property for a substantial amount of time.⁹

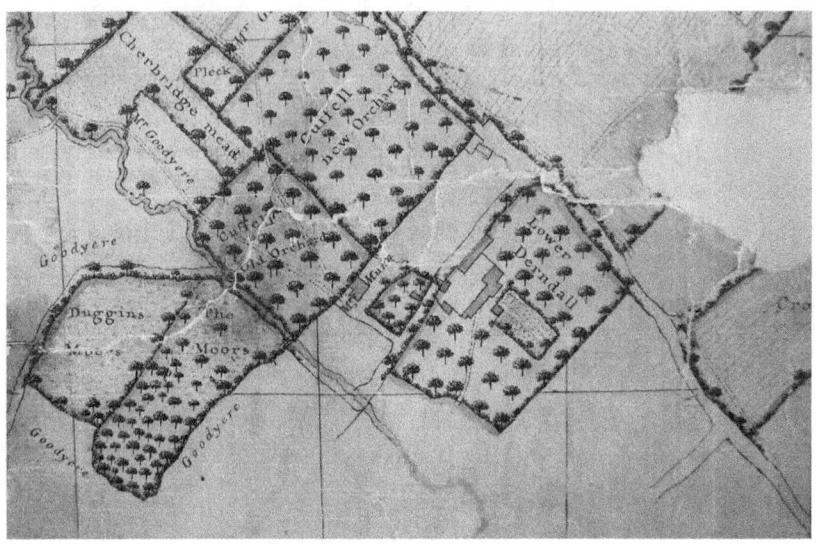

Lower Derndall in *c.* 1755, taken from Isaac Taylor's map. The brook can be seen at the top left of image, travelling down to the lower centre towards Wellington (HARC BN81).

Derndale was mentioned (in a bundle of Canon Pyon manor leases) from 1560 to 1631, the tithes from which were to be paid to the lessee of the manor, but they do not mention Brockton or Eston Folyatt. In these leases, Derndale's tenant is named as Thomas Apeynam/A Beynham (between 1560 and 1589) and he paid the annual rent of thirteen quarters of wheat. Thomas had signed the lease for 29 years, in place of his father John Apeynon.¹⁰ In 1590, Thomas's daughter Ann and her husband William Smith took the lease for their lives and the lives of their son Richard and his wife Ann.¹¹

The next lease in this bundle is dated much later at 1663 and is a 21-year lease to Thomas Berrington. However, the 1649 survey of the manor records the lease of the messuage of Derndale being held by him since 1617 'with all lands, messuages, leasowes, pastures … with the appurtenances'. We will meet Thomas Berrington again, in the chapter on maintaining law in the parish. Born around 1585, he married Eleanor Willoughbie in 1609 in a somewhat dramatic fashion. By the time he died (between 1666 and 1668) the couple were living at Little Pyon.¹²

The Chapter Act book of 1616 confirms this Derndale lease and adds that the premises were lately in the tenure or occupation of Thomas Blunt, and that the lease was for the term of the lives of Thomas and Eleanor Berrington and James their son.[13] A useful description of the messuage and lands at Derndale survives in the 1649 survey:

One messuage conteyning five bayes	5 bayes
2 barnes and one beast house conteyning	7 bayes
1 garden and one orchard cont	1 acre 2 roods
1 cottage conteyning	2 bayes
Arable land belonging to the said cottage and	
1 ridge of old land conteyninge	3 acres
Arable land in severall fields conteyning	95 [acres?]
And five and twentie acres of pasture divided into small p[ar]cells as followeth vizt:	
The high Moores conteyning	4 acres
Wall Green conteyning	4 acres
Little moore conteyning	1 acre 2 roods
The Marsh marsh and hoppyward	5 acres
One close called Vuthills cont	4 acres
The New Tyndings cont	2 acres 2 roods
One p[ar]cell inclosed in Millfield cont	1 acre
One p[ar]cell inclosed in Harrill hill cont	1 acre
One p[ar]cell inclosed in Horfell field cont	2 acres
And of meadow ground sixteene acres and one roode as followeth vizt.	
The ffrensh meadow cont	2 acres
The Berge moore cont	4 acres 2 roods
One little meadow by Bar'sby Croft cont	5 acres 2 roods
The broad meadow cont	4 acres[14]

In 1672, a new 21-year lease was agreed with Thomas Berrington, grandson of the above Thomas but by 1676, Richard Witherston had taken over the lease and the Witherston family continued as leaseholders well into the 18th century.[15] Being a holder of various lands throughout Herefordshire, it is unlikely that the Witherstons lived at Canon Pyon and probably sub-let the property as the Berringtons had done before them.

During the second half of the 17th century, tanning works were begun at Lower Derndale. No mention is made in the 1649 survey and the earliest record discovered, as yet, is in March 1683/4 when William Pyfinch leased a messuage, tan house and two orchards in Derndale to William Hornblow of 'Deirndall', tanner, for 50 years. As part of the terms of his lease, Hornblow was to pay any taxes due and 'repair, maintain and sustain the messuage, tanhouse, tan pits and barne, hedges, ditches, fences and not cut down, sell or dispose of any fruit trees'.[16] The tannery therefore seems to have been well established by this date.

The property stayed in the hands of the Pyfinch family until around 1712, when John Duggan, tanner, and Anne his wife released the messuage lying in Lower Dearndall 'lately purchased of William Pifinch' to his youngest son Richard Duggan. John and Anne kept a part of the land for themselves and for Anne's future security:

> John Duggan and Anne his wife to accept to themselves … that part of the garden that adjoins to the tanhouse and the house wherein the said John Duggan do now inhabit and dwell from the roadway to the east corner of the barn of the said demised premises, straight over to the little lane adjoining to the bigger orchard belonging to the said demised premises and that part of the garden shall remain to the said John Duggan and Anne, their heirs and assigns…. And the said Richard Duggan do covenant to and with the said Anne Duggan that she shall have the two little romes for her use on the west side of the said demised premises if she has occasion to make use of them, during the term of her natural life, the one rome adjoining to the chimney and the other adjoining to that.[17]

An interesting connection can be made in an indenture of 1707, relating to John Duggan's cottage, whereby William Pyfinch (and others) 'bargained and sold to Charles Tucker… the cottage where Thomas Trillo lived and his mother, now in the occupation of John Duggan, situated in Dearndall'.[18] The Trillo cottage can be traced to a mortgage to secure £30 in an indenture dated 10 April 1655 between Thomas Trillo of Dearndall, yeoman, Frances Trillo his mother and John Phillips of Canon Pyon, yeoman. The tenement or cottage where Thomas Trillo lived was in Derndale.[19] Two years earlier, Thomas's parents William and Frances Trylloe secured £24 for a 'little close of land containing by estimate half an acre in Dearndall in Canon Pyon, lying between the highway and the orchard of Rowland Gardner', probably the same piece of land which was recorded in the 1649 survey of the manor which he held 'freely' with a cottage in Dernedall and Brockton for the yearly rent of 1s. 4d.[20]

In 1717, the Duggans released the property to the Munn family…'except part of the garden', probably the same part as John and Anne Duggan had held for themselves.[21] Another look at the image of Lower Derndale from the *c.* 1755 map shows a building with 'Mr Munn' written by it. There is a similarity between the Duggan's description of their part of the garden and the map image (bearing in mind the difference of 40 years). This cottage could therefore conceivably date to 1649 or earlier. Many years later, in 1772, Aspasia Munn left the reversion of her 'freehold messuage tenement etc, situate in Lower Dearndale' to Thomas Jay, tanner of Dearndale, and his heirs forever.[22]

To summarise, although the exact location of Brockton is unclear and pre-17th century research might be enlightening, it is certainly connected with Lower Derndale

Lost townships and changing names

and the brook, whereas Eston Folyatt is almost certainly the former name of Upper Derndale. Eston Folyatt is likely to be connected with earlier Foliot family members who had connections with Hereford Cathedral.

COLWALL

Colwall was always associated with Nupton in manorial records between 1563 and 1640. The Institute for Place Name Studies interprets the meaning of the place name Colwall, near Malvern, as 'col (Old English) coal, especially charcoal' and 'wella (Anglian) a spring, a stream'. *The Dictionary of English Place Names* proposes the same Old English components but meaning 'cool spring or stream'.[23] Although Canon Pyon's Colwall may not have the same origin of meaning, it might nevertheless provide us with a clue to begin the search. Isaac Taylors map of *c.* 1755 shows two fields, Lower Coal Pits and Coal Pits Orchard, on opposite sides of the lane between Nupton and the Buttas; there was also a cottage and garden close by which no longer exists. This site is on the side of a slope and not far from the stream earlier known as 'Welsh brook'.[24] However, further work on earlier records would help with locating Colwall as there is little evidence in 17th century documents apart from the name. Even a terrier of 1569 only mentions 'Colpets' the field, not Colwall.[25]

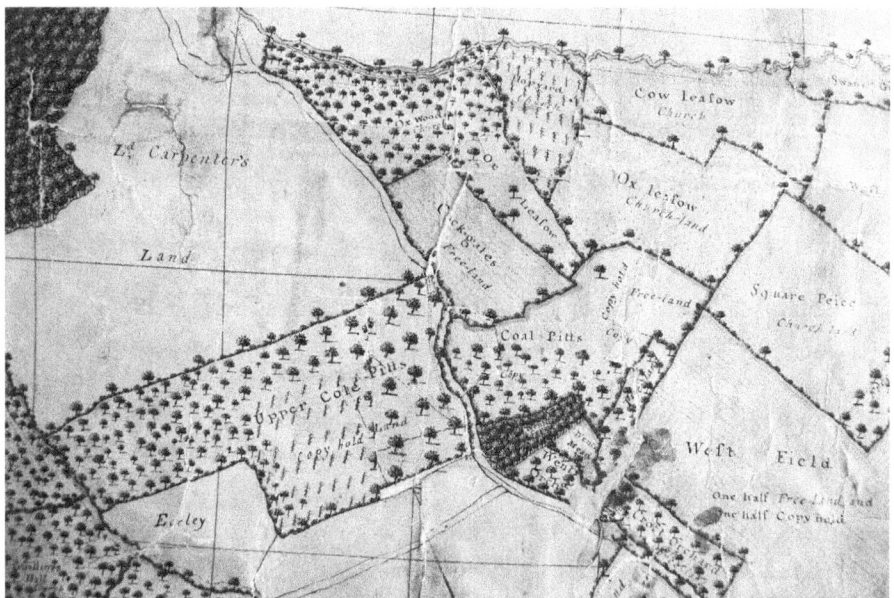

Detail from Isaac Taylor's map of *c.* 1755 showing Coal Pitts and Upper Cole Pitts fields on opposite sides of the lane. Nupton is off the map on the lower right of the image (HARC BN81).

ESTHOPE/EASTHOPE

Esthope was associated with Fulbridge in manorial records between 1563 and 1640 but whereas Fulbridge still exists, the name of Esthope has disappeared.

A terrier of the demesne lands of the manor describes the Canon Vallet as 'lying between Byrles Comon on the west and Esthops Hill on the east'.[26] The vallet is on Westhope Hill and though the later map of Isaac Taylor shows Westhope Common to the east, it likely that Esthope was even further east than this and became incorporated into Westhope common by *c.* 1755. The terrier, dated 1569, describes Esthope as 'William Cnapps [Knapp's] copyhold' and on it stood a mease house containing four rooms in which William lived, a barn with three rooms and an 'ote' barn of two rooms. With it was forty acres of arable, a ley, rough land and two acres of vallet, all lying to the northwest of the mease.[27] Other lands are listed but only the above seem to be associated with Easthope.

William probably had a son or nephew named Henry who had inherited the customary land from him for at the manor court of 16 October 1618 it was presented that Henry Knapp had died since the last court and had held 'one messuage, two virgates and about one nook of customary land with appurtenances in Esthope'. A heriot of the best beast was due to the lords - in this case, one brown coloured ox - and it was decided that his son, another William Knappe, was his heir.[28]

There is a large time gap to the next reference to Easthope; in 1663 a surrender dated 4 August (and presented at court 26 April 1664), by Elizabeth Knapp, John Digges and Dina his wife was for:

> a messuage called Eastehope, and all barnes, stables and all other out houses with the appu[r]tenances there belongingwith on[e] grove or toft all w[i]ch lands are now in the poss[ession] of Elizabeth Knapp, to have again to Elizabeth Knapp for her life and afterwards to Richard Coxe of Ledbury clothyer and Anne his wife and to the suis of Richard according to the custom of the manor... [for the] chief rent of 20s.

Just two years later on 17 April 1666, Elizabeth Knapp's death was presented to the court and Richard Coxe was found to be the next heir to the copyhold estate of one messuage and two yards of land.[29]

In amongst the manorial court surrenders, admissions and other documents is an undated paper entitled 'Quote how the land which Hugh Smallman bought of M[a]ster Richard Cox of Ledbury and of John Digges lieth bounden'. This mentions land of Ralph Darnell lying next to 'all those severall p[ar]sells [of arable] land belonging to a messuage in easthope late the lands of William Knap w[i]ch sd p[ar]cell of lands by est[imation] 4 acres'.[30] Ralph Darnell purchased Lawton's Hope in 1647[31] so the paper probably dates from between 1647 and 1670, the latter being when Richard Cox's will was proved.[32]

Soon after 1670, the holding at Easthope became occupied by the Bennet family. A surrender and admission at the manor court of 31 March 1674 records:

> To this court came Richard Bennett sen Joan/Johanne his wife and Henry Beaven in their own persons and surrendered one messuage called Easthope and twelve acres of arable land belonging to it and two meadow closes containing three acres and six acres of pasture with all and singular the appurtenances within the manor. For the use and behoof of Richard Benney and Richard Bennet jun[ior] and Lawrencia Benny and the heirs of Richard Bennet according to custom. Admitted and Richard Benny made fealty. Rent 2s 9d. Fine £6.[33]

Note the alternating use of the 't' and 'y' in the surname Bennet; this also occurs in some other manorial documents. Joan Bennett was formerly the wife of James Beavan and Henry may have been her son. In the 1649 manorial survey, Richard Bennett, then of Hereford, held a mill and a nook of customary land in the manor, in the right of his wife Joane formerly the wife of James Beavan. By the time of a suit roll dated 1677 for 'the township of Eastehope and fulbridge', William Bull, Richard Benny and Wrangford Hille were listed as residents so the Bennys/Bennets were still there.[34]

Almost twenty years later, the will of John Fletcher of Lawton's Hope was proved (1696). He bequeathed to his wife Elizabeth all his estates, including the 'rights and titles to the copyhold lands of the farm commonly called Bennetts Farm, adjoining Lawton's Hope'.[35] It is likely that the name of Easthope had fallen out of use and the farmstead had become known by the family's name; certainly by 1706 Easthope is no longer mentioned with Fulbridge in the suit rolls.

Finally, in a manorial court roll of 1720, Elizabeth Fletcher's niece Elizabeth Harcourt requested to be admitted to land lying in Lawtons Hope 'formerly the land of Richard Bennett'.[36] In summary, the farmstead at Easthope was in the occupation of the Knapp family in the late 16th century and it then passed through the Digges, Coxe and Bennett families, finally becoming absorbed into the lands of Lawton's Hope by the end of the 17th century.

SMETHLEY

This settlement was associated with the reputed manor of Lawtons Hope and was spelt Smethley or Smithley, sometimes referred to as Smirley. It was an ancient place, being listed in a manorial rental of *c*. 1400 as Smethely.³⁷ Not a great deal of information has been uncovered from 17th century records, but it is believed to have been located in the level area on top of the hill above Lawton's Hope. The 1649 survey mentions that the inhabitants of Smythley owed suit of court; they must attend the manorial court along with those of the other townships. At this date it was held by Francis Pember, esquire, who 'holdeth freely the Towneshippe of Smythley of the Lord of this manor.' He did not know of any other service due to the lords of the manor but paid the yearly rent of 1ˡⁱ 3ˢ 3ᵈ ob [£1 3s. 3 ½ d.]³⁸

In a 1676 interrogatory (preparatory questions for completing a glebe terrier), there was a question about Smethley:

> Do you not know or are you not pursuaded that the Township of Smeathley ye grounds thereunto belonging that the teith of it belongs to the vicar... can you conceive of this ground called Smeathley?

The answer was that the vicar had the tithes and 'the lands are by estimacion 30 or 40 acres'.³⁹ As with Colwall, little documentary evidence remains of Smethley by the 17th century, though the two items above suggest that it was still regarded as a township.

LITTLE PYON/THE BRICK HOUSE

Not a township but a farmstead, the house known as The Brick House still exists but was previously associated with a place called Little Pyon.

The two names appear together in a number of 17th century documents. The first example is an interrogatory of 1676 to the churchwardens, required from time to time in order to complete a terrier of the glebe lands, tithes and profits belonging to the vicarage of Canon Pyon. They were asked if they knew of any 'ground about the Brickhouse or Little Pewn where the teith is likely to cause controversie between the vicar [and] the farmer of the great teiths'.⁴⁰ Curiously, the churchwardens did not answer this question.

The second example is from Thomas Berrington's will, proved in 1687, in which he leaves to his son Thomas

> ... £20 a year for his maintenance, to be taken from rents and profits of the messuage at Little Pyon which I now inhabit called and known by the name of Brick House, until he shall reach the age of 21 yrs.⁴¹

This, in particular, suggests that Little Pyon was a piece of ground or area on which was built the Brick House.

Lost townships and changing names

In the same year, and quite possibly in response to the death of Thomas Berrington, a disagreement involving a seat in the parish church resulted in a church court case.[42] Such disagreements were fairly commonplace at the court; the seating position in church conveyed a family's all important social status in the community and the rights to certain pews were often attached to particular properties in the parish. Custom also played a huge role in the right to ownership and if it were to be broken, for example if the family left the parish or did not use the seat for some time, the right could be lost forever. In a similar fashion, the rights to an aisle or chapel in an ancient church must be proved by continuous occupation *and reparation* 'from time immemorial'.[43]

Thomas's widow, Mary Berrington, was defending her right to a particular seat in the parish church. Dated 1 July 1687, it was proposed:

> ... that the seat now in controversy for these 10: 20: 30: 40: 50: and 60 years last past and before and since and from time to time dureing all the time whereof the memory of man is not to the contrary has been always accompted reputed and taken to belong and appertain to a certain ancient messuage or tenement within the parish of Canon Pyon aforesaid commonly called and known by the name of Little Pyon wherein the aforesaid Mary Berrington now dwells and inhabitts And the owners or occupiers of the aforesaid messuage ore tenement and the lands thereunto belonging dureing all the time aforesaid have by themselves or servants constantly as often as they came to the parish church of Canon Pyon aforesaid to hear divine service and sermon upon Sundays and holy days satt in the seat aforesaid peaceably and quietly in right of the aforesaid messuage or tenement and have dureing all the time aforesaid constantly rep[ai]red the same as often as occasion required noe person or persons whatsoever claiming or p[re]tending any right title or interest thereto save only the own[er]s and occupiers of the messuage or tenement afores[ai]d untill the aforesd John Colville and Mrs Scilly now dec[ease]d some few years since p[re]tended an interest therein and intruded into the s[ai]d seat and new built the same as he p[re]tends.... All which by the confession of him the s[ai]d Mr Colville was done without any lawful authority.

John Colville was claiming the right to the seat but Mary Berrington claimed a far more ancient right.

Witnesses for the case were interviewed and they were chosen for their longevity of age and memory:

- George Whetstone, aged 54, husbandman of Wellington (for the last 4 years but born in Canon Pyon)
- Thomas Jones of, aged 70 or thereabouts, yeoman of Canon Pyon (for the last 40 years but born in Trwerne, Radnorshire)

Canon Pyon

- Richard Jones, aged 64, yeoman of Canon Pyon, (where he was born and had lived for the most part since birth), parish clerk for the last 20 years or above
- Hugh Smallman, aged 64, husbandman of Canon Pyon, (where he was born and had lived for the most part since birth)
- William Knapp, aged 64, husbandman of Canon Pyon (where he had lived for the space of 60 years or thereabouts, born in the parish of All Saints, Hereford)
- William Botchett, aged 55 or thereabouts, water miller of Eaton Bishop (where he had lived for the space of 2 years and before in the parish of Bridge Sollers for 8 years, born in the parish of Kings Pyon).

From their statements a picture of the situation emerges. John Colville had married Anne Celey, heir and daughter of Richard and Catherine Celey and when Ann died, the properties and lands in Canon Pyon passed to him. Mary Berrington was the widow of Thomas Berrington and the daughter of Sir John Barnaby and she lived at Little Pyon.

The chapel or chancel containing 'the seat in controversy' was known variously as Little Pyon Chapel, Mr Berrington's Chapel, or St Michael's Chapel. It was 12ft x 10ft and part of the wall of the church. Enclosed from the main body of the church by wainscot and rails, it contained a large pew and one or more benches. The Berrington family had sat on the pew for divine service and sermons and the servants 'and young people' sat on the benches 'without disturbance' for many years. There was a coat of arms of the Berrington family painted on the east wall of the chapel, described as 'being 3 white grey hounds with garlands about their necks'. This had been removed when the church was whitewashed a few years previously but may have been re-painted. The parish clerk believes that two children of Thomas Berrington the elder were buried in the chapel.

In the time of the 'unhappy wars' (Civil Wars) the Berrington family went to live at Monmouth and left the Little Pyon estate in the hands of tenants. It was alleged that Catherine Celey had a pew made and put in the chapel during that time. William Botchett believed that his father, a joiner, may have made the pew as he was apprenticed to his father, worked with him for many years and thus recognised his work. The original pew may have been removed. For some time following, the Celey family then used the pew for divine service and sermons 'without disturbance' and since Catherine Celey's death, John Colvile continued to do so.

Later, Thomas Berrington the elder did 'give them some disturbance and forbid them to sit there' but they continued to do so (they may or may not have had permission). About a year before the court case, the parish clerk had unlocked the church and allowed

Lost townships and changing names

Thomas Berrington the younger and Anthony Chambers inside, the latter putting 'a lock on the seat in controversy' and informed Mr Colville not to come to the seat anymore. The seat had remained locked ever since, except when the Berringtons came to sit there for divine service.

There are, of course, slight differences in the witnesses' details, depending on who had recruited which witness; they all, however, declared that they supported both parties and wished only for 'right to prevail'.

The Little Pyon estate had, from the 13th century, supported a prebendal stall in Hereford Cathedral which had been founded on a rent charge of £2 7s. 8d.[44] The prebend was also known as Piona Parva or Pionia Stephani and is likely to be relevant to the origin of the chapel in Canon Pyon church.[45]

The Berrington family had lived at Little Pyon at least from the first decade of the 17th century. Recorded in the Heralds' Visitations of 1634, the 'Arms of Berrington of Little Peon' were *'sable three greyhounds courant in pale Argent each gorged with a collar studded and ringed a bordure Gules, in chief a crescent for a difference'*.[46] Even without knowledge of armorial bearings, the three greyhounds with collars are recognisable from the witness's description.

Arms of Berrington of Little Peon, as described in the Herald's Visitation of 1634.
The description of those in the church did not include a crescent (which denotes a second son) so this may or may not have been present. In colour, the greyhounds would have been white (*argent* is silver) on a black background with a red border to the shield. Colour must have been used to paint the arms in the church as the walls were periodically whitewashed, rendering white greyhounds invisible (unless they were simply painted using black outlines).
Digital artwork by Phil Smith, 2022.

Also included in the Visitations volume are those who had attempted to have arms recorded with the Herald but without success:

> Wee whose Names are here underwritten beeing lawfully summoned before the Haralds of Armes Deputed for the County of Hereford to make p[roo]fe of our Armes and Gentry doe hereby Acknowledg ourselves to have noe right or Inter[e]st in Armes or Gentry…

Canon Pyon

Amongst the list from Grimsworth hundred is one Richard Selley. Could this be Catherine Celey's husband and an indication of an earlier attempt to enter the realm of the gentry? As the 'recognised badge of the gentry', arms were a crucial step in this process.[47] The Celey/Seley family (spelt variably Sylly, Silley, Seley, Celey) had been in Canon Pyon for a number of generations.

Regarding the messuage or estate of Little Pyon, there is one revealing section in the statement of George Whetstone ('this deponent' in the following statement) who states:

> ... that there was an ancient messuage or tenement within the p[ar]ish of Canon Pyon called Little Pyon, part of which was taken down before this dep[onen]t's remembrance and the rest within twenty years last past and near the place where the said ancient messuage stood was erected a house or tenement called the Brick House by some of the Beringtons ffamily as this dep[onen]t has heard but the said Brick house was built beyond this dep[one]nt's remembrance.

So the Little Pyon house had disappeared by the 1660s but the Brick House was built close by sometime before this (according to George Whetstone).

On the tithe map of 1840, a field called Little Pyon is located a short distance to the south of the Brick House but on Isaac Taylor's map of *c.* 1755, a field named Little Pyon Field is in a completely different position, immediately north of Brick House. The exact location of the earlier house at Little Pyon is thus not yet identified.

THE NEW INN/NEW END

The stretch of main road through the village, roughly from Crown House to Sizebrook, is known as New End. It has been said locally that the village originally centred on the church but when stone was being quarried at Westhope, workers and carriers would stop at the inn along the main road. Eventually a new settlement developed which became known as New End, being about ¾ to 1 mile from the church. However, it is the relationship between New End and a place called the New Inn that is the subject of this section.

The two places names seem to have been used for the same region during the 19th century and this is where we need to start. Beginning with the census returns, in 1841 there were seventeen families living at New Inn, with occupations such as schoolmistress, agricultural labourer, blacksmith, mason, tailor, shoemaker and an individual of independent means. Sizebrook and the Nags Head had their own entries and there is no mention of New End.

In the 1851 census return, there were also seventeen families at New Inn with a similar mix of occupations. Many of the families were the same as those in 1841 but also included were a wheelwright, a stonemason and a 'loader at mill'. The Nags Head and Sizebrook entries were separate but there was a New Inn S Brook (Sizebrook?) and a New Inn Brook entry. There were also some entries for 'Highway' in between the Crown and New Inn.

By 1861, there were no entries for New Inn but eighteen households for New End, with many of the same family names that were at New Inn in 1841 and 1851. So at some time between 1851 and 1861, the name New Inn appears to have fallen out of use and was replaced by New End (at least by the census enumerators).[48]

From 1813, parish registers often gave the residence of individuals (in general terms such as Canon Pyon, Westhope, Nupton or Derndale) and between this date and 1836 a number of baptisms were recorded of children of New Inn residents, some of the families being recognisable in the later census returns. So we can safely assume that New Inn was a region of Canon Pyon, apparently along the main road through the village, but how did it get this name?

In 1790, an indenture between Thomas Walwyn, gent, and Mary Wenland of Warham conveys to the latter:

> ... several messuages or tenements and farms commonly called The New Inn and Kinford farms in Canon Pyon and then in the occupation of Thomas Walwyn Hereford, Joseph Oven and John Tunstal together with the mill buildings, several pieces or parcels of arable land, meadow pasture and woodground ...[49]

Further back in time, in June 1724, another deed gives us more information. This time a Bargain and Sale between Edmund Adys of Lyde Arundel, gentleman, and Richard Poole of Barrs Court, Hereford, gentleman, with Francis Woodhouse of Mordeford, gentleman, for The New Inn at Canon Pyon, and lands belonging. The main property is described as:

> ... the New Inn, situate at a place called The New Inn wherein George Knapp doth now dwell and hath for 3 and 20 years last past, along with adjoining appurtenances, estimated 4 acres.[50]

The New Inn was thus also a building, with four acres, as well as a region or area. Was it a farm or an inn, or both? As well as the four acres, substantial amount of other land was part of this sale, summarised below:

- About 20 acres in Half Comers Field (Yew Tree Gobbett 7 acres, 3 acres belonging to Kinford, 3 acres heretofore Gayleys land and 6 acres in several parcels in the same field)
- 16 acres in Hassell Field (a common field) in several parcels
- 8 ½ acres in Claylands
- 1 ½ acres late Gayleys land and 5 acres in the same field in several parcels
- 8 parcels in Rye Field (a common field), c. 7 ½ acres
- 1 acre called Long Fryday
- 6 parcels in Lower Millfield, c. 7 acres
- 3 parcels in Upper Millfield, c. 9 ½ acres
- ⅛ acre in Upper Millfield where smith's shop lately erected, together with smith's shop
- Closes called The New Enclosure, the New Meadow, the Barn Meadow
- A meadow near Scarlett's
- A parcell in Lower Mill Field
- A medow called The Canvas
- 3 closes on Perry Tree Plock
- Close called Foulbridge Green
- A pasture called Oxe Leasow
- Rough woodland called Coxhill
- A parcel of land called [Bl]anchs Acres enclosed out of Half Comer Field

…and also:

> … a smith's shop and tenements etc belonging to it, in the last 23 yrs, lying in the parish of Canon Pyon and now in the possession of George Knapp and James Preece tenants or undertenants and heretofore several times bought and purchased and from several persons by Eward Adys in Canon Pyon, and cottage or dwelling now in the possession of Charles Andrews.

The many parcels of lands are typical of deeds in Canon Pyon at this date and earlier. Some of these fields can be identified on the 1840 tithe map, some possibly on the c. 1755 map and many are in the area established as the New Inn.[51] The earlier map provides another clue as it marks New Inn at the location where the Crown public house once stood, now Crown House.

This is at the northernmost end of the area established as the New Inn. Was mapmaker Isaac Taylor indicating this as the beginning of the area of New Inn or was he labelling the buildings (which seems more likely)? There are other references to New Inn further along the road on the same map including New Inn Meadow which is

Lost townships and changing names

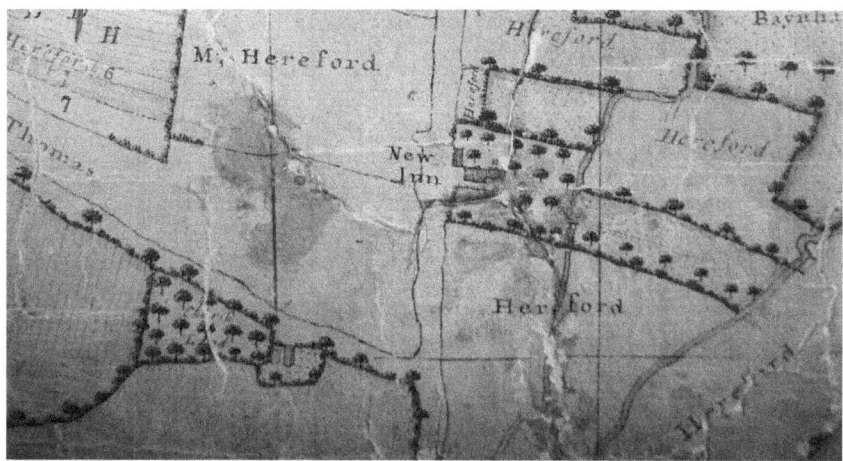

New Inn marked on the map of *c.* 1755 at the location of present day Crown House. The road to the church is at the lower left of the image (HARC BN81).

marked on the land now occupied by the new houses at Pyon Close. On the left side of the road between the Nags Head and Derndale are several New Inn fields marked on the 1840 tithe map. Confusingly, on the same 1840 map, New Inn is marked on the Kinford lane, close to the Nags Head.

In 1724, at the time of the deed previously mentioned, George Knapp had been the tenant of The New Inn and a smith's shop for twenty-three years. The landowner Edmund Adys was from Pipe or Lyde Arundel although he had held land in Canon Pyon from at least 1693 when he was in disagreement with John Colvile over land in the parish (probably the same Colvile who had contested the Berrington's pew at the church in 1687).[52] In 1717, seven years before Adys sold The New Inn, an abstract of his estates was recorded by the Forfeited Estates Commission, he being a 'popish recusant'. Along with lands in Pipe, Adys's statement included:

> All that freehold messuage or tenem[en]t with the buildings gardens orchards and severall lands closes meadows pastures and severall parcels of arable and ffeild lands and grounds unto the said messuage or tenement belonging with their app[ur]ten[an]ces called by the name of the New Inne ffarme formerly Gayles farme or tenem[en]t now in the holding of George Napp scituate lyeing and being in the village or hamlett of New Inne and in the p[ar]ish of Canon Pyon in the County of Hereford and alsoe two and twenty acres and an half or thereabouts of arable land held by me by lease for one and twenty years under the Custos and Vicars of the Cathedrall Church of Hereford used or enjoyed with the said ffarme and nowe alsoe in the holding of the said George Napp lyeing also in the p[ar]ish of Canon Pyon in the County of Hereford all which

> said freehold land and ffarme and alsoe the two and twenty acres and a halfe of arable leaseland as aforesaid for severall years past and are now in poss[ess]ion and occupation of the s[ai]d George Napp as tenant at will to me the said Edmund Adys or those clamieing under me at the yearly rent of £40.[53]

The rent for the 'two and twenty acres and a half of arable land' payable to the Custos and Vicars was 'ten bushells of good wheat and a couple of hens yearly'. This land is probably the Priests Close and twenty-four acres which was granted to Adys by the Custos and Vicars Choral in 1700 and which had formerly been granted to Richard Gayley.[54] This document confirms the New Inn as an area or 'hamlet' and moreover, gives us new information; that the farm was formerly known as Gayles (or Gayley's) farm. The land was freehold and at the time of the statement it was mortgaged to a Mr John Harris.

A 19th century abstract of title to 'freehold estates called New Inn or Kinford Farm and to Kinford otherwise Kennett Mill ...' cites an indenture of 1705 between Adys and Harris.[55] The statement 'New Inn *or* Kinford Farm' (my italics) could be misleading. Although connected in deeds and they may well have been part of the same holding (land along the main roadway through Canon Pyon is known to have belonged to Kinford), there is no other evidence to suggest that New Inn Farm and Kinford Farm were one and the same. Kinford is not far away from New Inn – just across two fields – but it is not in the area between the Crown and Sizebrook.

Returning to the 17th century, references to the New Inn are few and relate to the area rather than the farm. For example, 'the road leading from Derndall to the New Inn' in a 1683 manorial court record, and scouring of the watercourses from 'the ffortre [near the church] to the New Inn' in a 1680 court record, both of these being different points on the road between the Crown and Sizebrook.[56] The likelihood of there being an inn at New Inn in the 17th century is very high but did the New Inn/Gayley's farm fulfil this role and was this the Crown Inn or another, yet unknown building?

The final clue is gleaned from the court case involving the vicar Thomas Bedford in 1686. Thomas Abraham gave evidence against Bedford and Ann Herring and his occupation was given as 'inn-holder' (see Chapter 4). He reported that Bedford and Herring behaved in 'a familiar manner' and that he 'hath often seene them togeather at this dep[onent]'s house scituate in Canon Pyon being a publick house'. In 1687, Abraham appears in the manorial court records being admitted to land in Canon Pyon and he was described as 'of the New Inn'.[57] Thus there was a public house at the New Inn at this date with Thomas Abraham as publican; its probable location was at the site of the Crown Inn.

SOME LOST HOUSES

Isaac Taylor's map shows a number of houses along the lane between Shire Glatt and the church. These include 'Baynhams House', 'Knaps House', 'Moors House' and also 'Vaut tree' near the vicarage. These houses no longer exist but were they there in the 17th century?

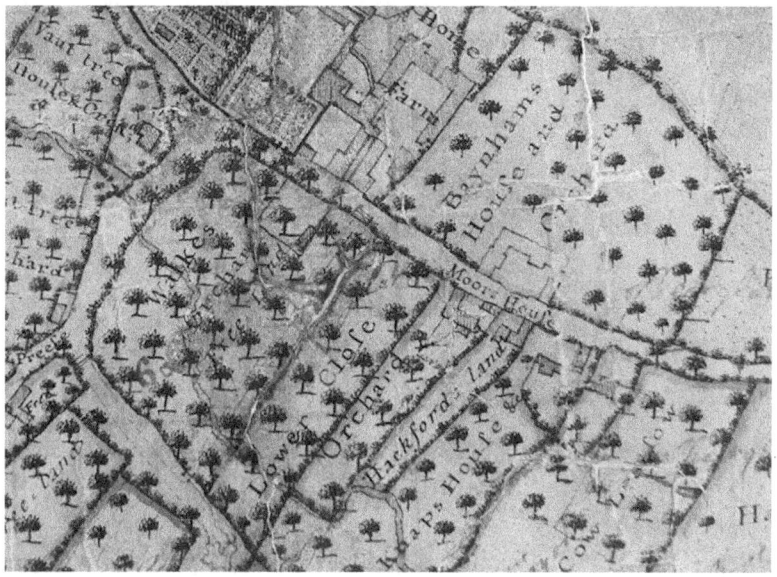

The lane between Shire Glatt (just off the map on the right hand side) and the church showing houses in *c.* 1755: Baynhams House, Knaps House, Moors House, Vaut tree (HARC BN81).

Moors House appears to have been situated approximately where the Great House Cottage is today and Baynhams House was on the opposite side of the lane in what is now a field belonging to the Great House. There were several Knap(p)s (Henry, George, William, John and Richard) living in the parish in the 17th century and also William Moore, all of whom are mentioned in the 1649 manorial survey.

Baynham's House looks to have been a substantial building and was close to Home Farm (now the Great House). It may have been the residence of George Bayneham who was recorded as a tenant in the 1649 manorial survey. He did not produce his copy of the court roll for the surveyors but had old copies from which 'it appeareth the land cometh anciently to him by descent'. This included two messuages and nine acres 'anciently the land of Thomas Holkins', a cottage in the tenure of Gwillim ap Griffith, a close called Lords Close and three acres of land in Rye Field called Turnors Land.[58]

Canon Pyon

Further down the lane, almost opposite Shire Glatt, was a property called Wilson's House, closer to the lane than the recently built house on the same piece of land.

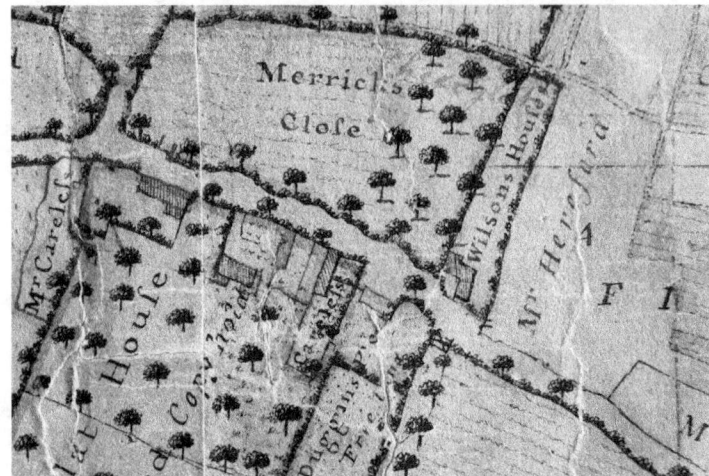

Wilson's House on the opposite side of the road to Shire Glat, *c.* 1755 (HARC BN81).

On the same map, another house is shown at Vaut tree orchard near the vicarage and at least four other buildings existed along the lane now known as Watery Lane. Whether they were all houses (maybe barns or animal housing), or even if they existed in the previous century, is not known. Few houses were named in the manorial records of the 17th century and were often known by their owner's or occupier's name (and could therefore change in time) or described in terms of their location.

A rare 1656 survival of a surrender in the manorial court mentions a house which could be a candidate for the Vaut tree or one of the Watery Lane houses:

> … one messuage with the outhouses garden and orchard contayninge about halfe an acre lyinge between the land [now] in the possession of George Baynham the younger and the vicaradge on both sydes wherein James Whettnoll and Phillipe Kirwood doe now inhabit …[59]

This was also one of the few known examples of apparent shared housing.

THE POUND

Definitely not a lost pound, its present location is where you might expect to find it in the 17th century; near the manor farm buildings, the church and other houses (which no longer exist). The *c.* 1755 map shows the pound in the same location as it is today. On the other side of the road there is a corner of a stone wall, in the same position as a rectangular feature shown on the map at the end of an avenue of trees.

Today's pound is stone built and roughly square in shape, with an opening at the back (in the corner closest to the church) and at the time of writing, plans are being made for restoration work to be done. The structure of the pound is Grade II listed and has been dated as 18th century or early 19th century.[60]

Location of the pound (same as today) on Isaac Taylor's map of *c.* 1755 (HARC BN81).

The earliest 17th century mention of a pound so far discovered is within the 'custom' section of the 1649 survey, where it is stated that 'the Lords are to repair the com[m]on pound'. There is no mention of the pound in the manor lease documents, so it is unclear whether the lessee was ever responsible for its maintenance or just the Dean and Chapter themselves.

The manorial court records do not mention the pound until a few years after the Restoration in 1660 but this does not mean that it did not exist. Before those entries, stray animals seem to have been catered for by individuals and sometimes the bailiff. A presentment of 15 October 1617 mentions strays in the custody of Richard Gailey. In October 1618 a stray brown chicken was in the custody of John Kinford and a red boar in the custody of Richard Sillye.[61] In April 1651, the jury presented that they knew of 'noe waves or strayes in any of the tenantes handes but one small st[ray?] shippe [sheep] in the handes of Olliver Gardner'.[62] As late as 1664, the homage presented 'one stray sheep in the hands of the bayliff, worth 5s.'.[63]

The first mention of a pound in the manorial records is in 1667 and between that date and 1674 it was mentioned regularly, along with other parish facilities. A typical entry is that of April 1673: 'Our highways, stocks, pound and butts are in repair and we have a crownet'.[64] But by April 1676, the pound was out of repair and was presented three times as such with the note that it was usually 'repaired by the lords', though not whether the work had been done.[65]

Canon Pyon

It should be said that today's stone pound may be of a later date than these entries but any earlier one was most likely to have been on or near the same site.

The 'front' wall of the pound in November 2019 (behind the church signpost) situated on the corner of the way to the church

NOTES

1 HCA 4735 doc 1 (extract of fines), HCA R10141, court rolls 1617-1620, HCA R1042, court rolls 1626-1642.

2 HARC R28/11090, Final Concord.

3 HCA 7001/2 f. 35.

4 HARC P64/7949.

5 HCA 4735.

6 HARC C11/1, Feoffment.

7 Mills, A. D., *A Dictionary of English Place Names* (2nd edition), Oxford University Press, 1998.

8 HCA 3151A.

9 For the Manorial Documents Register see https://discovery.nationalarchives.gov.uk/manor-search, accessed 15 July 2020.

10 HCA 4718/1.

11 HCA 4718/2.

12 TNA PROB 4/14997, proved 27 June 1668.

13 HCA 7031/3.

14 HCA 7001/2 pp. 47-48 and 66.

15 Cooke in *Collections towards the History and Antiquities of the County of Hereford, in continuation of Duncumb's History*, London, 1886 (the hundred of Grimsworth), states that Henry Gardner held the lease at the Restoration (1660), later George Gardner and then the Rev. Richard Waring; the latter is recorded in a lease of 1739 held in the Cathedral Archives.

16 HARC R28/11143.

17 HARC R28/11146.

18 HARC R28/11141/5.

19 HARC R28/11141/1.

20 HARC LCC Deed 11,1522, 7 June 1653 & survey, HCA 7001/2 p. 33.

21 HARC R28/11147.

22 HARC R28/11149, Copy of will, proved 18 April 1772.

23 https://www.nottingham.ac.uk/research/groups/ins/resources/kepn.aspx accessed May 2020, also A. D. Mills, *A Dictionary of English Place Names*, Oxford University Press, 1998.

24 Paul Hipkins, *A Welsh Survival in the land of Pyon*, Presidential Address, 2016, Transactions Woolhope Club.

25 HCA 7001/1.

26 *Ibid.*, Edward Broughton's lands (Woods).

27 *Ibid.*, William Knapp's copyhold.

28 HCA R1041.

29 Both 1664 surrender and 1666 presentment are in HCA 4735.

30 *Ibid.*, undated but estimated between 1647 and 1670.

31 Cooke, *Collections…*, p. 74.

32 TNA PROB 11/333/184.

33 HCA 4735.

34 HCA 4736, suit rolls.

35 TNA PROB 11/431/366.

36 HARC G87/10/23.

37 HCA R745/2, including the townships of Wotton, Colewall, Upton, Estonfoliot, Brotton, Smethely, Westhope.

38 HCA 7001/2, f. 33.

39 HARC HD2/2/6 and 7.

40 HARC HD2/2/6.

41 Hereford Deanery, proved 8 February 1687.

42 HCA 5384 Colville v. Berrington 1687/8.

43 Smith, Philip Vernon, *The Law of Churchwardens and Sidesmen in the 20th century*, London, 1903, p. 74.

44 Cooke, *Collections......*, p. 74.

45 'Prebendaries: Piona Parva', in *Fasti Ecclesiae Anglicanae 1066-1300*: Volume 8, Hereford, ed. J. S. Barrow (London, 2002), pp. 53-54.

46 Siddons, Michael Powell (transcribed and edited by), *Visitation of Herefordshire 1634*, Harleian Society, London, 2002, p. 98.

47 Campbell, Mildred, *The English Yeoman in the Tudor and Early Stuart Age*, Merlin Press Ltd, 1983, reproduced and printed in Great Britain by Whitstable Litho Ltd, Whitstable, Kent. (First published 1942 by Yale University Press), p. 35.

48 Census returns viewed on www.findmypast.co.uk.

49 HARC AP39/27, Indenture.

50 HARC QRD/7/20, Bargain and sale, 25 June 1724.

51 Fields on this map, *c.* 1755, which did not belong to Anthony Sawyer's estate were usually not named but often assigned as 'Mr Hereford's land' etc, Hereford being owner of Kinford lands at the time.

52 TNA C5/302/3, Chancery court case, Adis v. Colvile.

53 TNA FEC 1/1162 1717, accessed from www.findmypast.co.uk, 27 July 2020.

54 HARC G87/10/22.

55 HARC AP39/386 Abtract of title of the late Thomas Carpenter Quick.

56 HCA 4735, Court Baron, 20 Apr 1683 and Court Baron 1 Oct 1680.

57 HCA 5430, Dean & Chapter v. Bedford and HCA 4735 manorial court records.

58 HCA 7001/2

59 HCA 4735, 13 November 1656

60 https://historicengland.org.uk/listing/the-list/list-entry/1081975, accessed June 2020.

61 HCA R1041.

62 HCA R1043.

63 HCA 4735.

64 *Ibid.*

65 HCA 4735, 3 April 1676, 18 October 1676, 20 September 1677.

3

Canon Pyon church and the 'rectory impropriated'

As lords of the manor of Canon Pyon, the Dean and Chapter of the cathedral in Hereford had the patronage of the parish church and as such they had the right to appoint an incumbent, subject to the Bishop's approval. However, the site and farm of the manor had been leased to a farmer since at least 1563 and the lessee had 'the nomination of the vicar when and as oft as it shall be void [vacant] …' providing the Dean and Chapter approved of the candidate.[1]

The terms vicarage, rectory and parsonage have all appeared in Canon Pyon records although it is unlikely that there were three buildings. The benefice of a parish could have been a rectory, a vicarage or a perpetual curacy though the latter will not be considered further as it does not apply to Canon Pyon. The all-important tithes, a tenth part of crops and produce of the parishioners, were entitled to be received by the rector or vicar. In the case of a rectory, tithes were paid to the rector and they were known as unimpropriated.

From the medieval period, many benefices were owned by the monasteries; they were entitled to receive the tithes and were known as impropriated benefices. The monastery would use part of the tithe - usually a third - to pay for someone to provide the spiritual care of the parishioners on their behalf, or 'vicariously', that person being known to us as the vicar. The tithes used to support the vicar were known as vicarial or small tithes. The rest, known as rectorial or great tithes, were reserved for the monastery. Great tithes were usually corn, hay and wool, whereas small tithes incorporated other produce, though there were local variations. When the monasteries were dissolved, their benefices were often sold to local landowners, known as lay rectors. In the 19th century, Cooke wrote:

> Canon Pyon is a rectory impropriated to the dean and canons of Hereford by Bishop Aquablanc [1240-1268], having a vicarage endowed with a rent charge of £300, five acres of glebe, and a parsonage.[2]

This description indicates that both a vicarage and parsonage existed (the latter is often termed a rectory in other Canon Pyon documents). The benefice at Canon Pyon was thus originally a rectory and was impropriated to the Dean and Chapter, and not a monastery in this case, in the 13th century.[3] The Dean and Chapter then provided a vicar who received the vicarial or small tithes, the great or rectorial tithes being kept for themselves. When the manor properties were rented to a farmer (known as the tithe farmer) during the 17th century and earlier, he was entitled to receive the great tithes and pay his rents in grain to the Dean and Chapter.[4] The tithe farmer also had the advowson of the church and could select a suitable candidate for the vicar's benefice, providing that the Dean approved of the choice.

This arrangement does raise the question of how the advowson of the church was dealt with during the time that Edward Broughton and George Vaughan both held manor leases (c. 1600/01). It is unlikely that they both agreed to have Phillip Knapp presented for institution to the benefice in around 1600, though joint presentation is not unknown, and this puzzle is thus not yet satisfactorily resolved. By the Restoration in 1660, presentation to the benefice seems to have returned to the Dean.[5]

The manorial survey of Canon Pyon of 1649 records that the tithe farmer paid rent for the rectory and rent for the demesne lands in one combined payment.[6] The portion for the rectory was annually:

> ... thirteen quarters of wheat at three shillings and sixpence the bushell and six and twenty somes of oats at twelve pence the bushell which rent doth amount in the whole to six and thirty pounds and eight shillings.

He was entitled to collect tithes from about a third part of the parish and about a sixth part of 'the fruit ... and of all the hemp and flax which is sowed in any part of this tything ...'[6]

No record of a house named the Rectory or Parsonage has been found in 17th century records. It may have disappeared by this time or more likely it was on or near the site of one of the three buildings currently close to the church (the Old Vicarage, the Court Farm or the Great House). Another possibility is that the house was renamed as we have seen with the Great House and Court Farm.[8] The most likely location would be close to the church and Court Farm and probably at the site of The Court.

In 1649, the vicarage itself (as in the institution) was 'worth £40 per annum ... it consists of some little glebeland, a vicarage house and barn, tithe corn of some home closes and the tithe of wool and lamb, some fruit and other small tithes.' As part of the privilege of owning the advowson of the church, the tithe farmer also had to pay the vicar in corn to the tune of thirty-two bushels of wheat and forty-two bushels of oats a year.[9] As Rosemary O'Day has illustrated in *The English Clergy*, incumbents depended on their tithe and glebe for their income and could be severely affected by the rising prices of commodities if their glebe land was minimal.[10] By the mid-1600s, the value of great tithes such as hay and corn had increased far greater than that of small tithes, benefitting the tithe farmer far more than a vicar with little glebe land. This is particularly true if the tithe had been commuted to a money payment (a modus) which remained fixed.

Although in 1649 the Canon Pyon vicar could expect to receive an income of £40 a year from glebe lands and tithes, any withholding of small tithes by the parishioners or the wheat and oats due from the tithe farmer could put the vicar in financial straits. When crops were taken in, the vicar was supposed to be informed so that the tithe could be agreed on site or the vicar could take his portion there and then. Confusion could easily arise when entitlement to certain tithes was not clear amongst those involved; inevitably, these arrangements often lead to disputes which kept the church courts busy.[11]

In such a case of 1681, taken up initially in the ecclesiastical court, the vicar Thomas Bedford, who was in debt to the tune of 9s. 4d., complained that the tithe farmer Charles Somersett did:

> … very unjustly and wrongfully carry away of and from the grounds of one Thomas George called by the name of the Co[m]mon Hills or Hareleather in the p[ar]ish of Canon Pyon 4 thraves of tythe Rye wich doe belong to the s[ai]d Mr Bedford, each thrave [worth] tempore decimabili [at the time of the tithe] 20s. And also 2 acres of tythe barley and oates of and from the s[ai]d grounds which were due to the s[ai]d Mr Bedford each acre worth 15s per acre.[12]

The libel sets out the complainants statement of the number of sheep, lambs, fleeces, milk cows, calves, hemp and flax that he (Bedford) believed had been pastured and 'grown' by Charles Somersett in the parish and on which tithes were due. The figures in the defendant's 'answer' were considerably lower, not only in the number of animals and fleeces but in their value. The huge decrease in Somerset's stock between 1680 and 1681 is intriguing (see Table 2).

Taking the lower values in Bedford's claim over the three years, the total value of tithable produce would be £65 5s. 0d. and the tithe due would therefore be £6 10s. 6d., whereas Somersett pleads the value at £28 8s. 0d. and the tithe would be worth £2 16s. 9 ½d. It may not sound like a very large difference but the modern day equivalent of these tithe amounts are (approximately) £746.78 and £324.75.[13] None of these figures include any of the corn tithes.

Bedford's claim	Number (in each year)	Value	Somersett's response	Number	Value
Sheep	100 (or at least 90)		**Sheep**	80 in 1679/80 but 9 in 1681	
Fleeces	100 (or at least 90)	2s 6d (or at least 2s)	**Fleeces**	80 in 1679/80 but 9 in 1681	1s 6d in 1679/80 but 1s in 1681
Lambs	80 (or at least 70)	3s 4d (or at least 2s 6d)	**Lambs**	20 in 1679/80 but 9 in 1681	2s 6d in 1679/90 but 1s in 1681
Milch kine	12 (or at least 10)		**Milch kine**	12 in 1679/80 but 6 in 1681	
Calves	8 (or at least 5)	13s 4d (or at least 10s)	**Calves**	12 in 1679/80 but 6 in 1681	7s (in all years)
Hemp and flax	Which he *'did plucke up and convert to his owne use'*	40s (or at least 30s)	**Hemp and flax**	Not mentioned	

Table 2. A comparison of the tithable animal 'produce' between 1679 and 1681, in the case of Bedford v. Somersett, 1681 (HCA 5460).

The case eventually went to the court of Exchequer, where Bedford claimed that for his maintenance as vicar of Canon Pyon he was due the tithes of corn and grain 'in or upon every such old severalls or inclosures and enclosed land as be not reputed or taken to be field lands within the parish'. This wording is virtually identical to a line in the glebe terrier compiled by the vicar Phillip Knapp in 1617.[14] He also claimed all small and lesser tithes of wood, wool, calves, lambs, cheese, milk, pigs, geese, hops, flax, hemp and fruit by virtue of custom to be paid in kind, but that Somersett had taken all the above for the last 7 years to the tithe value of £15 for each year.

In Somersett's answer to the Bill, he cites his lease from the Dean and Chapter (as an extension of George Vaughan's lease) and often refers to his property as the parsonage impropriate; we can assume that the parsonage and the rectory are one and the same. He states that, as part of his lease, he was to pay the vicar thirty-two bushels of wheat and forty-two bushels of oats and that all tithes of corn, hay, grain, fruit, hemp, flax, hops and clover growing on what are known as the 'field lands' were due to himself, as they had been by ancient custom and for at least 60 years past. This does not contradict Bedford's claim for tithes from 'non-field lands'. Somersett also stated that tithes of corn, grain, hay, hemp, flax, hops, clover, wool, lambs, geese, pigs and all others from the demesne lands were also his 'by force and vertue of the same indenture'. This partially contradicts Bedford's claim for the small tithes. Neither George Vaughan's lease nor that of Edward Broughton mentioned 'field lands', only tithes of corn and hay of the parish of Canon Pyon, Derndale and an ambiguous 'all other tithes with the custom fines ...'.

However, Somersett did believe that tithes arising from 'the severalls (being not field land) and also all the small tithes arising from all the parishioners (excepting the occupiers of the parsonage and demesne lands)' belonged to the vicarage and that these were not usually paid in kind but by *modus decimandi*, a payment in lieu of tithes.[15]

The 'severalls' were probably the 'home closes' mentioned in the 1649 survey though which specific fields they are is not clear. The 1840 tithe map shows two fields, Upper Severals and Lower Severals, lying at the top of the Nupton lane (on the right when facing away from the village) just before it branches for Nupton Farm and the way to the Buttas and thus quite close to the current vicarage. The earlier map of *c.* 1755 only shows a small part of these fields as 'The Severals' with other enclosed fields around them. Cavill describes 'severals' and variations as meaning 'land in private ownership, in contrast to strips in common fields'.[16] The 'field lands' Somersett referred to may thus have been the open fields which still existed in Canon Pyon in the 17th century; these fields were divided into strips or portions, leased and worked by a number of customary tenants of the manor.

As well as tithes, the vicar was also entitled to Easter offerings, a payment from every parishioner for the supply of communion bread and wine at Easter. In the same ecclesiastical court case, the vicar declared that Somersett had:

> ... in his family besides himself and his wife in the parish of Canon Pyon aforesaid 4 com[m]unicants for every one of such co[mmun]icants he ought every year at the feast of Easter have paid 4d: and for himself and his wife their accustomed offerings and for a garden a penny according to an ancient custom time out of minde heretofore used observ[e]d and kept w[it]hin the s[ai]d parish.

The garden penny was another modus payment in lieu of tithes which had been agreed for garden produce. Once established as a custom, a modus payment was virtually

Canon Pyon church and the 'rectory impropriated'

impossible to change and if used extensively in a parish could lead to a significant decrease in the value of an incumbent's income. Harvest time would have been a test of neighbourly relations; as well as the physical labour of the task, parishioners wished to keep as much of their produce as possible whilst the vicar needed to gather in everything that was due to him. Conversely, the tithe farmer farmed his own land and gathered tithes due to him but also paid corn to the vicar and the Cathedral church at Hereford. Although the outcome of the above tithe case is not known, Thomas Bedford was soon to become embroiled in more serious personal matters to add to his woes; these will be discussed in his biography in the next chapter.

Out of his income, the vicar had to pay first fruits and tenths to the Crown as a form of taxation. First fruits were all the profits of the first year of an incumbent's entry to a benefice, whereas the tenth was paid annually.[17] He was also expected to maintain repairs of the vicarage (which always seemed to be in a state of disrepair) and incumbents could inherit a badly maintained vicarage from a predecessor. Three years before the tithe case, Bedford had complained that the vicarage had not been maintained properly for 40 years.[18] Furthermore, the vicar had to pay rent for the churchyard; in 1649, 'the Vicar holdeth the churchyard of the Impropriator of the Rectory by the yearly rent of 1s. 8d'.[19]

Churchyards in the 17th century rarely had stone walls or headstones, the latter appearing occasionally from the middle of the century onwards. Even by *c.* 1755, when Isaac Taylor produced his map of Anthony Sawyer's estate (the tithe farmer at that time), a picture of the church reveals nothing of fences or headstones, though there may be some artistic licence in this picture.[20]

Drawing on Isaac Taylor's map of *c.* 1755, showing Canon Pyon church and churchyard (HARC BN81).

Canon Pyon

Insufficient churchyard boundary fencing was a common complaint in the 17th century and fences were regularly broken and dug up by animals, so much so that burials near the building were often preferable to near the boundary fences.[21] On 18 January 1671, the vicar Thomas Griffithes certified that Richard Bennet had repaired his part of the churchyard fence after he had been presented by the churchwardens for not doing so.[22] A number of other similar notices survive, all post 1660, and in the spring of 1685 Roland Eckley was presented for his part of the fence not being sufficiently repaired to 'keepe out swine horses or other cattle'.[23]

Each year churchwardens were elected from amongst the parishioners, the custom being that one was chosen by the vicar and the other by the parishioners.[24] The presentment was a report made by the churchwardens in response to 'Articles of Inquiry' made by the bishop or his representative from Hereford. They recorded the state of the church building, the books and vestments, the churchyard fences and the vicarage house and outbuildings. The churchwardens were also required to inform on whether the minister conformed to the doctrine of the Church of England and whether (or not) the parishioners also conformed. If there were any who did not attend church or were believed to be dissenters they were recorded, as was any misbehaviour in church or dubious morality in the parish.[25] Miscreants would later be called to attend the church court and answer the 'charges' made (this will be discussed further in Chapter 5). The list of possible failings and misdemeanours was extensive and an over-diligent churchwarden might well make himself unpopular with a parishioner or two.

Although it was the tithe farmer (in place of the lord of the manor) who had to maintain the chancel of the church in good repair, the parishioners were responsible for the 'ornaments' of the church; the fittings, bells, books and vestments. If the churchwardens presented these things to be out of repair, they would be ordered by the church court to put things right. This involved making an assessment for the amount of 'lewne' (loan) required to be paid by each parishioner and subsequently collecting the said loan.[26] In another 1681 church court case involving Charles Somersett, in which the churchwardens had not been able to collect his portion of the loan, we gain some insight into the process. In the year up to March 1681, the church of Canon Pyon:

> … wanted repa[ra]cons in Tyle in Tymber in stone in paveing in Lime in whitening in glass, in Bells and divers other disbursem[en]ts for books for the charges and expenses of the s[ai]d churchwardens in the execucon of their office and for sev[er]all other things appertaining and belonging to the repa[ra]con and restoracon of the s[ai]d church and the ornaments … amounting in the whole to the summe of £11 10s. 3d.[27]

It was the custom that the 'sworn churchwardens ... for all the time whereof the memory of man is not to the contrary' would 'from time to time with the consent of the parishioners or the major part of them ...' place a public notice of a meeting for parishioners 'and every of them should meet at a certain time and place to be indifferently rated and ceased by the said churchwardens'.[28] This was done and the inhabitants were assessed according to 'the quantity and quality of their several lands goods and chattels which every one of them hold and possess within the said parish'. Somersett was assessed for [Canon] Pewne (10s.), for part of the Court (9s.), for the Moores and Hopwards (1s. 3d.) and for two plocks at Foulbridge (6d.).[29]

It is not clear why Somersett withheld his share of the loan, though the court case between himself and the vicar Thomas Bedford did not help matters. There was also a general dissatisfaction at the tithes and 'loan' system, particularly by dissenters who felt disconnected from the established church. Somersett came from a Catholic family and may have resented the payments, though there is no written evidence of this. No-one else appears to have been charged with non-payment of the loan and we can assume that most people did pay their dues.

In spite of all the good works completed in 1680, it was not long before the process had to begin again. After a visitation in 1689, churchwardens William Yeomans and William Bluck were:

> ... to receive orders to amend the Church being much out of repair, to p[ro]vide a cusion for the pulpitt, a Bible a Com[m]on Prayer Book p[re]sented imp[er]fect and to putt the rest of the ornam[en]ts of the Church in good order, p[re]sented to be but indifferent'.[30]

Between the parishioners, the tithe farmer and the vicar, and overseen by the church court, the church and vicarage should have been kept in a reasonable state of repair. It was not always so, particularly from the middle of the century onwards. From this time onwards, religious dissent became more established nationally and evidence of this in Canon Pyon is considered in the next section.

QUAKERS IN THE PARISH

Protestants who did not conform to the established Church of England have been known by various names, but 'sectaries' and 'dissenters' are used here, as they are most relevant to the findings in Canon Pyon. 'Sectary' was a term used in the Civil War and Interregnum period for the more radical of the non-conformers. After the restoration in 1660 the term 'dissenter' was used for both sectaries and for those who, having previously attended the parish church, then refused the ministrations of the newly restored Episcopal Church. Many of these followed the newly ejected clergy, some of whom had begun their own gatherings.[31] Those who refused to attend the parish Church services were also known as recusants.

Historians find the term 'puritan' more difficult to define but there were certain common characteristics. They believed in predestination (those chosen by God were already destined for Heaven and could not fall from grace) and were often zealous, deploring images and rituals and desiring to reform church and society without the episcopacy. They referred to themselves as 'godly' or 'the elect' (never as puritan) and were Sabbatarian, devoting Sundays to worship and prayer.[32]

Puritan groups of the 1600s included the Presbyterians, Independents and Separatists or Baptists (many of which have altered their doctrines since those early days). As yet, no evidence has been uncovered to suggest any such groups were in Canon Pyon in the 17th century but there is evidence of a small number of Quakers living in the parish. Quakers believed that they received personal messages from the Holy Spirit and that these were more important than the will of God. Puritans did not ally themselves with Quakers, these 'followers of the spirit'.[33] These are, admittedly, over-simplifications of the nature of dissenting groups, all of which were continually evolving their belief systems, joining together then parting ways again.

The Canon Pyon Quakers were few in number but appeared to remain resolute. In May 1686, a churchwardens' presentment gives the names of Quakers in the parish - the widow Oven, her son John Oven and her daughter Hester Oven and also Richard Bull. The churchwardens also reported that they knew of 'no other sectaries in our parish, but some ... that refuse to pay their Easter dues to our minister'; these were Walter Probart, [----] Collyar, Walter Cooper and William Clark.[34] This refusal is not necessarily an indication of dissent (there may be some other grudge with the vicar, or a simple case of poverty) though it is a common cause of non-payment. Quakers refused to pay tithes or church rates for the reparation of parish churches or even to use the established ministers for marriages and burials and thus escaped paying fees. They would not swear any oath and refused to remove their hats 'by way of homage to man' all of which resulted in fines or distraint of their goods and excommunication by the church courts.[35]

Besse's *A collection of the sufferings of the people called Quakers* records numerous cases of persecution of and violence against Quakers in Herefordshire between 1656 and 1683, mostly in Leominster, Ross and Hereford. In one of these incidents in September 1676, people in a Quaker meeting in Hereford, having been attacked by a 'rude rabble' on several days, were 'tendered' with the Oath of Allegiance and Supremacy. This was an oath of loyalty to the Crown and Church of England and on refusing to swear, they were promptly sent to gaol. One of these was William Oven, very likely connected with the Oven family of Canon Pyon.[36]

A number of other documents record the Oven family members as Quakers. William and Joanne Oven, possibly with two of their children, were at Kings Pyon in November 1671.[37] The couple continued to be presented regularly as Quakers in the church court records throughout the 1680s, by that time being 'of Canon Pyon', and were listed as excommunicates. By 1683 William had died and Joanne was recorded with a John and Mary Oven.[38]

William's last will and testament was proved on 13 November. He was described as a yeoman and the inventory of his goods is quite extensive, including 'eight oxen, eight cows and a bull, thirteen young beasts of several sorts, three mares and four colts, seventy sheep and swine of all sorts'. Being October (when the inventory was made), there was grain in the barn and 'wheat, rye, barley, pease and pulses and hay in the house' as well as butter and cheese and 'corn now growing on the ground' for the next year's crop. There were bedsteads, table boards, chairs, a press, a chest, linen, brass and pewter and the total value of his belongings amounted to more than £219.[39] Quakers were often severely persecuted financially but no documentary evidence of this has been found in the Ovens' case and the inventory is certainly not what you might expect with persistent persecution.

On 5 June 1699 the *birth* of James Oven, son of John (a hubandman) and his wife Jane, was recorded in the bishop's transcript of the Canon Pyon parish register.[40] It is remarkable for being the only birth recorded amongst all the baptisms since the start of the existing transcripts in the 1660s. The Oven family continued in their Quaker faith well into the next century; John Oven of Canon Pyon recorded the birth of their son Joseph, this time at the Leominster Meeting, in 1713 and there were many others in the 18th century Quaker records.[41] The family were still in Canon Pyon in the 19th century.

In the early days of the Quaker movement most of the Friends (as they styled themselves) met at a private dwelling house. No direct evidence has yet been found of a house or place in Canon Pyon where the Quakers might have met in the 17th century but they may have travelled to Almeley or Leominster where there were established meetings. The Friends attending those meetings often came from outlying villages and often carried local, sometimes devastating news with them. Quakers often dispensed charity in the face of disaster, evident in the following entry taken from the record of a Society of Friends meeting at Almeley:

Canon Pyon

> The 12th of the 9th m[on]th 1683 then disburst (by ye order and consent of Friends) two shillings to a poore widdow of ye parish of Cannon Pian whose house and Barne with Graine was consumed by fire; as was signified by the hands of many witnesses.[42]

The widow may not necessarily have been a Friend but it is highly likely that the Oven family and other Canon Pyon Quakers knew her and had some involvement in the decision.

There is some evidence of Quaker meetings in Canon Pyon in the next century, in 1723 and 1724, probably in the house of a Friend. In a manuscript volume of *'Sufferings of Friends for Tythe…'* it was recorded that in the 'Canon Pion Meeting' on the 22nd of the 5th month 1723 (this month is July in pre 1752 Quaker terms):

> Distrained of Jno. Drew alias Dunn of ye parish of Webly by vartue of a warrant from Wm. Lamb and Morgan Eavens Justices one iron pott and potthooks by Joseph Rich and Jno. David constable worth 11s 6d, the demand being 3s.[43]

It was common for goods to be taken in lieu of tithes and the value of goods taken was often far in excess of the sums required. The hapless John Drew/Dunn also had a goose and some corn taken in the next month, again recorded at a meeting at Canon Pyon. At a further meeting in 1724, Abraham Hughes had hay, corn, wheat and peas taken. Although it is not stated where Hughes was from, there is a marriage in the records of the Friends Meeting house in Almeley in 1713 between Abraham Hughs, son of John Hughs of Landegly, county Radnor and Sarah Oven, daughter of John Oven of Canon Pyon.[44] Although these events are a little later than the focus of this work, they illustrate that Friends were meeting, at least occasionally, in the parish by this time.

Occasionally, there are other clues to religious groups in the parish. In 1688, John Turbervile left an intriguing bequest in his will:

> I give and bequeath unto my daughter Rachell Powell eleven acres of pasture ground for the term of threescore yearse and ten If shee shal so long [s] live being a member of Lautons hope….[Lawton's Hope].[45]

Was this perhaps a conventicle or meeting house? A John Tubervile was presented by the churchwardens in 1660/1 for 'unreverently wearinge his hatt upon his head in the church in the time of Divine Service'.[46] We have seen that refusal to remove the hat is a habit of the Quakers but there may be more to this than we can know. Immediately

Canon Pyon church and the 'rectory impropriated'

after this entry, three lines of text are vigorously, but at the same time carefully scribbled out and cannot be read.

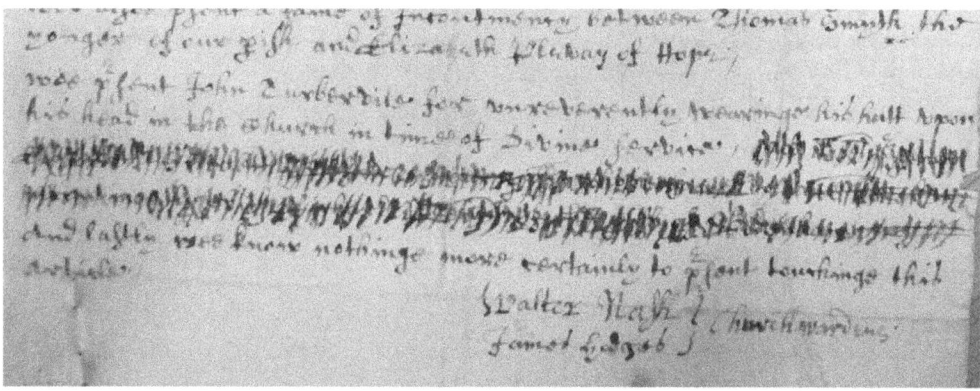

John Turbervile's presentment for not removing his hat in church, and the scribbled out lines following (HCA 4589).

It is also notable that this presentment was for the year 1660 when Charles II was restored to the English throne. In Canon Pyon, Thomas Bedford was ejected from his living at the vicarage and Thomas Griffithes restored. There are thus at least two other possible reasons for John Turbervile's rebellious action in church.

Disrupting a church service was a powerful way of making a protest in the 17th century. Although there were some who were moving away from the established church, most parishioners still attended their parish church and thus provided an audience. The hat-wearing is a relatively simple method but far more disrespectful than we can imagine today. As well as reporting such behaviour in church, the churchwardens were well within their rights to deal with offenders:

> They may pull off the hats of those who obstinately refuse to take them off and may gently lay their hands on those who disturb the performance of any part of divine service, and turn them out of church.[47]

Although written much later (early 20th century), the little handbook from which the above quotation is derived, states that 'the duties of the churchwardens have remained the same through the ages'.[48]

The link between Lawton's Hope and a meeting house is a tentative one; is there more evidence in the fields and buildings of Canon Pyon? There is a field marked on the 1840 tithe map, called 'In Meeting House Field', which appears to have been part of the bigger 'One Acre Field'.[49] It is located on the left side of the road between Kinford and Westhope (roughly where the Bulmer-owned orchard is today) and a fairly short walk from Lawton's Hope. It was owned (in 1840) by John Plevy who was part of a non-conformist family belonging to the Leominster Moravian with Protestant Episcopal Church in the late 18th and early 19th centuries.

Furthermore, a building called The Meeting House, between Lawton's Hope and Westhope, was occupied in 1851 by schoolmaster William Yapp and his wife and brother in law, but no earlier information has been discovered.[50] It may have been the house mentioned in a 20th century account by Ernest Patrick who lived in the village; he recalls that a house in Westhope, called The Meeting House, was demolished and a new mission room built.[51] The earlier (*c.* 1755) map by Isaac Taylor shows the large field (called 'One Acre Field' in 1840) but it is not named and there is no indication of 'In Meeting House Field'.[52] It seems likely, therefore, that the field name and meeting house did not come into use until the late 18th or early 19th century. Nor does it help with the possible link between Lawton's Hope and a meeting house.

ROMAN CATHOLICISM IN THE PARISH

A small number of followers of the Catholic faith resided in the parish during the 17th century. They appear to be mainly from the 'gentle' families and most probably had a long family association with the 'old faith'. 'Catholic recusant' was the name given to Catholics who refused to attend the Anglican Church services. Some became exiles, leaving England by choice or force. Others, most difficult to identify and quantify, were the so-called 'church papists'; those who still attended their parish church and kept their commitment to the old faith a secret.[53]

This may have been the case with James Berrington of Little Pyon, who was brought before the church court in 1621 'for not standing up at the saying of ye beleiefe'. Having confessed it was true he was admonished and probably paid a fine.[54]

According to Cooke, during the Civil Wars James Berrington (also of Little Pyon and probably the grandson of the above) 'had his lands sequestrated by the Parliamentary Committee on the suspicion that he was a concealed papist a conclusion he was enabled to confute by a personal conference with his accusers'.[55] In 1686/7, the witness statements in a case involving a church pew revealed that the Berrington family had left Herefordshire to live at Monmouth during the Civil War years.[56] Although no reason is given in the court case for this move, there are at least three other factors which may not be coincidental: there was a strong Royalist garrison at Monmouth, the rich and influential Catholic Somerset family lived at nearby Raglan Castle, and many Catholics supported the Royalist cause. The Canon Pyon Berringtons were also related to the Bishopstone and Winsley Berringtons, known to have Catholic sympathies.[57] James Berrington's aunt Katherine had married George Vaughan of Canon Pyon and later Robert Lochard of The Byletts, Pembridge - the Lochard's too were known to be a Catholic family. That Berrington managed to 'confute' the accusations of being a concealed papist is puzzling.

The Vaughans' daughter Judith had three husbands, two of whom (Walter Baskerville and William Lochard) were known to be of the Catholic faith.[59] William Lochard's estates were also sequestrated during the Civil War and he compounded for them at £50 a year.[60] Judith's daughter Katherine's third husband was a Somerset, part of the aforementioned family who held Raglan Castle in Monmouthshire and who were connected with the Jesuit college at Cwm on the Herefordshire, Monmouthshire and Gloucestershire borders.[61] The above families were all connected by marriage and those from Canon Pyon were associated with the manor lease or in the case of the Berringtons, nearby Little Pyon.

Hibbard discusses this intermarriage and network of family ties amongst the gentry, known as the 'Catholic connection', in terms of a protective unit and that there was little evidence at the county level of excessive persecution on a religious basis and even a marked civility between Protestant and Catholic.[62] Perhaps those who suffered sequestrations of their estates would not have agreed with this view. For those with 'means', persecution could also come from the direction of the ecclesiastical courts, as we have seen in the case of James Berrington.

There is a gap in the records between the 1630s, when the ecclesiastical court's Acts of Office books cease, and the restoration of the monarchy in 1660 when the books and churchwardens' presentments reappear. These later presentments add local insight to the proceedings - thus, in 1661, it was recorded:

> Wee doe p[re]sent that Mrs Judeth Barneby, Mrs Bridget Lochard, Mr Anthony Lochard, Alice Pike widdow, John Pike, ffrances the wyfe of Ralph Nash doe not repayre to church to divine service or administracon of the sacraments, but whether they be popish recusants or sectaries wee know not'.[63]

Judith Barneby was the Judith previously mentioned (she married John Barneby after the death of her husband William Lochard) and there is no surprise to see the Lochards mentioned in the presentment. Although being obliged to make a report on absence, it does not seem likely that the vicar and churchwardens would be clueless about the religious leanings of the local gentry, nor any parishioner for that matter, in a small parish. The denial may therefore lie in a reluctance to cause trouble for neighbours; some of the parishioners would be sub-tenants and servants of the gentry families, or possibly family of others being presented. One of the churchwardens signing this presentment was Walter Nash, though as yet a family link has not been established between him and Frances Nash or her husband Ralph. The latter was probably the Ralph Nash who was buried at Canon Pyon 19 Jul 1671 and Walter was buried in October the following year.

The first known record of Alice Pike, also presented, is from a rent roll of 1650 which records that she was to pay three shillings.[64] Widow Alice Pike also appeared in the Militia Assessments of 1663 and she was assessed at £5 10s.[65] She was presented two years later at the manor court for 'breaking the pain for the keeping of goats' and was on the suit roll for 1667.[66] In January of the same year Charles and Catherine Somersett surrendered land at the manor court, to be re-entered by themselves and Judith Barneby; the document mentions some exceptions including 'a tenement or cottage occupied by Alice Pike, widow'.[67] That Alice was a sub-tenant of the Somersetts is not evidence that she kept the same faith, but it does draw attention to a relationship with the family and her possible loyalty.

The last known record of Alice is from a Hearth Tax exemption certificate of 1672 when she is listed, along with many others, as a widow receiving alms.[68] She does not appear on a suit roll for the year 1676 (but there is a George Pike), or on another suit roll covering 1678-1684 (no Pikes at all).[69] Alice had been a widow for a long time; it is probable that she herself died between 1672 and 1676, though no burial record has been found for her as yet.

Around the same time (1676), Henry and Sarah Pleavey were reported at Birley as 'reputed papists', but at the foot of the document is a note in a different hand recording that they did not live at Birley but in the parish of Canon Pyon.[70] Two years later, Thomas Bedford vicar of Canon Pyon, wrote a note to the registrar at the Cathedral church, to be sent with Thomas Pike:

> That the bearer hereof Tho: Pike of the p[ar]ish of Canon Pyon and Henry Plevai of ye said par]ish and county of Hereford are poor men maintayning themselves and their famelys as wee concieve only by their labour is certified by us ...[71]

The note is signed by the vicar and Bartholomew Walter, a churchwarden. Although there is no explanation for the note, it is possible that the two men had been presented by the churchwardens for a 'notifiable offence', quite possibly recusancy, and may then have been facing fines. Alternatively, this may be a certificate with a view to exemption for the hearth tax. As well as Henry Plevai/Pleavey, it is notable that another member of the Pike family is involved.

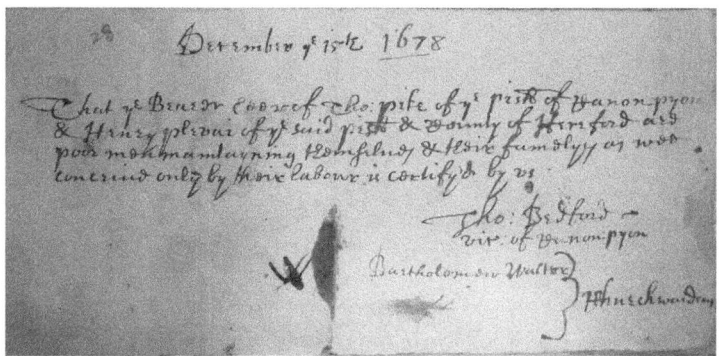

A note from Thomas Bedford, vicar of Canon Pyon, to the Registrar, confirming Thomas Pike and Henry Plevai to be 'poor men', 15 December 1678 (HCA 4664/28).

In 1672, Charles II instigated what became known as the Test Act; 'an Act for preventing Dangers which may happen from Popish Recusants'. Anyone in civil or military employment had to sign an Oath of Supremacy and Allegiance, which they could do at the Quarter Sessions in their own county. They also had to read a declaration denying 'transubstantiation in the Sacrament of the Lords Supper or in the Elements of Bread and Wine' and prove that they had received 'the Sacrament of the Lords Supper according to the Usage of the Church of England'. Refusal to comply meant the loss of their position. There were some provisos for protecting pensions and hereditaments of peers and at the other end of the social scale, parish constables, overseers of the poor, churchwardens and manor bailiffs were exempt (providing they had no qualifying civil or military office). This Act was followed by another in 1678, after rumours of a popish plot, this time extending the rules to peers.[72]

A character reference for Canon Pyon resident Wrainfort Hill survives at Hereford Cathedral Archives.[73] It is not dated but is amongst others from 1670-1676 which are catalogued as certificates of church attendance. The reference was written by the vicar Thomas Bedford and in fact did not mention the church at all:

> These are to certify whom it may concerne that Wrainfort Hill of Canon Pyon is reputed an honest and peaceable man, not at all inclyn'd as far as I am able to guess to disturbe the publique peace.

The vicar's use of the words 'reputed' and 'guess' suggest that he may not have known Hill that well and as Bedford had only returned to Canon Pyon in 1673, this might also help to date the document. Bedford noted that he had received 2s. 2d. for this service, further suggesting that Hill most likely paid for this reference for a specific purpose.

Canon Pyon

In 1680, both Rainford Hill and Charles Somersett appear in the Papist Oath Rolls in Hereford's Quarter Session records.[74] This was a precursor to Hill (forename spelt variously as Wrainford/Wranfort/Rainford/Wrainford) undertaking duties as churchwarden in 1681 and signing the copy registers which were to go to the Diocesan office. As churchwardens were not required to sign the oath purely for that role, Hill may have been involved in some other (as yet unknown) public office.

In a later churchwardens' presentment, dated 20 May 1686, the following are named as 'papists': Charles Somerset Esquire, Mrs Mary Somerset, Mr Francis Lochard, Mrs Brodford, Thomas Pike, Anne Ross and Sara Plevey.[75] We have already met the Somersets and Lochards, Thomas Pike and Sara Plevey. The identity of Mrs Brodford is a bit of a mystery, but the use of the title 'Mrs' would suggest a reasonably high social status and she may have been an acquaintance of the Somersets or Lochards. Anne Ross also had a connection with the Somersets; she made a will which was witnessed by Charles and Elizabeth Somersett. She may well have been a servant of the Somerset household, for after leaving legacies to her brothers, she instructs 'to do this in my master hand Mr Somerset eleven pounds and Mrs Hall of the grange six pounds the which I hope they will pay in a year time'. The inventory of her goods lists two bonds, one with Charles Somerset and the other with Elizabeth Hall, of the amounts given above.[76]

THE END OF BEING 'PRESENTED'

At the Declaration of Indulgence in 1687, penal laws against protestant dissenters and Roman Catholics were suspended and lists of 'offenders' disappear from the churchwardens' presentments. Dissenters and Roman Catholics in Canon Pyon were few, the former centred on the Quaker Oven family and the latter associated with the minor gentry families leasing the manor lands. The majority of the population had been and remained part of the Anglican Church.

Michael Watts' research into the number of dissenters shows that by the early 18th century, only 2.4% of the estimated Herefordshire population size of 41,440 were either Presbyterian, Independent, Baptist or Quaker.[77] Research into Herefordshire's Catholic community by Wendy Brogden indicates that there were only three or four gentry family members in Canon Pyon who were regularly presented as Catholics between 1580 and 1640, along with a small number of associated non-gentry parishioners.[78] From general observations in the presentments from *c.* 1660 to 1690, this did not seem to have changed significantly.

NOTES

1. HCA 4720/1,2,3 & 5, leases 1563 – 1631.

2. Cooke, William Henry, M.A., Q.C., F.S.A, *Collections towards the History and Antiquities of the County of Hereford, in continuation of Duncumb's History*, by William Henry Cooke, London, 1886 (the Hundred of Grimsworth, p.1).

3. See note 2 in Chapter 1, regarding impropriation.

4. HCA 4720/1,2,3 & 5, leases 1563 – 1631.

5. HCA 7031/3, Chapter Act Book, f. 185.

6. Demesne - the part of the manor not held by tenants but kept for the profit of the lord of the manor, or in this case the tithe farmer.

7. HCA 7001/2, ff. 55 &56.

8. HARC BN81, map of Anthony Sawyer's estates.

9. HCA 7001/2 ff. 57 & 62.

10. O'Day, Rosemary, *The English Clergy; the Emergence and Consolidation of a Profession, 1558-1642*, Leicester University Press, 1979, pp. 173-175.

11. Tarver, Anne, *Church Court Records – An introduction for family and local historians*, Phillimore, 1995, pp. 100-101.

12. HCA 5460, Bedford v. Somersett, 1681.

13. www.nationalarchives.gov.uk/currency-converter (accessed 15 Jul 2020) note that values are compared between 1680 and 2017 and the site does point out that the conversion provides a general guide, not a statement of fact.

14. HARC HD2/2/4 & 5.

15. TNA E112/412/184, Bedford v. Somersett, bill dated 11 Nov 1681, answer 28 Apr 1682. My thanks to David Lovelace for bringing this to my attention.

16. Cavill, Paul, *A New English Dictionary of English Field-Names*, English Place Name Society, 2018, pp. 374-5.

17. O'Day, *The English Clergy....*, pp. 176-7.

18. HCA 4664/32, 1678.

19. HCA 7001/2, f. 38.

Canon Pyon

20 HARC BN81.

21 Cressy, David, *Birth, Marriage and Death: Ritual, Religion, and the life-cycle in Tudor and Stuart England*, Oxford University Press, 1999, p. 466.

22 HCA 466/5.

23 HCA 4665/8; HCA 4664/40, 44, 53; 4655/9-11; 4654 & (Eckley) HCA 7002/1/8 Easter 1685.

24 HCA HD7/24, churchwardens' presentment 20 May 1686.

25 HCA 4589 (1660), 4593 (1673), 4596 (1678) and HARC HD7/24 (1686); the HCA references contain presentments from other parishes as well as Canon Pyon.

26 A loan (often spelt lewn or lewne) was not as we know it today (ie an amount that is paid back); it was an amount that was paid as a contribution.

27 This amount would be the equivalent of £1317.60 in 2017, www.nationalarchives.gov.uk/currency-converter accessed 24 Sep 2020.

28 Cessed – rated, taxed or assessed.

29 HCA 5456 (custom) and 5455 (assessment), Churchwardens v. Somersett, 1681.

30 HARC HD4/1/203 p. 59, Court Book.

31 For a discussion of the various terminology see *The Dissenters (from the Reformation to the French Revolution)*, Michael R Watts, Clarendon Press, Oxford, Reprint 1999, p1.

32 For two useful examples, see Spurr, *John, English Puritanism 1603-1689*, Macmillan Press Ltd, 1998, pp. 3-3, Defining Puritans and Dougall, Alistair, *The Devil's Book; Charles I, the Book of Sports and Puritanism in Tudor and Early Stuart England*, University of Exeter Press, 2011, pp. 3-5.

33 *Ibid.* p. 7.

34 HARC HD7/24.

35 Besse, J.A., *A collection of the sufferings of the people called Quakers*, 1753, Chapter 1, pp. 1-2, (causes of sufferings) accessed from Open Library 21 Aug 2020.

36 *Ibid.*, Chapter 18, p. 259.

37 HARC HD4/1/187, Consistory Court book.

38 HCA 7002/1/8, Acts of Office 1682-1718.

39 Proved Hereford Deanery, 13 Nov 1683.

40 HARC MX14 Bishop's transcript, Canon Pyon.

41 TNA RG6/1015, 5 Jun 1713.

42 HARC A85/4.

43 HARC A85/1a-f.

44 TNA RG6/1015, Quarterly Meeting (image viewed on www.findmypast.co.uk Jul 2020.)

45 Proved Hereford Deanery, 7 Jul 1688 (written 15 Jun).

46 HCA 4589, Churchwardens presentment for 'the yeare last past 1660 made the 17th day of May 1661'.

47 Smith, P. V., *The Law of Churchwardens and Sidesmen in the 20th century*, London, 1903, p. 77.

48 *Ibid*. p.6.

49 HARC BR39, Canon Pyon tithe map, 1840.

50 Census HO107/1979/359/4.

51 HARC Pamphlet 396: *Canon Pyon: Some Notes of What Has Happened Over the Years 1850-1915* by Ernest Patrick.

52 HARC BN81, map of Anthony Sawyer's estates.

53 On church papists, see Baker, Geoff, *Reading and Politics in early modern England: The mental world of a seventeenth-century Catholic gentleman*, Manchester University Press, 2010, p. 4.

54 HARC 7002/1/3, Acts of Office, 12 May 1621.

55 Cooke, *Collections* ..., p. 73.

56 HCA 5384 Colville v. Berrington 1687/8.

57 Ross, David, *Royalist, But ... Herefordshire in the English Civil War, 1640-51*, Logaston Press, 2012, pp. 19-20.

58 *Ibid*., p. 20.

59 HARC HD4/1/184, 16 May 1636, Walter Baskervile was 'detect[ed] that he had a child borne and baptised in the howse of Robert Lochard, gent, ... and not brought to the church at all', charged with being a papist recusant.

60 Cooke, *Collections*..., p. 72.

61 Ross, *Royalist But…*, p. 20, also Brogden, Wendy Elizabeth, *Catholicism, community and identity in late Tudor and early Stuart Herefordshire*, 2018 (thesis, University of Birmingham) https://etheses.bham.ac.uk/id/eprint/8483/5/Brogden18PhD.pdf (accessed May 2021).

62 Hibbard, Caroline M., *Early Stuart Catholicism: Revisions and Re-Revisions*, originally from the Journal of Modern History 52, pp.2-3, University of Chicago Press, March 1980, accessed from https://hdl.handle.net/2142/811, (Illinois Digital Environment for Access to Learning and Scholarship) May 2021.

63 HCA 4589, Churchwardens' presentment, 17 May 1661.

64 HCA R1043, Apr 1650 – Apr 1651.

65 Faraday, M. A., *Herefordshire Militia Assessments of 1663*, Royal Historical Society, London, 1972, p. 74.

66 HCA 4735, 30 Mar 1665 and 15 Apr 1667.

67 *Ibid* Jan 1666/7.

68 TNA E179/119/509/48, 19 Oct 1672.

69 HCA 4736.

70 HARC, Act Books, HD7/18 (25 Mar 1676) and confirmed (13 Aug 1676) in HD7/19 that they had lived at Birley but now at Canon Pyon.

71 HCA 4664/28, 15 Dec 1678.

72 Charles II, 1672: *An Act for preventing Dangers which may happen from Popish Recusants.*', in Statutes of the Realm: Volume 5, 1628-80, ed. John Raithby (s.l, 1819), pp. 782-785. British History Online http://www.british-history.ac.uk/statutes-realm/vol5/pp782-785 and *An Act for the more effectuall preserving the Kings Person and Government by disableing Papists from sitting in either House of Parlyament*, in Statutes of the Realm: Volume 5, 1628-80, ed. John Raithby (s.l, 1819), pp. 894-896. British History Online http://www.british-history.ac.uk/statutes-realm/vol5/pp894-896 (accessed June 2020).

73 HCA 4662/1.

74 HARC Q/RO/31, Quarter sessions.

75 HARC/ HD7/24.

76 Proved Hereford Deanery,10 Mar 1689.

77 Watts, *The Dissenters…*, Table XII, p. 509.

78 Wendy Elizabeth Brogden, *Catholicism* …, Map IX p. 107 and discussion p. 108/also p. 112n.

4

The clergy of Canon Pyon 1600 to 1707

There are few biographies for the many clergymen whose working lives took them no further than a parish church. Sometimes there is little to be discovered about them other than a name but for the six who took care of the cure of souls in 17th century Canon Pyon, some record of their lives remains and is collated here.

Before the beginning of the 1600s, there had been a drive to improve the education and scriptural knowledge of parish clergy and from around the 1630s, many more of them held a university degree. Not only was more knowledge expected, but a greater emphasis was placed on pastoral care and the teaching and instructing of parishioners; no longer was it sufficient to simply deliver the sacraments by a relatively uneducated clergy. This may have had the effect of raising the status of the clergy to a profession but the value of their livings did not necessarily increase in tandem with this status which often lead to resentment.[1]

At the start of the century, the advowson (or right to choose the incumbent) was a part of the manor lease, provided that the Dean approved of the candidate, but at some point after the restoration patronage appears to have reverted to the Dean and Chapter. The Canon Pyon vicars and their parishioners, and even sometimes the Dean, did not always manage a respectful and caring relationship. As we saw in Chapter 3, the vicar was also a farmer and a tithe gatherer, leading to endless conflict for some and a reputation for the clergy to be litigious. Although well within their rights to take parishioners to court for their dues, the impact on lay attitudes to the clergy could be profound, particularly up to the period of the Civil War and Interregnum. Set within a background of increasing anticlericalism in the 1640s and 1650s, many clergymen found themselves having to defend the system of the settled ministry. Religious groups such as the Independents and the Quakers did not feel the need of a church hierarchy though opinions on the right course of action ranged from reform to total abolishment.

Canon Pyon

The laity grew more disaffected by church discipline but it was the parish clergyman who bore the brunt of ill-feeling. He had to instigate the presentments, read out the court's citations in church and ensure that penances were performed. He was at the forefront of an increasingly hated institution. Add to this the impact of the war on food supplies and tithe revenue and clearly it was a tough period for the clergy.[2]

Even by the end of the century, clergyman William Nicholls felt compelled to write *The Duty of Inferiours towards their Superiours in Five Practical Discourses*.[3] For the clergymen, Nicholls discussed why parishioners should love, maintain, obey and respect them. The defensive nature of the book in the matter of the clergy belies the publication date of 1701. Its content could easily apply to 50 years or more before this and suggests that attitudes had not changed much by the end of the 17th century. Noticeably, the author had little to say about a clergyman's duty to his 'inferiors'.

How well Canon Pyon parishioners were ministered to in the years between 1646 and 1660 is debatable; it was a time of disruption, lack of documentation and harassment for clergy and parishioners alike. The following work is therefore open to future development if (or when) more information comes to light. As is usually the way, harmonious relationships rarely find their way into public record and evidence of strife is easier to find.

THE CHURCH BOARD

The starting point for discussing the 17th century Canon Pyon vicars has to be the board mounted in the porch of St Lawrence's church.[4] The board lists the known incumbents of Canon Pyon but a comparison of the information of 17th century incumbents with that given by 19th century historian Henry William Cooke reveals some differences.[5]

There are also a number of inconsistencies between the information given by both sources and the history that has emerged from research. Note that in the following biographical works, the dates in brackets after each name refer to the time it is believed that the incumbent was either at Canon Pyon, or instituted to the living (but not necessarily resident).

PHILLIP KNAPP/E (c.1601 – 1639)

This vicar was the longest serving of the ministers in the 17th century. Although the church board tells us that he was vicar from 1605, he was in Canon Pyon earlier than this. In a will proved in 1601, Oliver Vaughan left 'to Phillip Knapp vicar of Cannon Pewne for my tythe wooll - 19s. 4d.'.[6] It is possible that Oliver Vaughan or his father

Year	Church board	Year	Cooke
1605	Philip Knapp	1605	Phillip Knapp
1639	Jonathan Dryden	1639	Jonathan Dryden
1645	Thomas Griffiths Ejected 1650	1645	Thomas Griffiths Ejected 1650
1651	Thomas Bedford Removed 1660	1651	Thomas Bedford Removed 1660
1660	Thomas Griffiths Restored	**1661**	Thomas Griffiths Restored
1672	Daniel Wycherley Rector of Whitney	1672	Daniel Wycherley, B.D. Rector of Whitney
1677	Thomas **Griffiths** **Replaced**	1677	Thomas **Bedford**
1682	Herbert Hook	1682	Herbert Hooke, M.A.
1700	Thomas Husbands, M.A.	**1708**	Thomas Husbands, M.A.

Table 3. A comparison of the incumbents' information given on the church board and in Cooke's work (differences in bold).

had a hand in Phillip Knapp's entry to the benefice of Canon Pyon as this privilege was part of the lease of the 'farm and site of the manor of Canon Pewne' which Oliver Vaughan's grandfather (also Oliver Vaughan) had taken out in 1569 and which had descended to Oliver (junior) in 1601.[7] However, confusion with the manor lease at the turn of the century means that the presentment may have been in the right of Edward Broughton, gentleman. Instinctively (and admittedly without evidence), the later clashes we shall see between Knapp and Broughton leads one to surmise that this is not likely to have been the case and that the presentment to the benefice was Vaughan's.

Knapp was probably a local man; a William Knappe was the bailiff for Canon Pyon manor from 1576 to 1577 and a Henry Knappe held a copyhold messuage in the manor from 1615.[8] Phillip Knapp also left legacies of land in the manor to Knapp family members who appear to have lived in the parish. There is no record of a university education nor any evidence of a family tradition of churchmen.

Canon Pyon

Phillip Knapp saw some major changes during his time of ministry; from the Calvinistic belief in predestination at the start of the century, to its rejection by Laudianists in the later 1620s and 1630s. Parishioners and clergy alike were expected to adapt. In 1604, new canons (church rules) were agreed and all those entering the ministry had to sign an acknowledgement that King James, who had come to the throne in 1603, was their leader both spiritually and in worldly terms and that the Prayer Book held nothing against the word of God.[9] By this date it is likely that Knapp was already in the vicarage.

The first decade of the 1600s saw much religious unrest, predominantly centred on maintaining the Protestant reformation. Nationally, the Gunpowder Plot of 1605 caused a wave of anti-Catholicism and Catholics were banned from public office. In the same year, the vicar of Allensmore in Herefordshire refused to bury a known recusant in the parish churchyard, which led to her being clandestinely interred there in the night, sparking what came to be known as the Whitsun Riots.[10] In the following year, the Oath of Allegiance was introduced requiring English Catholics to acknowledge the king's sovereignty and reject the pope's right to depose or attack him or his kingdom.

Within this backdrop of local and national events, the relationship between Knapp and at least one of his parishioners was less than ideal. In June 1608 Knapp was summoned to the church court, having been presented by the churchwardens for 'that he dothe not [take] divine service every Sunday and holydaye in dai time neyther upp[on] Tuesdayes Wensdayes and Frydayes'.[11] This was directly against the law set out in the 1604 Canons which stipulated that 'the Common Prayer shall be said or sung distinctly and reverently' on Sundays and Holy days. So too, the litany was to be read after the tolling of the church bell on Wednesdays and Fridays 'whereunto we wish every Housholder dwelling within half a Mile of the Church, to come or send one at least of his Household fit to joyn with the Minister in Prayers'.[12] With a widespread parish such as Canon Pyon, this may not have included as many parishioners as one might imagine.

The churchwardens at the time were Edward Broughton and John Kinford and at the same court session they presented that the church wanted tiling and the chancel needed paving. Knapp appeared in court twice more and in February 1609 another appearance was set for Easter but nothing more is contained in the Act books for this case.[13]

In 1610 Knapp inadvertently became involved in Canon Pyon's own 'plot', although at face value it does not appear to have had anything to do with religion.[14] Edward Broughton, lease-holder of at least part of the manor at the time, brought a case against James Berington whom he accused, along with other 'riotous and disorderly persons', of plotting and kidnapping his step-daughter Elinor Willoughbie whilst he was away from home. This was apparently done with a view to marrying her to James Berington's son Thomas and gaining a sizeable estate.

The case is described fully in Chapter 5 but the events relating to Phillip Knapp are considered here. According to Broughton, the 'riotous and disordered persons' did 'repair and assemble themselves together at the house of one Philipp Knappe, clerk', it being the next house to Edward Broughton's, thus making the vicar a witness and a defendant. Although Broughton did not accuse the vicar of being directly involved in the kidnap, he nevertheless implicated him in the plot, stating that the vicar bore him some hatred. Knapp admitted 'that there have been diverse suits in law' between himself and Broughton but denied any knowledge of a plot. He was adamant that 'he did not receive or entertain any of those the defendants' on the night of 30 October last (1609) but that they did go to his house the following morning 'without his consent' and 'for what intent or purpose they hither come he knoweth not'. Furthermore, he denied wishing that Elinor 'should be stolen away or the plaintiff's estate weakened' and that he:

> ... told James Berrinton ... about St Peters day last that the report went the plaintiff Edward Broughton had put away his daughter because of the said James Berringtons son... the said James Berrington then mentioned he would not marry his son unto the plaintiff's daughter for any thing.

By chance, the vicar of King's Pyon also became a witness in this case.[15] Edward Sampson (50 years old, clerk, of Kings Pyon) had gone to the house of James Berington 'to speake with him about his owne business' but James' daughter had told him that her father had gone to Canon Pyon. The vicar went to find him at Canon Pyon but instead found Thomas Berington 'at Philip Knapp's house' and Berington did not know where his father was. There were others sitting around the fire but 'finding the said Phillip Knapp to be in bed [he] dep[ar]ted within one quarter of an hour from the said company and from the said Phillip Knapps house'. He also denied knowledge of any plot 'for the taking away of the said Elinor'.

Although no law suits have been found, the sour relationship between Canon Pyon's vicar and the tithe farmer did not improve. Broughton and another named Gayley were brought before the church court for making a noise in the churchyard during a christening; the vicar sent out his clerk to 'bidd them speake softer' but they continued with the noise.[16]

At the same church court, Broughton 'and his man James Whetnoll' stood accused of laying 'violent hands on Sr Philip Knappe vicar there in the court house on the court

Canon Pyon

day being the xxviijth day of Marche' (1611). A few years previously, a Richard Gayley had been before the church court for 'immodest behaviour towards the minister', though we are not given any further details.[17]

Away from strife, and as part of his duties, the vicar was required from time to time to compile a terrier listing the glebe lands belonging to the vicarage. One such terrier of 1617 was compiled by Knapp:

> A true Terrier of all the Glebe lands and tithes and other possessions belonging to the Vicarage of Canon Pyon sett lying in being in the County and Deanerie of Hereford taken by the vicar of Phillip Knap the now incumbent there. George Baynham, Francis Clarke churchwardens Thomas Wotton John Scarlett Sidemen and John Kinforde one of the chiefest men of the parish the tenth day of May 1617.
> There belonging to the vicarage of Canon Pyon a dwelling house containing ffour Bayes or Rooms, a katchin containing ij Rooms a Stable all clad with Tyle. A Barne containing three Rooms One other Room for Catle Two Rooms for Sheep One Room for Swine, all which are covered with Straw. There belongeth also to the said Vicarage a Garden, a meadow containing by estimation two acres, a faire Churchyard, A small Orchard containing by estimation a quarter of an acre known by the name of Safron Close And about Ten acres of arable Land. There belongeth also to the said Vicarage xxxij bz [32 bushells] of wheat due and payable yearly at the feast of All Saints from the Canon Bakehouse in Heref[ord]. And forty ij bz [42 bushells] of Oates due and payable also at the feast of All Saints yearly from the Parsonage Barne in Canon Pyon. There belongeth also to the said Vicarage all manner of Tythe of all old severalls which are not reputed and taken for field grounds. All the Tythe Wood of the parish Except the Tythe wood of the Canon Vallett Herbage Mortuaries Oblac[i]ons and Privie Tythes
> By me Philip Knap
> the now Incumbent[18]

This document contains one of the few references to sidesmen that have been found for this parish. Originally called synodsmen but by the 17th century known as side- or sidesmen, their role was to assist the churchwardens in their tasks.[19]

With the death of King James in March 1625 and the succession of his son Charles I, any hopes for religious stability were soon dashed. Charles became closely associated with Archbishop Laud and together they promoted the reform of the church in the manner of Laudianism, rejecting predestination. One aspect of this change was to have altars moved to the east end of churches and rails added to prevent any 'profanation'. Bishops themselves were revered by Laudian enthusiasts and the authority of the church and clergy paramount. Laudians wished to see the 1604 canons followed in full, including the use of the surplice, the sign of the cross and kneeling at the altar, which some saw as a reversion to pre-reformation days. Baptism as a sacrament also became controversial. The high ceremonialists believed in the importance of baptism as a 'sacrament of regeneration' whereas Puritans looked for ways to make the ceremony simpler, believing that only God can wash away sins, not water or the sign of the cross. If the parish registers for Canon Pyon survived, we may have been lucky to find some hint of Knapp's opinions but unfortunately that is not the case.

He did, however, show some tendencies to be strict with his parishioners. In April 1626, Knapp was brought before the church court for 'putting back' Margerie Gardner from the communion; presumably this means preventing her from taking communion.[20] The month previous to this, Margerie herself had been summoned to the church court on the charge of being 'illegitimately impregnated' by Hugh Yeomans, to which she confessed and was given three days penance. Knapp's extra punishment landed him in trouble but he 'subjugated himself' to the church court and was dismissed with an admonishment.

Two years later, in December 1628, Knapp was charged with refusing to marry Daniel Holder and Joan Kinford, even though they had a licence from the Ordinary.[21] When he appeared before the court a couple of months later, no explanation for this was recorded but he believed it was not his fault. The judges expressed their belief in him and dismissed him with a warning that he would be fined if it happened again.[22] The marriage did eventually take place as Daniel and Joan Holder appear in a court case in 1638 involving other members of the Kinford family, but whether or not it was at Canon Pyon is unknown.[23]

Throughout the years 1629 - 1640, King Charles embarked on a personal rule and managed to damage relations with and alienate himself from Scotland, Ireland and his own Parliament.[24] But by 1638, the tide was turning against Laudianism. People began to see bishops as provocative and the Laudian clergy as giving the king unlimited power. Thankfully perhaps, Phillip Knapp did not witness the country slide into Civil War; he wrote his own will in April 1639 and it was proved in London in January 1640.[25] The religious preamble at the start of his will is very simple: 'I bequeath my soule into the hands of the Almighty my Creator and Redeemer And my bodye to be buryed in Christian Buryall.'

His final service to his parishioners were the legacies of 6s. 8d. 'to the reparation of Canon Pewne church' and 6s. 8d. 'to the poor of the parish of Canon Pewne'. He did not name a wife or children of his own and his executor was a nephew but he left legacies to the children of his brothers Richard and Edward and to their children. He had lived to a good age; his witness statement in the court case of 1610 gave his age as about 59 and therefore in 1639 he would have been around 88 years old. Certainly he was relatively wealthy, leaving lands and tenements 'which I purchased of Simon Jeffreys' to his nephew and namesake Phillip Knapp and an annuity to a great-nephew of the same name. His niece Anne Knapp received land, sheep and two cows named Tadge and Blewe. With no immediate dependants, he seems to have been able to maintain a reasonable standard of living.

Although the burial registers have not survived for this date, by chance we have a personal memory of where he was buried. Almost 50 years after Knapp's death, a disagreement about a pew or seat in the church resulted in a case in the Consistory court. One of the witnesses, 64 years old parish clerk Richard Jones, had the following observation recorded in his interview on 27 September 1688:

> ....above 40 years since he rem[em]bers a grave made there for the interment of Mr Philip Knapp vicar of the s[ai]d parish but some excepcons being made thereupon it was filled up again and he the said Mr Knapp was buried in the high Chancell of the said church.[26]

The 'filled up' grave was in the chapel or chancel belonging to Little Pyon, or the Berrington family. The near burial of the vicar there does not seem particularly relevant to the court case and no other witnesses mentioned it but because Richard Jones thought to do so, we know that Philip Knapp was laid to rest in the chancel of the church in which he served for so long.

Members of the Knapp family continued to live in Canon Pyon throughout the 1600s and those who left wills were generous towards the poor of the parish and the church. Widow Anne Knapp, in 1643, left:

> ... £5 for a clarke to remain forever and the increase and yearly profit to be distributed in wheaten bread by the overseers of the poor and the churchwardens, one half on St Thomas' day next before Christmas and the other half on Good Friday yearly forever.[27]

In 1646 William Knapp, yeoman of Canon Pyon, wrote his will and left 20s. 'to the poor of Canon Pyon', 10s. 'towards the reparation of the church', to be used within one year of his decease and, more unusually, he left 'to the minister of the parish, part of one 'timber try' for the reparation of the vicarage house'.[28] William's will was witnessed by Jonathan Dryden, the vicar who took over the ministry of Canon Pyon after Phillip Knapp's decease.

JONATHAN DRYDEN (c. 1640 – c.1646)

This vicar holds a unique position in Canon Pyon history; he was the incumbent when Civil War broke out. Although there is some evidence that he may not have been resident, he witnessed a parishioner's will and his daughter married a local man so this is unlikely to be the whole story. Assuming he did minister to the parishioners, it was during the most testing of circumstances including the involvement of some of his family in wartime events in Hereford. Eventually, Dryden left the parish 'under a cloud'.

Dryden came from a relatively well-to-do background and was probably Canon Pyon's most illustriously connected incumbent, certainly of the 17th century. He was a cousin (once removed) of John Dryden the poet and great-uncle to author Jonathan Swift although Swift never knew him. Born at Northampton in 1601, Dryden became a Cambridge graduate (B.A. in 1621/2, M.A. in 1625) and began his career at Hereford.[29] He was collated in August 1627 to the prebend of Withington Parva by the Bishop of Hereford, Francis Godwin, a relative who also collated Thomas Swift (Jonathan Swift's father) to the living at Goodrich.[30]

Jonathan Dryden married Martha Vaughan on 7 February 1627 at St Owen's church in Hereford[31] and was later instituted to the rectory there (in 1634).[32] He had already been presented to the living of St John's in Hereford in February 1629/30[33] (for which he received dispensation in 1635) followed by an institution to the rectory of Whitney in 1640, this time presented by the lay patron Sir Robert Whitney, Kt.[34] This plurality might further suggest that when Dryden was instituted to Canon Pyon (around 1639-1640 but this is unclear) he may not have been resident, at least not to begin with.

Dryden was not a man to lead the quiet life of a rural parish vicar and his achievements continued long after the death of his patron Bishop Godwin in 1633. He was officiating at the consistory (church) court in Hereford in 1635[35] and in 1638 was one of the commissioners who examined witnesses in a 'cause of scandalous words provocative of a duel' in the High Court of Chivalry.[36] Having originally dealt with cases regarding coats of arms, by the 1630s the Court of Chivalry heard causes of defamation involving gentlemen; the intention was to prevent the disastrous effects of duelling.[37] Although the court met at Westminster, the plaintiff's depositions in the above case were taken by Dryden and his associates 'in the hall over the new market house in Hereford' between 28 and 30 Aug 1638.

By then, the political situation between King Charles and Parliament had intensified. In 1640 Archbishop Laud was imprisoned and Parliament were committed to reversing the Laudian 'reformation' of the previous decade. The beloved aspects of their worship came under attack and altar rails, surplices, prayer books and images were destroyed by zealots. Churchwardens were required to remove such items from their churches; even crosses, stained-glass windows and fonts were targeted. Such iconoclasm was at best disturbing but at its worst violent, destructive and frightening for the local people.

Robert Harley, Kt., M.P. for Hereford was himself responsible for some of this destruction.[38] He also most likely commissioned the 'puritan survey' of the ministry of Herefordshire which was returned to him around 1642. The entry for Canon Pyon names Mr Dreyd (probably Dryden) as the 'vicar non resident and prebend of Hereff[ord]'. This is the main evidence (other than circumstantial) we currently have that he was not resident in Canon Pyon. Whilst Mr Dreyd[en], whose family background was strongly Protestant, escaped the scathing criticism of the author of the survey, many other vicars were not so lucky. Hence Mr Griffiths, vicar of Kings Pyon was 'neither constant p[r]eacher nor of good life'. Indeed, the whole of Grimsworth hundred (Canon Pyon's hundred) underwhelmed the survey's author, who remonstrated that 'there is not one constant and conscionable p[r]eacher' amongst them. Stretford hundred (Kings Pyon's hundred) faired only marginally better as there were 'but two constant and conscionable p[r]eachers'.[39] These judgements, of course, were based on a Puritan's point of view.

By 1644, Royalist forces were 'spread across Herefordshire's northern parishes taking free quarter and demanding food, shelter and fodder for their horse'. Although half-hearted attempts were made to stop the raids, the plundering continued. In March 1645, a group of people from Broxash hundred (which includes the nearby parishes of Bodenham, Marden and the Suttons) formed what became known as the Herefordshire Clubmen in an attempt to protect their properties and food supplies. They clashed with Royalist soldiers and dismissed an attempt to draw them to the Parliamentary side. The arrival of Prince Rupert's troops, who 'plundered every parish and house' and dealt harshly with the clubmen, signalled an end to their protest.[40]

It was not, however, the end of free quartering or plundering; the siege of Hereford by the Scottish army in the summer of 1645 lead to even more raids. Miles Hill's pamphlet, published in 1650 (using reports he had gathered in 1646) gives information about the value of goods taken from one hundred and six Herefordshire parishes by the plundering of the Scots army.[41] Seventy parishes did not return information and Canon Pyon is not mentioned but the impact of hungry soldiers scavenging through the countryside should not be underestimated, particularly for parishes only a few miles away from Hereford.[42]

Possibly related to these events is an entry in the 1649 survey of the manor of Canon Pyon:

> And likewise there is demanded by vertue of an order of plundered ministers by Mr Jonathan Draydon minister of Cannon Pyon bearing date July the eight one thousand six hundered fortie and six the sum[m]e of fifty pounds out of the rent corne payable out of the said Rectory being a preaching minister.[43]

Originating in Dec 1642, the Committee for Plundered Ministers was created to help ministers who had been 'plundered by the royalists'. Later, it also became the remit of the Committee to 'find vacancies for deserving ministers' and eject 'unsuitable' incumbents.[44]

Is it possible that the Royalists in Hereford had plundered the vicarage, thus driving Dryden or the occupants of the manor away so that he had not received his annual payment of wheat and oats? Or that the Committee had found him an alternative living? According to Cooke's list of vicars, Dryden had left the Canon Pyon benefice by 1645 but as he witnessed the will of William Knapp of Canon Pyon on 10 December 1646, he was either still there or had returned and spent at least some time in the parish.[45] Rizzo states that he became the minister at St Giles, Camberwell, Surrey, and there is evidence that he was the vicar there from 1650.[46] There is thus a gap of four years which are unaccounted for, between about 1646 and 1650.

Whatever the details of the circumstances, Dryden and his family left Herefordshire probably sometime between the latter two dates. Sadly, he only lived a few more years and ended his days in Camberwell. He signed his will on the 24 November 1653 and was buried three days later at St Giles; his burial stated that he was the vicar of Cam[berwell].[47] In his will, proved in February 1653/4, he described himself as a 'minister of God's word at Camberwell'. His soul he bequeathed 'into the hands of my blessed redeemer whoe purchased it with his blood secondly for my body I bequeath it to the dust from whence it came to be buried in the church of Camberwell'.[48]

Dryden's eldest son Jonathan was studying at the time and was to receive his father's books and papers as long as he continued to study, though Dryden feared that his son would not be able to continue 'God forbid' because of his father's death.

A few years before, Dryden's daughter Martha had married William Karver. The Karvers were a Herefordshire family, living at the Buttas (or Butthouse) in the parish of Kings Pyon but just across a field or two from Canon Pyon church. William and Martha also went to live at Camberwell but William died not long afterwards and was buried on 10 February 1650/1 at St Giles' church.[49] He left a nuncupative will recorded in 1650 and proved in September 1653 for which Dryden had executorship. The will describes Karver as 'late of the Buttas but departing this life at Camberwell'. Karver left his house and money to Martha, who was 'great with child'.[50]

Canon Pyon

Martha returned to Herefordshire to live with an aunt and uncle in Mordiford. Tragically, she also died two years later and left a will which was written in August 1652 and proved the following May.[51] She left money and goods to her Dryden brothers and sisters and requested that 'the rest of my goods att Camberwell under lock and key there' be distributed amongst them by the discretion of her parents, her father being the executor of her will. Sadly, there is no mention of a child. As Dryden himself died soon after, his poor widow Martha who had lost a daughter, son-in-law and husband in such a short space of time, was left to deal with the all of the administration.

Although Dryden had left Herefordshire, he had retained several properties in the county. He left a house in Hereford, a house and lands at Tupsley and a 'little house in Whitney'. He was also very well connected; he had named his wife as executrix but was painfully aware of the task in hand and stated that:

> I desire to employ Doctor Edward Alderne and my worth[y] cosen and noble frend Captaine Thomas Alderne whom I humbly desire to assist my wife in this business…[52]

Dr Alderne was an Oxford graduate, a lawyer and an 'active Royalist' in Hereford during the Civil Wars.[53] His brother Thomas was a merchant in London and later became Victualler to the Navy (in 1655, two years after Dryden had died).[54] It was probably in London that Thomas Alderne had met Dorothie Rowe and they had married at St Helens, Bishopsgate in London in 1648.[55] She was the daughter of Owen Rowe, an Independent, haberdasher and one of the signatories of the death warrant of Charles I.[56] A third Alderne brother, Daniel, played a pivotal role in the capturing of the city of Hereford by the Parliamentarians. Although a Royalist, he was disillusioned and along with another officer of the Hereford garrison, gave information to Parliamentarian Colonel Birch through another disaffected Royalist Sir John Bridges. In December 1645, using information and accomplices supplied by the two officers, the Parliamentarian army were able to enter and take the city. A pamphlet was later published relating the tale of the subterfuge, which may have been authored or informed by Alderne.[57]

After this event, Sir Robert Harley attempted to place ministers whom he considered able, godly and preaching into Herefordshire churches. It was around this time that Jonathan Dryden had left Canon Pyon but whether it was by choice or ejection has not been discovered. His brother-in-law, Dr Thomas Swift, who was an outspoken Royalist, *was* removed from his livings as vicar of Goodrich and then rector of Bridstow in 1647.[58]

Thomas Alderne himself died just four years after Dryden and his will was proved in 1657.[59] Dryden's appeal to his 'worthy cosen and noble frend' was not in vain; Alderne left a £15 annuity towards Dryden's son's maintenance at university. He also bequeathed to Mary, Frances, Constance, Robert and Henry, children of Martha Dryden (Dryden's widow) £20 apiece which cousin Francis Griffith was to use for their benefit until they reached the age of 21 or were married. The most striking feature of Alderne's will is his evident commitment to the Independent church, and in particular to relieving the poor. Forty pounds was:

> …to be disbursed amongst the poorest people of Master John Goodwins church according to the direction of the Pastor and officers thereof. Unto twenty such poore Christians as my executors shall thinke worthie of Charitie – 20s a year. To twenty more such Christians as Master John Goodwin shall think worthie of Charitie – 20s apeece. And to twenty such poore Christians as my Mother Rowe shall think worthie of Charitie – 20s apeece. Twenty pounds in monie to be distributed amongst the poore of the parish of Hackney according to the discretion of William Spurstowe and my Father Rowe and to the poore of the parish of Coleman Street tenn pounds to be distributed amongst them according to the discretion of Joseph Sibley and Master Thomas Weaver.

John Goodwin, vicar of St Stephens, Coleman Street (London) was an incumbent who had been removed from his living by the Committee for Plundered Ministers in 1645 for refusing to baptise and administer communion to all parishioners. Afterwards he and his followers set up an Independent church in Coleman Street.[60]

Referring back to the 1649 survey of Canon Pyon manor (and in light of the Alderne family connection), Jonathan Dryden's claim of £50 from the Rectory's rent corn, 'being a preaching minister', takes on a new significance. Preaching and an enthusiasm for sermons was a characteristic of the Puritans and 'preaching ministers' were supported by the Committee for Plundered Ministers. Would Dryden have fulfilled Sir Robert Harley's requirements of an 'able preaching and Orthodox Minister'? The evidence would seem to be in favour of this and it is therefore unlikely that he was forcibly removed from his Canon Pyon living. There could also be some other reason, as yet unknown, for him leaving Canon Pyon; perhaps there was simply nothing left to keep him there. He would have lost the prebend of Withington (as did all prebendaries around 1646) and possibly also Whitney, his patron being the ardent Royalist Sir Robert Whitney.

In 1646, the minster of St Giles, Camberwell was the 'godly' John Maynard, installed by the Puritans but who was so unpopular that the parishioners petitioned to remove him.[61] It is quite possible that Dryden's connections with the Aldernes and the London Independents helped to secure him the position at Camberwell to replace Maynard.

It seems fitting that after all the complications of his and his family's life during the Civil Wars, Dryden's son Jonathan completed his studies, became ordained as his father wished and had a long career in the church.[62]

THOMAS GRIFFITHES AND THOMAS BEDFORD INTRODUCED

The fortunes, or otherwise, of these two ministers were hopelessly entangled in the 'politics of religion' during the Civil War and the Interregnum. The chronology of their ministries, according to Cooke's list, was Thomas Griffiths 1645-1650, Thomas Bedford 1650-1660 and Thomas Griffiths again 1661-1672.[63]

Ejecting clergy from their benefices and replacing them with 'improved versions' was a common occurrence in the 1640s and 1650s. It has been estimated that 2,300 ministers with Royalist or Laudian leanings were removed before 1649 and they were replaced by clergy with a whole variety of beliefs and ideals.[64] Hereford Cathedral fared no better than the parish churches, all the canons, prebendaries and vicars choral having lost their livings at that time.[65]

Neither of these clergyman have left much of an imprint in the paper record between 1645 and 1660 but the times were not conducive to record-keeping for the Dean and Chapter, the properties and assets of the Cathedral having been sequestered by Parliament's administration in 1646. The dean was ejected from his post, the bishop imprisoned and the canons and prebendaries removed; normal service was not to resume until the Restoration. Both Griffithes and Bedford were to return to the parish at a later date, but what has been discovered about their earlier time at Canon Pyon follows next.

THOMAS GRIFFITHES (1645 or 9? to 1650)

There are a number of entries for Thomas Griffiths/Griffithes in the Clergy of the Church of England database for Canon Pyon and Kings Pyon between 1629 and 1673.[66] He seems to have begun his career at Kings Pyon in 1629 and also married Dorothy Bridges there on 25 April 1631. They baptised at least five children at Kings Pyon between 1632 and 1638.[67]

Both Cooke and the church board show Griffithes being at Canon Pyon by 1645. Canon Pyon's register for this date has not survived but that for King's Pyon has and it offers some interesting, if frustrating, clues. There is extensive damage on some of the pages for the 1640s; some of this is probably rodent damage but part of it is deliberate (cutting).[68] The damage in the register looks as if a piece of the parchment page may have been cut out, starting at the top left corner when viewing the 1648 page (see the image opposite).[69]

The clergy of Canon Pyon 1600 to 1700

The entry on one of the damaged pages is for January 1648 and the handwriting matches that in the previous years. Although Griffithes' signature is not visible on the 1648 page, it is for the previous years thus it is fairly certain that this is Griffithes' work. The next visible entry (on the same page) is for 1662 and in a different hand. In the 1640s the new year would not begin until 25 March (and this is observed on earlier pages in the register) so the last entry before the damage is actually January 1649, the month that King Charles I was executed.

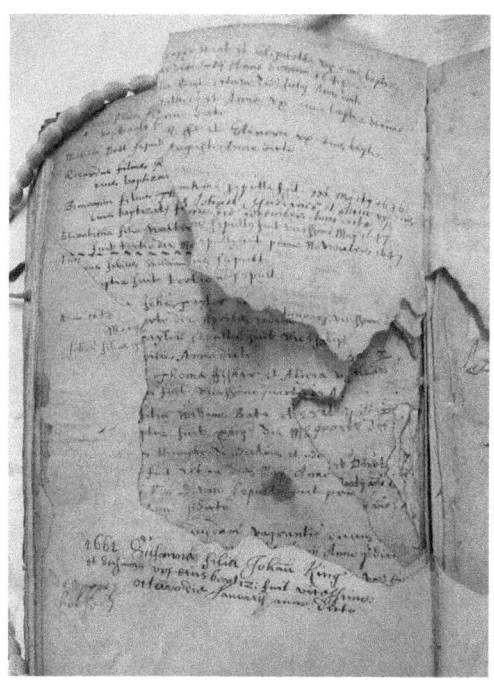

The damaged Kings Pyon register between entries for 1648 and 1662 (and in some pages either side) (HARC AF77/1).

Thomas Griffithes was not averse to making his feelings known in writing, as we shall see in the second part of his story from 1660, and with that in mind it is not unreasonable to surmise that he may have written something in the register. Sadly, whatever was in that space has been lost forever, so it remains unproven.

It does, however, show that Griffithes was still at Kings Pyon at the beginning of 1649. Could he have been incumbent at Canon Pyon at the same time or did he leave Kings Pyon for Canon Pyon? Griffithes was probably the Kings Pyon vicar noted in the 'puritan survey' of 1642 as being 'neither constant p[r]eacher nor of good life' but no evidence has been found that he was removed by the Parliamentarian administration.

The most important clue occurs when vicar Hugh Sontley was instituted to King Pyon in 1666. The position was noted as vacant due to the resignation of Thomas Griffithes, described as the late incumbent though his date of resignation is not given.[70]

The 1640s had seen changes that will have grieved many vicars. Bishop Laud was executed in 1645, the Church of England had no leadership to speak of and Parliament had begun to sell off the lands of bishops, deans and chapters. In the parish church, the Directory of Public Worship was to be used instead of the Book of Common Prayer. Weddings were to be conducted in church again but 'without any further ceremony' and the use of the ring regarded as non-conformity. Although this decade saw a greater freedom of religious choice than ever before, to some (perhaps true of Griffithes) this was abhorrent. To others it meant a chance to follow their 'liberty of conscience'.

Locally, however, the pressure on people was still intense. Charles had arrived in Hereford on 18 June 1645 and it was decided that a new army was to be raised, 2,000 of the men to be from Herefordshire. Many deserted at the first opportunity in spite of the threat of execution if caught.[71] In addition, there was particularly heavy taxation between 1646 and 1648 and much free quartering of soldiers, who often abused their providers and demanded or took whatever they wanted.[72] Loyalty to either side must have been short when life was made so difficult.

Griffithes may have had both the Kings Pyon and Canon Pyon livings at the same time or he may have left Kings Pyon shortly after January 1649. Another possibility is that he stayed and did not officially resign until much later. He was certainly in Canon Pyon in May 1649 as he is mentioned in the will of Lewes Griffithes, a labourer of Canon Pyon, who bequeathed to his daughter Catherine '£1 1s. 6d. that lyeth in Mr Thomas Griffithes hands, minister of Canon Pyon'.[73] In the 1649 manorial survey, it was stated that 'the vicar holds the churchyard … by the yearly rent of 1s. 8d.' and indeed, Griffithes appeared in the Canon Pyon manorial court roll (in a rent roll undated but attached to records between April 1650 and April 1651): 'Mr Thomas Griffiths for the churchyard … 0 1 8' (1s 8d).[74] These are the last known records of him at Canon Pyon until his return in 1660.

Griffithes' marriage to Dorothy Bridges may have ensured his family did not go without sustenance during tough times. Her father was Thomas Bridges, gentleman, of Morcott (Moor Court, between Pembridge and Lyonshall) who had left her and her sisters £100 apiece in his will of 1630, with Morcott descending to her brother Bodenham Bridges. Thomas and Dorothy Griffithes appear as witnesses in at least three Chancery cases in support of the Bridges family between 1633 and 1657 and probably remained in close contact during the years between 1649 and 1660.[75]

THOMAS BEDFORD (*c.* 1650/1 - 1660)
According to the church board (and Cooke), Thomas Bedford replaced Thomas Griffithes and remained in the post until the Restoration. No written evidence of him has been found during this time and he does not appear in the Clergy of the Church of England database for these dates, although this is known to be incomplete. This is the most difficult time for records at the Cathedral and the years between 1650 and

1660 are a particularly meagre time in terms of surviving documentary evidence in the parish. Admittedly, it is therefore an assumption that Bedford was minister in Canon Pyon for the ten years between 1650 and 1660 and is based on Cooke and the church board, both of which are not necessarily accurate.

The Church of England Clergy Database has an entry for the ordination of Thomas Bedford as a deacon on 17 July 1660 and a priest on 18 July. Could this be the same Bedford who was at Canon Pyon in the 1650s, seemingly before his ordination (perhaps as a curate)? The database also has an unlinked entry for him in the curacy of Hentland and St Weonards in 1668.[76] This is likely to be the right person as Thomas's wife in Canon Pyon was named Deborah and a Thomas Bedford and his wife Deborah baptised a son Benjamin at St Weonards in 1662 and a daughter Deborah at Hentland in 1670.[77]

During the 1650s, new Acts came into force including the Toleration Act of 1650, which abolished the requirement to attend the parish church. Recusancy laws were also repealed and new religious groups, which had appeared in the 1640s, now proliferated. Members of these groups began to refuse to pay tithes and preferred to hear lay preachers, both of which mortified the clergy. Since the Church of England had been abolished, the parishes were left to manage as best as they could. Private baptisms, formerly only used in the case of a sick child, had begun to increase in the 1640s and then flourished in the 1650s. In 1653, secular weddings were allowed and banns during the Protectorate (1653-1660) were to be publicly read in the market-place.[78] Many parish registers are devoid of entries at this time.

After the death of Oliver Cromwell in 1658 and later the resignation of his son Richard, the political tide turned again and there was talk of restoring the monarchy to Charles II. Finally, in May 1660, Charles II was welcomed back to England and the Crown. If Bedford had been at Canon Pyon this signalled the end of his ministry, at least for the time being.

THOMAS GRIFFITHES RETURNS (1660 - 1672)

The Chapter Act book records Griffithes presentation to the living of Canon Pyon on 29 August 1660 by the Dean Herbert Croft.[79] This was just before the September Act for the 'Confirming and Restoring of Ministers' whereby those in post were confirmed unless a previous clergyman was alive and wished to return to the living. This 'early' return has also been observed in neighbouring Radnorshire, where six out of the ten known ejected clergymen were removed before the September Act.[80]

Griffithes may have been in neighbouring Kings Pyon for the last few years but now he had returned and he was aggrieved. At the end of a churchwardens' presentment

Canon Pyon

'for the year last past 1660 made the 17th day of May 1661', Griffithes made his feelings known in writing:

> I Thomas Griffithes minister of Can[n]on Pion doe p[re]sent that the kitchin of the vicaradge house there is out of rep[ar]acons by the default of Oliver Crumwell of Damnable memory Wroth Rogers, Thomas Raulins, Beniamin Mason and others
> Tho: Griffithes [signed][81]

This statement by Thomas Griffithes might indicate that the previous incumbent Thomas Bedford had not in fact been resident at the vicarage and maybe the property had been ransacked by soldiers.

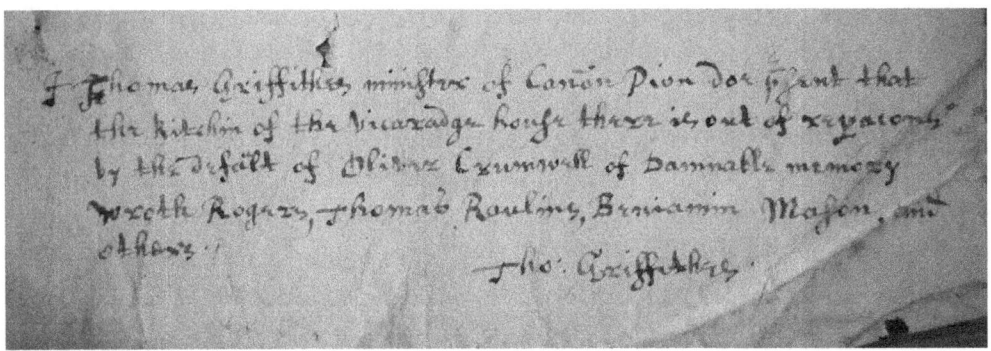

Thomas Griffiths blamed 'Oliver Crumwell of Damnable memory' and others for the disrepair of the kitchen at the vicarage in the 1661 churchwardens' presentment (HCA 4589).

Wroth Rogers, a native of Monmouthshire, had been in the New Model Army. He was a Puritan, a committed Parliamentarian and became Governor of Hereford in 1648. He was promoted to colonel and charged with the task of keeping Herefordshire 'in line with the new republican regime'. Thomas Rawlins succeeded Miles Hill (one of the surveyors of Canon Pyon manor in 1649) as county treasurer and was 'in charge of the cathedral funds from 1646-49'. He was accused (with others) of dishonesty in 1649. Benjamin Mason's role in events is less clear, though there was a captain of that name in the Parliamentary army and he was in Hereford.[82]

Whether Griffithes had any personal interaction with these men or whether he singled them out simply because they were Parliamentarians in the county is not known. It is possible that the vicarage's kitchen had been ransacked by soldiers searching for supplies in the late 1640s. The 1617 terrier of the glebe lands (see the section on Phillip Knapp) lists the 'kitchin' as a two-roomed building, separate to the four-roomed dwelling house, a common practice to avoid loss of the whole property in case of fire. In the same presentation of 1661, the churchwardens reported that:

> ... we want a Com[m]on Prayer booke and a Surplice and also we p[re]sent that our chancel is somewhat out of repair being to be repaired by John Barneby and George Sawyer esqrs but they are now about repairing it And the kitchin of the vicarage house wants some reparacon ...

Without the guardianship of the abolished Dean and Chapter, standards of maintenance had fallen. The Book of Common Prayer had been replaced (and probably many destroyed) by the Directory of Public Worship in January 1645 but was re-instated soon after the restoration.

The next few years of Thomas Griffithes' ministry were markedly different to his earlier time at Canon Pyon. The Act of Uniformity of 1662 was the first of a series of Acts which lead to severe persecution of dissenters and non-conformists, despite the fact that Charles II had promised religious freedom. This Act was uncompromisingly strict in the use of the Book of Common Prayer by clergy, and parishioners must once again attend their Church of England church and pay tithes; other denominations were banned. Many people did go to church but some also attended other meetings; if caught they faced fines, seizure of goods and sometimes imprisonment.

Griffithes appears in a scattering of records between 1662 and 1671. He signed the bishop's transcripts (copies of parish registers) between these dates, is listed in the Militia Assessments for 1663 for £26 6s. 8d. and for one hearth in the Hearth Tax of 1665. He also appears in a manorial suit roll of 15 April 1667 as 'Mr Thomas Griffits'.[83]

A more unusual survival is a certificate, written and signed by Griffithes, of the banns and marriage of Thomas Dugmore and Rebecca Mason on 3 June 1667.[84] The parish register for this date has not survived but the Bishop's Transcript has and this marriage does not appear in it, which may explain why this record was created (though not why the marriage was omitted in the first place). Thomas and Rebecca Dugmore baptised their first child at Canon Pyon church in March 1667/8.

The last glimpse of Griffithes was in 9 November 1670 when he witnessed the grant of administration of the goods and chattels of Phillip Yeomans to his widow Elizabeth. Griffithes himself died in 1672 and he was buried at Canon Pyon on 18 September. Based on his career details, he must have been between 64 and 70 years old when he died. He did not leave a will but his wife Dorothy was granted the administration of his estate on 15 February 1672/3. Also signing this administration document was a Benjamin Griffithes of Canon Pyon, gentleman.[85] An inventory of his goods survives although it is very faint; it contains numerous household items including a 'frine pann

Canon Pyon

1 grediron 1 dripping pann and 1 apple roaster – 0 5 0' (value 5 shillings). He also had a mare and a colt worth £3 15s., books and manuscripts worth £5 and wool worth 15s. (possibly tithe wool) and the total value of his goods came to £55 2s. 4d. He died before the copy of the parish register was sent to the diocesan office that year so it was signed by the churchwardens Thomas Steephens and John Kinnersley. Ironically, when the same two churchwardens signed the next churchwardens' presentment on 11 January 1672/3, just four months after Griffithes' death, they reported the vicarage house and kitchen to be 'out of repair', almost 13 years after Griffithes himself had complained of the same.[86]

A certification of banns and marriage at Canon Pyon by Thomas Griffithes, 3 June 1667 (HCA 4663/9).

DANIEL WYCHERLEY (1672-1673)

The church board and Cooke both suggest that this vicar was at Canon Pyon from 1672 to 1677 but evidence for this is contradictory. Copies of the parish registers sent annually to the diocesan office were signed by Thomas Bedford from 1673 onwards yet the Chapter Act book had recorded, on 24 September 1672, that:

> Dr Wycherley clayming a statute right to the vicaridg of Canon Pyon now vacant upon the death of Mr Griffiths late incumbent he the said Dr Wycherley be collated therein at the next generall Chapter.[87]

It is not clear if he was ever actually presented to the living. On the same date in 1672, he was recommended to the prebend of Hinton, whilst already a prebendary of the Cathedral. He was obviously very highly thought of:

> We having taken notice of the worth, piety and orthodox learning of our trusty and wellbeloved Daniel Wycherley Dr in Divinty and one of the prebendaries of that our Cathedral have thought fit hereby effectually to recommend him to your choice …

Another record, in the Diocesan Call Books, tells us that Thomas Bedford was returned to the Canon Pyon benefice from 12 July 1673.[88] In which case Daniel Wycherley may have only been at Canon Pyon for a short time and quite possibly was completely non-resident. Along with Jonathan Dryden, he was one of the most highly qualified of the 17th century incumbents listed on the church board, but Wycherley spent the least amount of time in the parish, being also the rector of Whitney and prebendary of Hinton until his death on 30 April 1677. The former Canon Pyon vicar, Jonathan Dryden, also held the prebend of Whitney and held a house in Whitney. As Dr Wycherley claimed a statutory right to the vicarage of Canon Pyon, there might be a connection (as yet unresearched).

THOMAS BEDFORD RETURNS (1673-1688)

By the time Thomas Bedford was instituted to the Canon Pyon living in July 1673 the Test Act of February 1673 had been passed. This Act was targeted at anyone holding a public office position and was not only an oath for Royal supremacy and allegiance but also a declaration against transubstantiation (transformation of substance of bread and wine into body and blood of Christ). The oath taker must also provide a certificate that they had received the sacrament in the Church of England. All of this was to prevent Roman Catholics obtaining positions of authority.

Of all the 17th century incumbents of Canon Pyon, Bedford has left the greatest paper trail in this, his second residency in the parish. More importantly, he left a permanent record of some aspects of his life in some letters to Dean George Benson, who had instituted Bedford to the living and was his Patron, and also to Griffith Reighnolds the Hereford Registrar (or Register) for the church court at Hereford. The first concerns two of his (un-named) parishioners in May 1678:

> There have been 2 of Mr Berringtons servants with mee since our presentment was put in by the churchwardens and have earnestly importun'd mee (if possible) to use my endevors to quit them of the trouble and charge that is now like to attend them being presented for neglecting to pay their Easter offerings. Now my address to you in their behalfe is the persons being poor and professing sorrow for their neglect That you would bee pleased to spare them and to strike them out of the presentm[en]t; they have promis't heerafter never to give the like occasion yet if you will have any thing of them pray informe the bearer in this case w[ha]t fee (if any) from them will bee expected; they are only presented not yet cited. I have noe more now but my love and service to you, in expectat[i]on of yo[u]r resoluc[i]on, I rest
> Yo[u]r ffriend and servant
> Tho: Bedford[89]

Canon Pyon

Easter offerings were used to pay for the communion bread and wine and were collected from each household. Non-conformists often refused to pay these dues although there is nothing to suggest that this was the case with Mr Berrington's servants. On 27 August in the same year Bedford was once again intervening on behalf of one of his parishioners in a letter to the 'Register':

> There is one George Phillips of our parish hath bin lately with mee and tells me that the Apparitour hath bin lately with him citeing him into the Dean's Court by vertue of a presentm[en]t th[a]t was put in by the ch[urch]wardens after Easter last, certainly in this there must bee a mistake; for I wrote the presentm[en]t and I know not for w[ha]t the said George should bee presented; therfore pray have recourse to the presentm[en]t that was put in by the ch[urch]wardens and rectify this mistake, I remember there was one Phillip Phillips presented a poor man of w[i]ch I think there will hardly any thing bee had of him should a procedure be made ag[ain]st him in Court; but for George I utterly disclaime any thing that might give an occasion to mee to put downe his name in the presentm[en]t therfore pray let not the poor fellow bee troubled without cause, this is all from
> Y[ou]r faithfull ffriend
> & servant Tho: Bedford[90]

Here seems to be a vicar with a care for his parishioners but why did he claim to have completed the presentment himself when it should have been the task of the churchwardens? Bedford wrote again on 2 October in the same year (1678) but this time on his own behalf and in his letter was a change of tone:

> I must acknowledge and thank you for yo[u]r patience ever since you have prest mee or rather importun'd mee to Reparacons the disadvantage th[a]t I receive my selfe by the delapidacons would bee Argum[en]t sufficient to prompt me to what you have soe oft enjoyn'd mee; besides my owne promises would obliege mee were there but a possibility in the case not to insist uppon what I have don[e] in this matter which is more I'm sure then have bin donne this 40 year but rather uppon w[ha]t I would doe if I could or uppon w[ha]t I am resolv'd to doe as soon as I can that is to put the vicarage house in sufficient repayre which to doe will cost more then 2 years proffitts at the annuall rent that the vicarage is at now: it would be less charge I'l[l] maintaine it to build a new house then sufficiently to repayre or to patch up the old one, which to doe by one that is in my condic[i]on would be as impossible as to build a castle in the aire: therfore pray excuse me yet a while till the world favours mee better then nowe it doe. I had seen you this day or before this time I had wayted uppon you to give you a more p[ar]ticular Account of this buisness but that I am unwilling to run myselfe uppon the hazard of a greater danger in soe doing then what I pr[e]sume might attend mee yet in exerciseing yo[u]r patience or rather in

The clergy of Canon Pyon 1600 to 1700

> depending uppon yo[u]r further forbearance. Pray bee not severe to mee: only a
> word to the wise at present I subscribe as in very deed I am
> Yo[ur] very much engaged though poor ffriend and servant
> Tho: Bedford[91]

This is an interesting letter for a number of reasons; it tells us something of the condition of the vicarage and that Bedford was being charged to make improvements but there is something else going on in his life for which he felt the need to plead 'pray be not severe to mee'.

In a further letter, dated 1 November, he again requested to be excused for his absence from court. He was hoping that his former letter might have saved him from the suspension that he had heard of but if not, he would beg a reversion. He continues:

> I have noe such slighty thoughts of any of you whatever some of you might
> have of mee; therefore I hope you will not condemn mee before you heer mee
> neyther in this nor in any other matters and to speake truly and more plainly
> then if the case were otherwise would bee convenient for mee heer to express,
> there is that ag[ain]st mee in the sheriffs office that obstructs my appearance if
> this will not satisfy at the p[re]sent I know not what will; I had rather trust my
> Ordinary with my living then the sheriffe with my liberty: therefore till such
> time that fortune favours me or rather providence provides for mee to quit
> myselfe in some measure of these frures and dangers that now attend mee I
> hope you will pardon mee if I appear not in publique for a while where and
> when I might bee like to bee surpriz[e]d and debared of my freedom which is
> now my choysest and almost sole enjoyment.[92]

So by November 1678 Bedford believed he was suspended and expected to be arrested. He wrote again on the 7 December to 'his worthy friend and patron Dr Benson the Revd. Dean of the Cathedral Church of Hereford' and once more pleaded for leniency in as yet un-named matters:

> … and now since I am as yet still in apprehension of the same danger let these
> lines I beseech you supply my room and apologize for a further excuse in that
> case as also let them serve to entreat your worship so far to favour me in this
> case as to give order to Mr Register (who I suppose of his own good nature
> will not willingly wrong me) that in the condition I am now in that no troubles
> in this matter attend me from your Court having so many at present upon me.[93]

The vicar must once again have been summoned to Court for in a letter dated 24 May 1679, he continued to make his excuses, writing that he 'cannot avoid it without hazzard of such inconvenience'. He seemed unsure of the reason for the summons and referred to 'that slighty notice that I have had on't that you expect me to appear to satisfy you why the repairs of the vicarage are not yet consummated'.[94]

But the repairs were only a small part of Bedford's worries. He was involved in a number of Consistory Court cases between 1677 and 1686. In 1677 he had taken out a cause against George Karver of the Buttas/Butthouse, in the adjoining parish of Kings Pyon, in a case of unpaid tithes.[95] The case persisted until 1681 by which time, as we saw in Chapter 3, Bedford had taken another cause against Charles Somerset, esquire, for non-payment of tithes.[96] Tithes were crucial to the life of the clergy, particularly if the glebe lands were small and there was a family to feed. Bedford was desperate; he was in debt to the Dean and Chapter for 9s. 4d. for 'yearly rent or tenth' and he took his case to the Court of Exchequer, maintaining that he had:

> ... carefully and honestly officiated and performed and still dothe officiate and performe the cure therein [at Canon Pyon] reading and preaching the word of God and instructing the people of the said parish ... for their soules health.[97]

Bedford merely wanted his rightful dues in tithes for his 'maintenance and livelihood' and accused Somerset of withholding them from him, as well as refusing to allow him to see Somerset's indenture of lease. This, he complained, 'deprived him of all means and ways to come to the knowledge of the said tithes due to him as vicar' (it did not; tithes due to the vicar were not mentioned in the lease, only the annual wheat and oats that Somerset was obliged to pay for the advowson of the church). Bedford pleaded 'custom'; that he was duty-bound to maintain the dues and rights of the vicarage and that he was 'like to be deprived of his said maintenance and livelyhood and utterly disabled to satisfye and pay the said yearly tenth due to his Ma[jes]tie...'. He continued, that he was a 'very poor man and hath a great charge of children' and could not contend with Somerset who was a 'person of great riches and wealthe and also of greate interest in the countrye att common law'. He begged the court for their 'accustomed clemencies towards all such as are oppressed'.

Somerset was not required to pay tithes to the vicar, only the corn mentioned above. He did have other property in the parish, on which some tithe *was* due to the vicar, but claimed that this had been paid (apart from some tithe of wool for which Bedford had refused the money payment). Scathing in his analysis of Bedford's character, Somerset:

> ... beleeveth the poverty which the s[aid] compl[ainant] hath suggested in himself and his family is much occasioned through his own improvidence and litigious temper beinge accompted troublesome to the neighbours in small trifles ...

The clergy of Canon Pyon 1600 to 1700

Furthermore, to Somerset's 'vexation', Bedford had begun several law suits against him over the previous years, suspended them for a year or two then renewed the same suits. As they would come to trial he would not proceed to the hearing. He had begun another case in the last year, at the church court, 'for tithes p[re]tended to belong to him' (probably the one set out in Chapter 3) but Somerset had made a complaint to the Dean and officers of the court, pleading costs and charges 'without any just cause' and they had dismissed the suits forthwith.

What had provoked this long-standing battle over the tithes by Bedford is a mystery, other than the obvious need for money. Somerset claimed that he had only been living in the parish for about 3 years, in a house with lands not belonging to the rectory (although he and his wife Katherine would have had the manor lease). Yet, for at least 5 years, Bedford had been pressing for the church court to inquire into the vicarial dues. An interrogatory dated September 1676 included twenty-five questions about tithes due to the vicar, many of which had the defensive tone now indicative of the hand of Bedford:

> Are not you persuaded also that as in all other parishes that I know of in this county or have ever heard of in this Kingdom That the teith wool and lamb and frught [fruit] and hops of the said parish doth not as well there as elsewhere belong to ye vicar?[98]

The answers to most of the questions in the interrogatory, which the churchwardens and other parishioners completed, suggest that in fact he was entitled to a reasonable amount of tithe produce (or money payment in lieu) which would have helped feed a family under normal circumstances. Maybe it was not enough to deal with serious repairs on the vicarage as well as personal debt.

Unfortunately for Bedford, things were about to get worse. By 1686 he was in more trouble with the church authorities. Accused of a number of misdemeanours, including adultery and the mistreatment of his wife and children, the Dean and Chapter brought a 'case of office' against him in the Consistory Court.[99]

Some of the papers of Bedford's case have survived and they offer further insight into Bedford's relationship with a few of his parishioners. The first is dated 20 August 1686 and it outlines the complaint against him. In March to August of that year, Bedford stood accused of:

> … not having the fear of God before your eyes [you] have lead a loose and scandalous life by being too intimate with and keeping in your house Ann Herring as your servant maid … to the great scandal of your ministerial

> function, the evil example of your parishioners and to the great grief, trouble and vexation of your wife and children ... Many of your parishioners of Canon Pyon made a complaint to the Dean and Chapter... orders were sent to you from the Dean and Chapter aforesaid to turn the said Ann out of your service, whereupon you pretended to turn her away ... for 2 or 3 days... [but then] committed the sole management of your house to her and will scarce allow your wife clothes.

It was declared that there was a 'public voice or fame' of his misdemeanours in the parish, essential to bringing a case of this kind to the court.

A week later, on the 27 August, Bedford made a personal answer in which he denied any wrong-doing although he confirmed that Ann had lived in his house as his servant. He also confirmed that he did receive a letter to the effect 'that unless I did turn away a notorious ill-named lewd female speedily, I must expect nothing less than a speedy suspension'. What then followed was a shockingly raw revelation of Bedford's relationship with his wife. He stated that as the letter did not mention Ann Herring by name, he thought it must refer to his wife 'who has so foul a disease upon her at that time, occasioned by her ill name and lewd living'. Although he did not think that the letter meant his servant, he did:

> ... for fear of the severe sentence of suspension put her away for some time but the busy time of harvest coming on and I not knowing where to get any other to provide for the necessaries of my self and family was forced to send for her again.

A further attack on his wife's character came when he declared that she wanted for no apparel 'but better she might have if she drank less brandy and smoked less tobacco, the extremes of which ... this respondent saith his poor vicarage cannot afford to allow'. Bedford completed his 'answer' by admitting that there was a 'public fame' in the parish of Canon Pyon, raised 'by some scandalous and envious persons and promoted by others of the same rank though very unjustly'.

Those desperate letters that Bedford had sent to the Dean in 1678 are now beginning to make sense. As well as fighting for possible unpaid tithes and living with an unhappy domestic situation, he was accused of immorality; all of which undoubtedly made him unpopular with some parishioners.

Neither did Ann Herring escape the Court's attention. On 24 September 1686 a libel was issued against her, charging her not only with adultery with Thomas Bedford but also with other men and with 'unseemly carriage of behaviour towards Mr Bedford's wife'. Her 'railing against and abusing' of neighbours' wives all added 'to the great scandal of your Christian profession and the evil example of others'. There was a 'public voice, fame and report' of her behaviour also but there is no 'answer' in the documents for Ann's side of the story.

Depositions (witness statements) were taken, ten of which survive amongst the papers. These statements (all against Bedford) would have been taken personally by the deputy registrar and later copied, read out in court and then signed by the witness and registrar.[100] The first five are by Deborah Bedford, Alice Davies, William Burcher (husbandman), George Bainham (yeoman) and Thomas Abraham (inn keeper), all of Canon Pyon. All of them state, in a similar pattern of phrasing, that there was 'a public voice, fame and report' within the parish of Canon Pyon and in adjacent parishes that Thomas Bedford and Ann Herring have 'committed the foul sin of adultery or fornication'. Alice Davies' statement is of particular interest as it provides some hitherto unknown information about Bedford's family. Her statement was taken on 4 October 1686 and she:

> … being a servant maid to Mr Wm. Bedford minister of Monkland father of Thomas Bedford, was sent upon a Saturday in the month of Aprill last was 12 months [April 1685] to the house of Mr Thomas Bedford by her said master to desire him to come on the morrow to preach at Munckland for her master who was then not very well.[101]

By the time she had delivered her message it was late in the day and it was suggested that she stay the night, which she did; her statement was based on her experience in the Bedford household that night. Only Alice and Deborah Bedford (Thomas's wife) made statements giving evidence based on actual observation of the alleged adultery, although this was nothing more explicit than the sharing of a bedroom. The others offered more circumstantial evidence or hearsay, such as seeing the pair at the 'drinking of ale together', going 'together to an ale house in this parish in a very familiar manner' or being seen riding together 'upon one horse', all of which would have been unacceptable behaviour for a 17th century clergyman, married or not.

Two of the witnesses reported that Mrs Bedford had often complained to them that she and her children were not allowed food and drink unless Ann Herring gave it to them and that she often requested relief from neighbours. Deborah herself admitted that her husband threatened her and that she been told to 'be beholden to the said Ann Herring' for 'what they had in this house'. The impression is that this inharmonious domestic situation had been going on for some time.

Another two of the depositions contained statements which were guaranteed to put Bedford in a bad place professionally. Because of the behaviour of the pair, 'many

Canon Pyon

of the parishioners of the said parish are much discouraged in performance of their duties in coming to church to hear divine service and sermon as formerly they were wont to do'.

By 26 November an additional five articles were brought against Bedford. The first alleges that he and Ann Herring had lived 'incontinently' between 1678 and 1685. The second was that he took his tithe geese and pigs to an alehouse 'to be dressed', did not allow food and drink in the house for his family and threatened to throw them out if they were not obedient to Ann. The next allegation was that he quarrelled with his neighbours, told them 'they have no souls' and assaulted Roland Eckley, one of his parishioners. The fourth allegation was that he had compiled the churchwardens' presentments and not mentioned that there were any 'bastard children' born in the parish when he had actually christened several. Finally, he had promised and sworn to 'vindicate the reputation of Ann Herring as long as you are worth a groat'.

Eight years was a long time for a minister and some of his parishioners to be at odds. This was also the first mention of any problem with Bedford's administrative duties. Between 1673 (the start of Bedford's ministry) and 1685, there were five christenings of illegitimate children recorded in the bishop's transcripts but no reports have yet been found in presentments between these dates.

The case continued in January 1687 with five further depositions in support of the new articles, given by Roland Eckley, gentleman, Ann Eckley, Ann Leath, Margaret Walter and Catherine Baynham. Three of the women reported that Mrs Bedford had come to them, begging for bread, and two said that she had asked to sleep in the 'hay mow' as she was afraid to go home. Ann Eckley's statement is notable in that she recalled a visit Bedford made to her father's house in order to collect his tithe wool. He had brought Ann Herring with him which had caused offence to Ann Eckley's mother who had promptly made her feelings known; insults were traded between Mrs Eckley and the vicar, part of the 'evidence' for the third article against him. The more serious allegation of assault was described by Roland Eckley (called 'this deponent' in the following transcript):

> ... that ab[ou]t September last there was a warr[ant] granted by one of his maj[est]ties justices of the Peace ag[ain]st the s[ai]d Thomas Bedford upon the complaint of his wife w[i]ch warr[ant] was delivered to Mr Wm. Town the Cheife Constable who desired this dep[onen]t to goe with him to the s[ai]d Mr Bedfords, w[i]ch this dep[onen]t did and meeting wth the s[ai]d Mr Bedford he the said Constable told him that he had rec[eive]d a warr[an]t ag[ain]st him and the s[ai]d Mr Bedford desiring to see the warr[an]t the s[ai]d Constable replyed that he would not shew him the warr[an]t but told him that contents thereof

and that his word was a sufficient warr[an]t wheruppon the s[ai]d Thomas called him rascall and bid him goe ab[ou]t his business this and the day following this dep[onen]t at the request of the Cheife Constable, brought the s[ai]d warr[an]t to the s[ai]d Thomas and showd it him: and the said Thomas thereupon fell upon this dep[onen]t and beat him w[i]th a staff giving him 2 blows upon the head; and this dep[onen]t closeing w[i]th him they fell down together and whilst they were down the afores[ai]d Ann Herring comeing to assist her s[ai]d m[aste]r struck him with the stone upon the forehead and wounded him grieveously. Therewith of w[i]ch wounds the blowes he was sick and ill a long time after.

Nothing further was recorded about the assault but Bedford was determined not to be defeated and he presented an 'answer' to the allegations. He refuted the evidence given in the statements of Deborah Bedford, Alice Davies, William Bircher, George Vaughan (this one is not amongst the papers), Thomas Abraham, Roland Eckley, Ann Eckley, Margaret Walter and Catherine Baynham, 'for that they [are] all some or one of them intimate friends and familiar acquaintances of Deborah' … and 'capital enemies' of Bedford 'who would if it lay in their power not only deprive him of his livelihood but of his life also'. He declared that 'no faith or credit' be given to the deposition of Alice Davies; that her description of the events on the night she stayed at his house was false (she had described Ann Herring going up two pairs of stairs to Bedford's room but there was only one). To further discredit her, Bedford described Alice to be 'a person excumated [excommunicated?] and of a very loose life and conversation and hath been suspected of a thief …'. Roland Eckley's character fared no better 'for he is a capital enemy of the said Mr Bedford and hath several times vexed and troubled him with suits of law and indictments' … and 'hath sworn falsely in this cause'.

Bedford revealed more of his domestic situation and it makes for uncomfortable reading. He and Deborah had lived happily together in marriage for many years and had several children but about 20 years before, his wife 'had proved disloyal and keeping company with foul diseased men … by which means she got the foul disease of the ffrench pox' (resulting in the evident rift between them). Bedford closed his 'answer' by admitting there is 'fame or report' in the parish of Canon Pyon or other adjacent parishes about himself and Ann Herring but that this was 'first raised and continued by the pretended witnesses aforesaid and their relations'.

Whatever the truth of the beginnings of this case, it appears to have descended into a tit-for-tat situation. During 1686, Bedford made a counter-complaint in a suit of defamation against Ann Eckley, wife of Roland, who (amongst other insults) accused him of giving his wife the pox. In July 1687, William Bircher was re-examined and stated that 'he knoweth but of one pair of stairs in the house' but that he had not heard of Alice (Davis) being a thief 'but hath known her live in good services', nor did he know of Roland Eckley being an enemy of Bedford. However, something had changed as he went on to state that 'he is no enemy to the producent [Bedford] nor wisheth him any hurt' nor that any of the others were enemies of him and if Bedford 'would forsake her [Ann Herring] they would all be very kind to him.' It is important to note that there were no witness statements in Bedford's defence and the purpose of the existing papers was to provide a case against Bedford.

The apparent softening of attitude came a little late. The last document in the bundle is a bill of expenditure dated 16 December 1687. There is no further information and the Court books for this date appear to be missing so the result of the case is not known, but two months after the bill of expenditure was made out, Thomas Bedford died. He was buried at Canon Pyon on 20 February 1687/8, his occupation being recorded as vicar. It may be that he had been ill for those last few months and the case was suspended.

Most curiously, at the very summit of high feelings in May 1686, a churchwardens' presentment was completed for the parish of Canon Pyon which recorded, 'our minister is a priest episcopally ordained and conformable to the doctrine and discipline of the Church of England'. It is not possible to know the true extent of feelings in the parish; with only ten witnesses (some of whom are related) and all of these 'against' Bedford, the evidence is inevitably biased. Also possible is that his own deposition may be exaggerated in order to strengthen the defence of his character and livelihood.[102]

Thomas Bedford's family had a tradition for church careers; his father William had matriculated from Brasenose College, Oxford, and was the vicar of Monkland from 1627, probably until his death in 1689. His will does not mention Thomas's family but a long inventory of his goods reveals him to have been comfortably well off.[103] Although there is no record of Thomas at Oxford, he had two brothers, James and William, who did attend; William went on to be the vicar of Eardisland in 1669.[104]

THOMAS GWILLIM (1687/8)

Thomas Gwillim, curate, signed the parish register copy for the final year of Thomas Bedford's ministry. Although, as curate, he does not appear on the 'church board' of vicars, this Thomas has left his mark in Canon Pyon history by one particular act. In a memoir of his life is the following:

> Tradition has preserved in his family an occurrence which took place in the early days of his professional career. He had the curacy of Canon Pyon in

1687, when the protestants were under tribulation thro' the Romish propensities of James 2d, whose memorable Declaration for "freedom of conscience" was ordered to be publickly read in all churches and chapels of the Kingdom. Mr Gwillim found in the reading desk at Canon Pyon this Royal Mandate, but instead of complying with the order he tore the hated edict to shreds in the presence of the congregation.[105]

There is no mention of the reaction of the congregation!

The Declaration of Indulgence of 1687 allowed freedom of worship again but also for non-Anglicans to hold positions of office. Many ministers refused to read it (Thomas Gwillim was not unusual) and certain bishops, who had petitioned the King against it, were gaoled and put on trial but later acquitted. In June 1688, the Queen gave birth to a son which meant there was now a Catholic heir, and this set the scene for what is usually called the Glorious Revolution.

Gwillim was, in later years, 'collated to the prebendal stall of Piona Parva' (Little Pion) in 1706 so it would appear that his career was not harmed in any way.[106]

HERBERT HOOKE (1688-1707)

The last of the 17th century Canon Pyon vicars, Herbert Hooke was baptized at Bridstow near Ross on Wye on 5 May 1663. He was the son of Christopher Hooke, vicar of Bridstow, and his wife Mary, nee Westfaling. Hooke came to Canon Pyon as a young man in 1688 having matriculated from Jesus College, Oxford in 1680 and gained his B.A. in 1683 and M.A. in 1686.[107] He cannot have been at Canon Pyon in 1682, which the 'church board' records, as he was still studying and Thomas Bedford was definitely in the living at that time.

Hooke was ordained deacon at Gloucester Cathedral on the 28 November 1686 and was presented to the Canon Pyon benefice on 25 June 1688.[108] Unfortunately, he inherited the continuing problem of repairs to the vicarage. Only the year after arriving at the vicarage, following a visitation in 1689, it was entered in the Court book 'Herbert Hooke, vicar [of Canon Pyon] for not repayreing the vicaridge house p[re]sented to be out of repair' and he was given a year to make reparations.[109]

As with most of our 17th century vicars, Herbert Hooke arrived in the parish at a time of great political change. The year 1688 saw William of Orange arrive in England with an army, with the intent of protecting the protestant faith and his wife Mary's rights as heir to James II. After sending his wife abroad and James himself later fleeing to France, the king was declared to have abdicated and the monarchy was now 'vacant'; William and Mary were offered joint rule of the country. In 1689, the Declaration of Rights set out the 'misdemeanours' of James II and later became the Bill of Rights, which included a clause disallowing the monarch to marry a Roman Catholic. William restored the Presbyterian government in Scotland, defeated James in battle in Ireland in 1690 and, with James in exile in France, brought an end to the revolution. Although laws against non-conformity were not repealed, those who had taken the Oath of Allegiance in 1678 were exempted from penalties. Dissenting clergy were free to minister as long as they signed thirty-six out of the thirty-nine Articles and 'dissenting' parishioners were also free to worship as long as meeting places were registered.[110] Baptists and Quakers were included amongst them but they still did not have full civil rights. This new tolerance must have made life easier for the vicar and churchwardens, who were no longer required to report dissenters and Catholics in the churchwardens' presentments.

Herbert Hooke married Penelope Stallard at Eardisland on 23 August 1696.[111] He remained the vicar at Canon Pyon until he died on 24 October 1707, at the relatively young age of 44. There is no record of any children and he left legacies to his sister and wife.[112] An inventory of his goods, taken by George Knapp and Ralph Bull included 'about half a load of pulse (value 5s.), about half a load of pease (5s.), three bushells of pease and barley (4s.), three bushells of rye (4s. 6d.) and four hundred of old hops (£6 – the largest value item on the inventory)'. At least some of this was likely to have been tithe produce as was 'about half a load of hay' at 6s. 8d., but no horse. Amongst the furniture items were a desk, a study of books, a clock, and 'two small looking glasses', essential items for a conscientious vicar and his wife.

Sadly, his last year would have been a stressful one; the Hookes were accused of using a young relative named Katherine Meredith as a servant.[113] They had taken her in, upon the request of her uncle John Stallard, to teach her to write and were promised payment for her keep. The problem seems to have begun when Katherine began to entertain suitors. The Hookes incurred expenses relating to numerous visits of men or friends who sometimes stayed, with their horses, for several days. Her final choice of a marriage match was met with considerable disapproval by the Hookes, who decided that if she proceeded with the match, they could no longer maintain her and she would have to pay all the board she owed.

Amongst the court papers is a bill of expenses for Katherine's living between October 1700 and June 1704, listing many items of haberdashery and clothing and including her four years of food and lodging, the total of which came to £71 8s. 9d. After their marriage, Thomas and Katherine Hill lived near the vicarage in Canon Pyon. The Hookes made their statement for the court in April 1707 and by October, Herbert had died - the second of the Canon Pyon vicars to have done so during a court case.

A REVISED 'CHURCH BOARD'

Before leaving the biographies of Canon Pyon's 17th century incumbents, it might be useful to summarise their dates in the parish in light of the current research (see Table 3).

Year	Name	Reason vacated
c.1600/1	Phillip Knapp	Died 1639
c.1640	Jonathan Dryden, B.A, M.A.	Left parish for Camberwell c.1645/6
c.1649-50?	Thomas Griffithes	Either ejected or resigned c.1649/50
c.1651?	Thomas Bedford	Removed 1660
1660	Thomas Griffithes	Died 1672
1672	Daniel Wycherley, B.A., M.A., D.D.	Probably non-resident, also Rector of Whitney & prebendary of Hinton
1673	Thomas Bedford	Died 1688
1688	Herbert Hooke, B.A., M.A.	Died 1707

Table 4. An updated summary of the 17th century incumbents of Canon Pyon

NOTES

1 O'Day, Rosemary, *The English Clergy; the Emergence and Consolidation of a Profession, 1558-1642*, Leicester University Press, 1979, particularly Chapter 14.

2 *Ibid.*, Chapters 14 and 15.

3 Nicholls, D. D., William, *The Duty of Inferiours towards their Superiours in Five Practical Discourses*, London, 1701.

4 Donated by G.F. Bulmer in 1920, as indicated on the board itself.

5 Cooke, Henry William, *Collections towards the History and Antiquities of the County of Hereford, in continuation of Duncumb's History*, London, 1886 (Hundred of Grimsworth), p. 75.

6 TNA PROB 11/98/316, proved 17 November 1601.

7 HCA 4720/2, Lease.

8 HCA R273, manorial account rolls 1576-77 and HCA 7001/2, manorial survey 1649.

9 The 1604 canons are still in use today and can be read online at https://www.anglican.net/doctrines/1604-canon-law/ (accessed June 2021.)

10 For a discussion on the events and people involved in the Whitsun Riot, see: Brogden, Wendy Elizabeth, *Catholicism, community and identity in late Tudor and early Stuart Herefordshire*, 2018 (thesis, University of Birmingham) https://etheses.bham.ac.uk/id/eprint/8483/5/Brogden18PhD.pdf.

11 HCA 7002/1/2, f. 24.

12 https://www.anglican.net/doctrines/1604-canon-law/ accessed 4/10/2021.

13 HCA 7002/1/2 Acts of Office 1608-1614, f. 3 & 4, 4,5 & & June 1608.

14 TNA STAC 8/68/23, Broughton v. Berington, 1610.

15 The Clergy of the Anglican Church Database records him as instituted to Kings Pyon in 1594, https://theclergydatabase.o/ all references accessed between April 2020 and September 2021.

16 HCA 7002/1/2 Acts of Office 1608-1614, f. 130 r&v, 1 June 1611.

17 HD4/1/162, Acts of Office 1605-6, 10 September 1605, f. 7.

18 HARC HD/2/2/5, a 1709 copy of the original HD/2/2/4 which is partly illegible.

19 Smith, Philip Vernon, *The Law of Churchwardens and Sidesmen in the 20th century*, London, 1903, p. 5.

20 HCA 7002/1/3, Margery Gardner, f. 184, Phillip Knapp, f. 187.

21 *Ibid.*, f. 301.

22 *Ibid.*, f. 301v.

23 Kinford v. Kinford, 7 May 1638, TNA C3/407/17 (Court of Chancery).

24 Charles I ruled without calling a Parliament, believing he had the right to do so under the Royal Prerogative.

25 TNA PROB 11/180/545, 5 April 1639, proved 29 January 1639/40.

26 HCA 5384, Colville v. Berrington, 1688.

27 TNA PROB 11/199/424, 24 June 1643, proved 17 February 1647.

28 TNA PROB 11/253/750, 10 December 1646, proved 30 April 1656.

29 Clergy of the Church of England Database: https://theclergydatabase.org.uk/.

30 Rizzo, B, *Swift's Favourite Cousin 'poor Pat Rolt'* – *and other relations*, News and Queries (Journal), Oxford University Press, December 1983, pp. 519-524; see also Clergy of the Church of England Database.

31 HARC, parish register 1626-1704, Film MX162.

32 Rizzo, *Swift's Favourite Cousin* …

33 HCA 7002/1/3 (my thanks to Wendy Brogden for locating this).

34 Clergy of the Church of England Database.

35 HARC HD4/1/184, June to November 1635 (further thanks to Wendy Brogden for this reference).

36 www.british-history.ac.uk/no-series/court-of-chivalry/279-harford-woodyatt, accessed 4 December 2021.

37 www.british-history.ac.uk/no-series/court-of-chivalry/intro-court, accessed Dec. 2021.

38 Spraggon, Julie, *Puritan Iconoclasm during the English Civil War*, The Boydell Press, 2003, pp. 84-85.

39 HCA 6450/3, *Transcript of A Puritan's Survey of the Ministry in the County of Hereford made and sent to Robert Harley*, M.P. for the County about 1642, being Manuscript No. 206 belonging to Christi College, Oxford, by F.C. Morgan 1959.

40 Ross, D, *Royalist, But … Herefordshire in the English Civil War, 1640-51*, pp. 89-96.

42 For graphical accounts of the hardships suffered by both soldiers and civilians in the nation, see Perkins, Diane, *The English Civil War; a people's history*, Harper Perennial, 2007, particularly chapters 15, 18 and 25.

43 HCA 7001/2, f. 56.

44 For the Committee of Plundered Ministers, see https://discovery.nationalarchives.gov.uk/details/r/C13564. The unsuitable were also termed 'scandalous' ministers and the Committee had the power to investigate suspected scandalous ministers, interviewing parishioners and gathering evidence and removing those who did not 'fit' with the religious policy of the time - see Parliament, Politics and People seminar, 29 June 2016, accessed June 2020 from https://thehistoryofparliament.wordpress.com/2016/06/29/parliaments-politics-and-people-seminar-gary-rivett-information-regimes-and-governance-in-the-english-revolution-parliament-and-the-case-of-the-committee-for-plundered-ministers/.

45 TNA PROB 11/253/750, proved 13 April 1656.

46 Rizzo, *Swift's favourite cousin*…. See also Blanch, W.H., *History of the Parish of Camberwell*, Vol. 1, 1875, Re-print, ed. Michael Wood, FamLoc Books, 2015 (for Dryden's burial).

47 London Metropolitan Archives, London, England; Reference Number: P73/GIS/125, image accessed on Ancestry June 2020.

48 TNA PROB 11/240/189, 24 November 1653, proved 10 February 1653/4.

49 London Metropolitan Archives, London, England; Reference Number: P73/GIS/125, image accessed on Ancestry June 2020.

50 TNA PROB 11/228/362, nuncupative will, proved 14 September 1653.

51 TNA PROB 11/229/118, 13 May 1653.

52 According to Rizzo, Alderne was a cousin of Dryden's wife Martha.

53 Ross, *Royalist, But* ..., p. 22.

54 Thesis: *The Administration and its Personnel under the Protectorate of Oliver Cromwell, 1653-1658*, by Bernard Spring, B. A., University of British Columbia, 1966, accessed online June 2020 from https://open.library.ubc.ca/cIRcle/collections/ubctheses/831/items/1.0104532.

55 Index reference accessed 30 Jun 2020 at www.findmypast.co.uk, marriage index, 11 April 1648, Also in Boyd's Marriage Index.

56 Rowe was put on trial at the Restoration and died in the Tower in 1661 - see Watts, Michael, *The Dissenters – From the Reformation to the French Revolution*, Oxford University Press, 1978 (reprinted 1999), p. 237, also British Civil War Project http://bcw-project.org/biography/owen-rowe accessed 15 June 2020.

57 Pamphlet entitled *A New Trick to Take Townes* - see Ross, *Royalist, But*..., pp. 117-124 for a description of the event.

58 Ross, *Royalist, But* ..., p. 132 (Note - Thomas Swift's brother-in-law was Jonathan Dryden, the cleric).

59 TNA PROB 11/265/496, proved 20 June 1657.

60 See Watts, *The Dissenters* ..., p. 120 for a discussion on the Independent church at Coleman Street. Thomas Alderne's father-in-law, Owen Rowe, was a member of this church (p. 237).

61 https://www.british-history.ac.uk/london-environs/vol1/pp68-121 accessed July 2021.

62 Clergy of the Church of England Database, 19 September 1663.

63 Cooke, *Collections* ..., p.75.

64 Spurr, John, *The Post-Reformation; Religion, Politics and Society in Britain 1603-1714*, Pearson/Longman, 2006, p. 134.

The clergy of Canon Pyon 1600 to 1700

65 For a discussion on the events at Hereford Cathedral at this time, see Aylmer Gerald and Tiller, John (eds.), *Hereford Cathedral – A History*, Hambledon Continuum, 2000, p. 102.

66 Clergy of the Church of England Database.

67 HARC AF77/1, general register 1538-1722.

68 My thanks to Liz Bowerman and the conservation team at HARC for their analysis of the damage to this document.

69 HARC AF77/1, general register 1538-1722.

70 HD5/2/23, 1674, Hereford Deanery Call Book.

71 Parker, Keith, *Radnorshire from Civil War to Restoration*, Logaston Press, 2000, p. 97.

72 *Ibid.*, p.p. 129-132.

73 TNA PROB 11/209/426, 30 May 1649, proved 16 October 1649.

74 HCA R1043, rent roll.

75 TNA C8/71/88 (1633), C8/121/58 (1657), C8/137/6 & C8/141/12 (1659). The latter refers to the will of Thomas Bridges of 1630.

76 Clergy of the Church of England Database; partially confirmed in Diocesan Call Book, HARC HD5/2/23/1677, along with his re-institution to Canon Pyon in 1673.

77 AB73/1, St Weonards Parish Register, 1624-1690 (with gaps).

78 For discussions about the rites of baptism and marriage during the interregnum, see Cressy, David, *Birth, Marriage and Death: Ritual, Religion, and the life-cycle in Tudor and Stuart England*, Oxford University Press, 1999, p. 296 & 306.

79 HCA 7031/3, Act Book.

80 Parker, Keith, *Radnorshire from Civil War*... pp. 233-4.

81 HCA 4589 churchwardens' presentments (includes other parishes in the peculiar of the Dean) 1660-61.

82 Ross, *Royalist, But*...pp. 136, 152-163 for all those named.

83 Faraday, M. A., *Herefordshire Militia Assessments of 1663*, Royal Historical Society, London, 1972; Hamden, J, *Hearth Tax Assessment for Michaelmas 1665 for Herefordshire and Comparison with the Herefordshire Militia Assessments of 1663*, transcribed by J. Hamden, 1984: https://www.woolhopeclub.org.uk/people/1665-hearth-tax and HCA 4735.

84 HCA 4663/9.

85 HARC, probate administration, Hereford Deanery, 15 February 1672.

86 HCA 4593.

87 HCA 7031/3.

88 HARC HD5/2/23/1677, Call books.

89 HCA 4664/46, 1 May 1678.

90 HCA 4664/35.

91 HCA 4664/32.

92 HCA4664/31.

93 HCA 4664/17.

94 HCA 4664/24.

95 HARC HD4/26, Instances 1677/1681.

96 HCA 5460, Bedford v. Somerset, 1681.

97 TNA E112/412/184, my thanks to David Lovelace for bringing this case to my attention.

98 HARC HD2/2/6-8.

99 HCA 5430 Dean & Chapter v. Bedford, 1686. The 'Office' business of the Court dealt with the spiritual discipline of the clergy and their parishioners and was also sometimes referred to as 'correction' business.

100 Tarver, Anne, *Church Court Records – An introduction for family and local historians*, Phillimore, 1995, p.18.

101 He was probably the William Bedford who matriculated from Brasenose College, Oxford in 1615, aged 20 and was incumbent of Monkland from 1627 (*Alumni Oxiensis: Oxford University Alumni, 1500-1886*, accessed from www.ancestry.co.uk, and see also HARC HD5/2/23 1674).

102 HARC/HD7/24, churchwardens Jo. Jones and Hugh Smallman.

103 Hereford probate 31 December 1689.

104 *Alumni Oxiensis: Oxford University Alumni, 1500-1886* – www.ancestry.com accessed July 2020.

105 HCA 7003/4/3 no 15, (*Biographical Memoirs of the Custos and Vicars admitted into the College at Hereford from 1660-1823, Collected from Public Records & private researches by a former member of that Society. By the Revd. William Cooke, Vicar of Bromyard, Rector of Ullingswick and a magistrate of Herefordshire.*)

106 Cooke, *Collections towards…*, p. 75.

107 *Alumni Oxiensis* …

108 https://theclergydatabase.org.uk/ accessed July 2021.

109 HARC HD4/1/203, p. 59.

110 Agreed in Elizabethan times, these Articles can be read online at churchofengland.org/prayer-and-worship/worship-texts-and-resources/book-common-prayer/articles-religion.

111 HARC MX185, bishop's transcripts.

112 Probate, Hereford, Deanery, 3 February 1707/8.

113 TNA C7/158/22, Hill v. Hoock. Thomas & Katherine Hill brought the complaint, possibly in response to a cause in Common Law brought by Herbert and Penelope Hooke. The bill of complaint has not survived but the answer by the Hookes has, along with the expenses list for 1700-1704. The Hookes denied any ill-usage and were emphatic in their explanation of the care given to Katherine whilst in their home.

5

'Our watch and ward have been duly kept': maintaining law and order

Life in seventeenth century Canon Pyon was governed by the rules of the manor and the church. They each had an ancient system for monitoring behaviour and reporting those deemed to have broken the rules, all with a view to maintaining order and upholding the moral character of the parishioners. In this chapter we consider the work of the manor and church courts and some of the individuals unfortunate enough to have had dealings with them. Some parishioners also had a brush with the civil court (the Quarter Sessions in Hereford) and others the national Courts of Equity and we will meet a few of these too.

Whilst the nature of this chapter might give the impression that society was oppressive and the people downright troublesome, it is probably far from the truth. The manor and church court proceedings relied upon parishioners informing on each other and although it is difficult to assess how much personality might have been involved, conversely there must have been many small transgressions that were ignored. Either way, those charged with making the presentments could themselves be in trouble if they did not show due diligence.

THE MANOR COURT
Manorial tenants would soon know the character of the steward employed by the Dean to manage the affairs of the all the manors in his custodianship (though more often than not it was the deputy steward who presided over the courts at Canon Pyon). Part of this official's job at the court was to oversee the maintenance of customs and encourage the system of self-regulation within the manor. Seasonal routines of the working of the manor's fields were to be followed by everyone, regardless of the social status of the lessee. Rules were laid down as to when ditches were to be scoured, hedges cut, fences and gates to be erected and when animals were to be kept out of certain

fields, all on the pain of a substantial fine if not done on time or not completed satisfactorily. Agreed and set by the tenants, these were often referred to as 'pains laid' and may be directed at an individual and a particular piece of land or at the parishioners as a whole.

Two types of courts were held which, by the 17th century in Canon Pyon, were nearly always combined into one event. The Court Baron dealt with upholding the customs of the manor, enforcing payment of rents and services due by the tenants and dealing with disputes such as debt and trespass between tenants. The bailiff, whose main task was to collect the dues for the lord, was appointed at this court. The Court Leet's responsibility was to oversee the frankpledge, often called the view of frankpledge, which involved a group of about ten households maintaining law and order in a mutually responsible manner.[1] This involved dealing with offences such as nuisances and affray and levying fines to those deemed at fault. Constables, sometimes known as petty constables, were appointed at this court.

In a letter to the Council of Wales and the Marches in 1633, John Grene on behalf of the Dean and Chapter, made a complaint about a bailiff at Canon Pyon manor and he provides us with a summary of the custom of the holding of the courts:

> [the lords of the manor] ... for all the time whereof the memory of man is not to the contrary, have had and used to have a Courte Leete and viewe of ffranke pledge to be held for and within the said manor before the steward of the said Courtes twice every yeare that is to say once within the moneth next after the feast of Easter, and once againe w[i]thin one moneth after the feast of St Michael the Archangell aswell of all the tenants of the said manor as of all the resi[d]ants inhabitinge within the said manor to doe such suite and service, and for p[re]sentinge of such defaultes and neglectes as doe belonge to a Courte Leete ...[2]

All residents within the manor, not just the tenants of customary land, were required to attend the manorial court. John Grene continued to explain that the custom for electing a bailiff involved tenants and residents nominating three of their number for the post. The three would then be presented at the court, and the steward chose one of them to be the bailiff. He was to gather rents, fines, amercements and 'perquisites', and to make accounts of them; reasonable literary and numeracy skills was a requirement for the post. It was the apparent failure of 'Thomas Birrington of Little Pewne' (Thomas Berrington of Little Pyon) to account for and hand over £30 to the Dean and Chapter, three years before in 1631, which was the cause of the letter.

Few manorial court records survive from the early 17th century but a short run of records dated October 1617 to May 1620 illustrate the election process:

- 15 October 1617: Edward Yeomonds, George Beynam, senior, and Richard Sillye presented and George Beynam elected.
- October 1618: Edward Yeomonds, Richard Silly and John Kinford presented and Richard Silly elected.
- 16 October 1619: Edward Yeomonds, John Kinford and William Mason presented and William Mason elected.[3]

One cannot help but wonder if Edward Yeomonds was relieved or offended at these results.

THE PETTY CONSTABLE

The duties of the petty constable of the parish or manor (as opposed to the high constable of the hundred) were seemingly never-ending, having to deal with anything amiss in the neighbourhood from affray, disputes, escorting wrong-doers to court, delivering warrants and ensuring any punishments set by the church courts were carried out. He was to report on Popish recusants, their children (over 9yrs) and their servants, but on the other hand he should be 'aiding his neighbours against unlawful purveyances'.[4] At harvest time, he should ensure that those owing services for 'mowing, reaping or getting in of corn or hay' turned up for duty and in Easter week that the parishioners chose new highway surveyors for the mending of the parish roads. Today's familiar '... and any other task' is not a modern concept; the Constable's Oath includes 'all other things belonging to the office of a Constable'.[5]

Petty constables were chosen and sworn in at the Court Leet, but they were also to be sworn in by the Justice of the Peace in Hereford. The constable must be 'apt and fit for the execution of the said office' and should have 'honesty, knowledge and ability' and be chosen from the 'abler sort of parishioners'. They should not be chosen by 'house' or other custom, though in practice this may have happened. The young, the old and the poor were exempt, as well as the clergy, physicians and attorneys. Constables were required to keep accounts of their expenditure and were reimbursed their costs at the end of the year so a certain level of education and wealth was important.

From the 1660s, with the survival of a greater number of the court records, it can be seen that constables were put forward from amongst tenants from the various townships of the manor, Westhope and Canon Pyon being the most common. Often several names were put forward and it is not always clear who had been selected for the post though sometimes the outgoing post holder is mentioned. Included here are also some pre-1660s examples:

- 1 April 1635: William Trilloe is sworn [as] Constable for the following year *[Will' Trilloe jur' est Cunstabul' p' Anno sequent]*.[6]
- 11 April 1651: Ordered that George Carpenter, Rowland Gardner and John Cox snr [senior] doe goe before some Justice of the Peace for this county to be sworne constables of the Peace for this parish within x [ten] days [next] ensewing ... and that then George Baynham, Rich. Edwards and Tho. Jay be discharged.[7]
- 12 October 1665: Returned for constables for Pewne [Canon Pyon]: John Phillips, Griffith Jones, Rich. Gayley; for Westhope: Philip Yeamans, Thomas Sely, Walter Nash (John Phillips and Tho. Syly selected, Rich. Morvan present constable).
- 17 April 1666: Returned for constables: Richard Burcher, Richard Gayley, Henry Knapp (Richard Gayley sworne Constable for Canon Pion in place of Richard Morvan.)
- 26 March 1668: George Scarlett being returned a fitt p[er]son to s[er]ve ye office of Constable for ye p[ar]ish of Canon Pyon did app[ear]e and was sworne Constable ...
- 3 April 1676: Returned for constables: William Gardner and Richard Gayley for Cannon Pion, John Symonds and William Bluke for Westhope (this last item crossed through).[8]

Constables signed a lengthy oath outlining their duties; despite the considerable responsibility they were unpaid and had to combine these duties with their usual occupation. They might be called upon by court officials, other parish officers and the parishioners themselves - it was unenviable task and not without its own risks.

In 1676, William Gardner had been elected a constable but then found himself in trouble. He had been directed to apprehend one Simon Cope 'being the reputed father of the bastard child of Elizabeth Millard' and bring him before the Justice of the Peace at the Quarter Sessions in Hereford.[9] Although Gardner did appear to catch the man, he then 'wilfully and willingly did permit and suffer the said Cope to escape and run away'. Whereupon the court demanded that William Gardner be brought before the court to show why he 'should not maintain the said bastard child for such his neglect'. Later, he was ordered 'to pay unto Elizabeth Millard the sum of 4d. a week from the day that the said child was born until such time as the said William Gardner shall find the said Simon Cope, towards the maintenance of the said bastard child'.

Canon Pyon

This seemingly harsh judgement was no doubt designed to ensure that constables took their duties seriously but also illustrates the general aversion to a person becoming a burden on the parish poor rates whenever avoidable. Gardner could have been fined 20s. by the Justice of the Peace but maybe the above judgement was an alternative. There does not appear to have been any further action on this case, nor a relevant baptism recorded in the bishop's transcript of the parish register for Canon Pyon.

PRESENTMENTS AT THE MANORIAL COURT

The presentment (report) by the homage or the jury at the manorial court reveals some of the requirements of the tenants and inhabitants in maintaining order in the manor and who might be fined for non-compliance. Thus, in a fairly typical presentment of 1665:

> P[re]sentmen]t of the jury of the manor of Cannan Pyon at a Court Leete and Court Baron held for the s[ai]d manor the twelth day of Octob[er] 1665
>
> *Imp[rimis]*. For tresons fellons or murders we know of none
> To the second article we saie not anie tenant died since last court and before we know not of anie but what were retorned
> *It[em]* Our watch and ward have been duely kept
> *It[em]* Our highwaies are in reparation and bridges and for stocks we have a sufficient ~~paire~~ [crossed through]
> We have butts but they are out of reparation and for bows and arrows we have none because they are out of use *vjs viijd upon each township* [fine in a different hand]
> *It[em]* We have not anie crowe net within our p[ar]ish as we know of *vjs viijd upon each township* [fine in a different hand]
> *It[em]* We know not of anie scoulds or evedropers within our p[ar]ish.
> *It[em]* We laie a paine of all that shall keepe goate or goats within our p[ar]ish except they keepe them upon theire owne ground and to put all those that are within the p[ar]ish awaie by the first of November this pain is a pain of thirtie nine shillings and six pence and so to keep them away.
> *It[em]* We laie a paine of ten shillings upon everie one that have not tined their hedges and gates that were to be done at Saint Michael about the corne field that it be done within three daies after this time.
> *It[em]* We lay a paine of 10s upon everie one that have anie gates or hedges about the pulse field to do it by the second of Februarie next sufficiently.
> We return for traunterie Edward Seabourne Thomas Steevens and William Clarke *vjd*
> and for faulte of court we refer ourselves to the list *ijd poore iiijd other*
> We retorne the pain of goats upon Arthur Taylor laid the last Courte for not putting his goates awaie.

[constables]
For Pewne : For Westhope:
John Phillips Philip Yemans
Griffith Jones Thomas Sely
Richard Gayley Walter Nash

[jury]:
Edward Monington Thomas Silley Wm. Plevey
Thomas Jones Oliver Gardner Wm. Staunton
George Baynham Philip Yeamans Wm. Gayley
Rich. Baynham John Mason George Scarlet
Rowland Gardner

It is commanded to Jo. Phillips that he come in before the first of Nov. next before one of his Ma[jes]ties Justices and be sworn Constable for Canon Pion under the pain of xxvjs viijd [26s. 8d.] upon notice to be given by Rich. Morvan the present Const[able].
Tho. Syly [jun?] Constable for Westhope
We present [for] bayliffs Oliver Gardner, Thos. Silly and Tho. Jones
Affur [assessed]:
Edw Monington }
George Scarlett}   Jur [sworn]

The presentments follow a similar pattern at each court and the set of questions or 'articles' which had been used can be fairly easily surmised from the answers.

Although fines for 'not using their bows and arrows' often appeared in the earlier 17th century presentments, by the 1660s the Canon Pyon butts are often 'out of reparation' and bows and arrows are rarely mentioned. Earlier in the century, whole townships in the manor were still being fined for not using their bows and arrows,[12] even though the importance of archers as part of the war machine had declined and use of the arquebus and other firearms had become more common.[13] The fines varied between townships, probably according to the number of households; Nupton, Westhope and Dearndall alias Eston Foliatt were fined 2s., Canon Pyon 3s. 4d. and Brockden and Derndall only 12d.[14]

In the previous century, the Herefordshire Musters for 1539 and 1542 include the names of several archers in Canon Pyon: Richard Mason, William Cooke, John Monyngton, William Goodman, Harry Sampson, Richard Leynam [Beynam?], Richard Silly, Roger Dymons [Symons?], William Gregge, John Symons, Edward Wotton, William Gardyn[er] and Thomas Gardyner.[15] Many of the surnames of these men continued into the 1600s in the parish and manor, as did many others who were named as 'billman' in the same musters. Although Queen Elizabeth abolished archery as a requirement for

Canon Pyon

the trained bands (local, part-time militia), bowmen continue to practice until the 1620s and the last known use of archery in English battle was during the Civil War in 1642.[16]

Some of the Canon Pyon archer family tradition can also be traced in the first quarter of the 17th century. A small number of the early presentments record fines to individuals for not using their bows and arrows (rather than the whole township as became common later). Those fined on 16 Oct 1619 were:

- For Canon Pyon: George Beynham jun., John Beynham, Simon Jeffreys, Phillip Knappe, George Leethe, Andrew Gardener, James Whetnall, Richard Whetnall, Robert Lochard, gent., Nathaniel Gailey, John Scarelett, and Henry Knappe
- For Nupton and Colwall: James Pritchard, servant of William Gregge, Thomas Berrington, gent., Thomas Davies, John Wolriche, servant of Thomas Berrington, gent., and William Pritchard
- For Westhope: Phillip Yeomands and Oliver Phillips
- For Brockdon and Dearndall: Phillip Gardener, John Wotton sen., and John Wotton jun.[17]

Another of the tasks of the parish constable was to have 'a Care for the Maintenance of Archery, according to the Statute'.[18] From medieval times, each township was required to have its own butts, but the location of those in Canon Pyon manor is not currently known. 'Butts' was originally the name of the mounds or earthen platforms which were often in matching pairs at each end of a field, usually on the edge of a settlement or sometimes near the church and sited on flat, level ground providing a long range for shooting. The butts originally provided a backstop to which a target was pinned but by the post-medieval period, coiled straw moveable backstops were in use with a white cloth target sporting a central black circle.[19]

Caution should be taken with field names containing 'butts' as this could also mean irregularly shaped remnants of a common field and nothing to do with archery. Two such named fields on the 1840 tithe map probably belong to this category; one is on a slope and the other is triangular in shape and neither would appear to be suitable for archery practice. On Isaac Taylor's *c.* 1755 map there is an enclosure called Bowcroft (on the other side of Longbridge, on the way towards Bush Bank). Tempting as it is to associate this field with archery, its shape is triangular - the shape a drawn bow would make - and this may be the only reason for its name.[20]

Trantory (trauntorie, trantorie and other various spellings) was another regular entry in the Canon Pyon court records throughout the century, along with the fine of 6d., which did not change between 1620 and 1680. Trantory was most likely the selling of goods, possibly ale or cider, outside of the proper market.[21] The same offenders appeared time and again so the fine seems to have been more of a tax than a deterrent. In a presentment of 31 March 1664, instead of 'trantory' it was reported that 'there are no regraders or fore stallores of the markets in our parish as far we know.'[22] Forestalling was the buying of produce before it reached the market; it was an underhand practice of self-preservation often associated with dearth years, along with engrossing (hoarding grain in cheap years to sell at a greater profit later) and regrating (buying produce at market and reselling elsewhere for a higher price).[23]

In a similar vein to trantory, there were rules around the selling of ale and short measures were likely to result in a hefty fine. Richard Gailey and Joanne Wever were both fined 20s. in October 1618, for not selling ale by the large English measure at the 'great market', according to a pain that had been set out at the previous court.[24]

Many of the 'pains laid' (fines that are set if the task is not complete) involved the maintenance of fences and gates around the corn and pulse fields, the cutting of hedges and the scouring of ditches. Westhope had an 'upper' well and a cistern or 'spout' further down the hill. In April 1651, a pain of 20s. was laid 'in the township of West Hope that no p[ari]sh[io]n[er] shall wash any buckinges or doe any offence to anoye the water but what they doe at the sesterne' (buckings were washing baskets).[25] In April 1664, the homage laid a pain of 10s. '… on the up[p]er well in Westhope that non shall wash any clothes [or] yarn there'. In the next year, the fine was only 6s. 8d. and clothes must only be washed at the 'cestorne or Lower Spout, for not spoiling the water', but by 1676 the fine for washing clothes at the upper well was 13s. 6d. The upper well must have provided drinking water for the Westhope residents and the lower one was used for washing clothes and 'buckings'.[26]

Another of Westhope's water courses was described in October 1666 with a view to its maintenance:

> We lay a paine of thirteen shillings fower pence of the township of Westhope that the ancient watercourse from Westhope down to the Widlands and from thence alonge the ancient watercourse into the longe meadow belonging to ffulbridge it to be scoured.[27]

A similar description six months later described this water course starting at the 'two appletrees' in Westhope's field. Remarkably, this same pain was set all the way back in October 1618; the Widlands is not mentioned at that time and the fine was 7s. but the two apple trees were at the start of the watercourse.[28]

Canon Pyon

Close to the well at Westhope stood a tenement (dwelling) with about half an acre. It was surrendered in 1683 by Thomas Silley and Hannah his wife to the use of Phillip Silley, an apothecary of Leominster (and probably Thomas's cousin), at the rent of 10d. a year. This is probably the same Thomas who was presented in March 1668, under pain of 30s., not to 'turn the water of a coorse from the holy well down to westhope'.[29] As yet, this is the only occurrence of the title of 'holy' well discovered in 17th century documents.

Canon Pyon's brooks were also subject to regulation by the manor court. The brook which runs through the parish via Wormsley and the Buttas to the church, turning abruptly to run down the hill to the present day village did not appear to have a name in the 17th century, although a few references have been found to 'the old broke' which may refer to this one. Isaac Taylor's *c.* 1755 map shows an area next to the vicarage called Vaut tree on which stood a house with an orchard. The house is no longer there, nor is the lower orchard planted with trees but the upper part of the land still has trees upon it (though not fruit). The name was still in use in the 1830s as William and Mary Jones of Votry or Votrey baptised three of their children at the church.[30]

Vaut tree with house (centre of image) and orchard, through which the brook runs, *c.* 1755. The vicarage and pound are the top of the image. (HARC BN81).

In the second half of the 17th century, Vaut tree occurred in manorial presentments as variations of fortie or fortrie. In April 1673, the homage laid a pain:

> ... that every one adjoining to their owne ground shall scower the brooke sufficiently from the weare at the forty down to the further end of Stantons meadow under paine of 20s before the tenth of June next.[31]

At the next court in September, it was reported that this was not done and 'we require the longer time for doing it'. In the following year, the pain was laid again but in October 1676, a new pain of 20s. was laid 'on the inhabitants of the township of Cannon Pion that they make a sufficient footebridge over the brooke at the fortree within a months time'. Amazingly, a wooden footbridge is still maintained over this part of the brook today, in what is now known as Watery Lane (Vautree lane perhaps?).

Agricultural tools are rarely mentioned in the presentments but between 1617 and 1619 there were three references to a *vannus*, Latin for a winnowing basket or 'fan'. In October 1617, Edward Knappe was presented for 'not hanging up the winnowing fan at the time of his harvest last autumn' (*non pendebat vannam tempore messis sue Autumni ult*).[32] A year later the widow Elizabeth Sillye was presented for the same offence, this time for not hanging up the fan on the gate of the 'meaninge glatte' on the old field 'according to the general pain'. In the third example of April 1619, the homage presented Richard Sillye for not hanging up the winnowing fan or cutting his hedges on the 'meaninge glatt in a certain field called hafcumber' (which his father William Sillye used to do) and he therefore forfeited the pain of 7s.[33]

The *vannus* was probably a shallow basket used for scooping up corn and tossing it in the air so that the chaff blew away on the breeze and the corn landed in the basket.[34] An alternative meaning is that it was actually a fan, used to blow the chaff away, but the *vannus* in these examples seems to have been kept outside and not in a barn, so a basket seems to be the most likely option. Later presentments (post-1660) mention the fields being 'rid', possibly meaning the clearing of remaining wheat before livestock were allowed in. A 'ridder or rudder' was defined in 1681 as 'the widest sort of sieve for the separating [of] the corn from the chaff' and could therefore have been similar to the earlier *vannus*.[35]

All three examples mention the 'meaninge glatt', one mentions the 'old field' and another the 'hafcumber' field. These two fields lay around the base of Pyon Hill, Half Comer (as it was known later) was around the southern and part of the eastern edge and Old Field on the west side (next to the road leading towards Leominster) and round to the north. This covers quite a large area of ground. A 1569 terrier of tenants shows that these fields had numerous tenants, each tenant's acres being scattered in different parts of the fields.³⁶ Showing similar patterns, but not as detailed, is the 1649 manorial survey.³⁷ It is safe to assume then, that between 1617 and 1619, Old Field and Half Comer would also have had numerous tenants.

A 'glat' was a gap in the hedge or fence and 'meaninge' may either be from the Old English *(ge)meane* - land shared or held in common - or possibly from land occupied by the lord of the manor (as in demesne).³⁸ The winnowing fan was thus supposed to be hung on the gate at the common ground (or possibly lords ground) between Old Field and Half Comer Field, for communal use amongst the tenants during harvest time, at least between those dates. No other references occur after this, although there are large gaps in the records until 1660. It is also likely that the place where the winnowing fan was hung changed according to which fields grew wheat in each particular year.

As well as land maintenance, presentments also included reports of misdemeanours involving the landscape and in particular the blocking of rights of way. In an undated presentment (estimated as 1650s) Thomas Silley was reproached for 'stopping up' a bridleway between Fulbridge and the way towards Leominster; such a path still exists in that location. He was fined 6d. and ordered to open up the bridleway before 25 December on pain of 20s. if defaulting. In 1664, Ralfe Nash was presented for 'enclosing up the church way from the dwelling house of Philip Yeomands now in the possession of William Griffithes' and this to be mended within three weeks under the paine of 20s. Although not to do with rights of way, an unusual entry of 1666 reported that William Trumper was caught 'laying hare pipes or gives for catching hares and catching one hare'.³⁹

Occasionally, tenants were presented for houses being erected without the statutory four acres attached, as happened in 1666 when two were reported, 'the one house inhabited by Richard Coole, the other inhabited by Simon Taylor upon Thomas Jays Hill near Dinmore'. The Erection of Cottages Act of 1588 was passed in response to large numbers of illegally erected cottages on waste or common land, built by people who believed they had the right to remain if they were unchallenged for one night. Four acres of associated land was to prevent squatters and others, as the land should be freehold or 'inheritance, lying near to the said cottage'.⁴⁰

There was a caveat to this law; churchwardens and overseers of the poor were allowed to 'erect cottages for poor people' provided they had written permission from the lord of the manor or by instruction of the Justice at the court sessions (with the lord's assent).⁴¹ This may have happened in the case of Richard Cowles in 1679 (is this the Richard Coole mentioned above?) when the sessions ordered 'the officers of Cannon Pyon to build a house for him and in the meantime build him an habitacon'.[42] There is no further information on this curiously worded instruction – perhaps basic, temporary accommodation was to be made whilst a more substantial house was built. It is likely that he would not have been allowed to lodge with another parishioner as this was forbidden in the same statute; 'There shall be no inmate, or more families, or household, than one dwelling in any cottage, made or to be made ...'.[43]

High on the list of priorities of the presentment was a report of any customary tenant who had died since the last court, what land they had held, if a heriot was due to the lord of the manor and who was next in line to be admitted to the property. When Henry Knappe died, it was reported at the court of 16 October 1619 under the township of Canon Pewne that he had a messuage (house and usually some garden) and about one virgate of land in Canon Pyon. The heriot to be paid was the best beast, in this case one brown cow. He also had a messuage, two virgates and a nook of land at Esthope and the heriot for this property was one glossy black cow. In the absence of parish registers for Canon Pyon at this date and no existing will, not only is this probably the only record of Henry Knappe's death (he died since the last court six months before) but his heir was named as his son William.[44]

Disagreements between customary tenants relating to the boundaries or responsibilities were also dealt with at the court. Hence, at a court on 1 October 1680, very precise instructions were given:

> ... it is comanded to John Kinersley gent., Rowland Gardner, William Gardner, Thomas Jones of Canon Pyon and Richard Benny five of the jury of this court upon Tuesday the second day of November next betweene the hours of 9 a clock in the morning and three a clock in the afternoon of the same day to goe and take a view for John Turbervile ... Mr James Price and John Mason concerning a husbandry way leading to old croft and to enquire out the right way and also to know to whom the hedg[e] doth belong that lyeth on the south side of the said croft. And likewise on the same day and time to go and take another view for Wm Nash in a matter between him and the said Mr Price concerning a way claimed by the said Wm Nash to his plock of ground called Hogmarsh to inquire out the right therof and how and when to be used. And then also to view and enquire for the s[ai]d Wm. Nash concerning a ditch and an elm in difference between him and William Bluck, And then also to view and enquire for the sd Wm. Nash concerning a meare hedge in difference between him and Thomas Dugmore and likewise on the same day to view and enquire for the said Wm Nash concerning the ditch he claims betwixt his [---] and John Masons fold ...

Canon Pyon

The 'viewers' were to report at the next court, which they did on 2 November:

> We whose names are here nominated viz. John Kinnersley, Rowland Gardner, William Gardner, Thomas Jones and Richard Benney being part of the Jury of the manner of Cannon Pion and appointed to take sev[r]all views in West hope we doe settle it as followeth -
>
> As concerning the husbandry way leading to the Old Croft William Gayley Richard Gayley Hugh Smallman doe testifie that they never knew any other way through John Masons fold and through the Gobbett belonging to Mr Price into the Old Croft according to the former course of husbandry.
> And as concerning the hedge on the south side of the Old Croft wee doe finde it to belong to Mr Price.
> Wee doe finde a way through the lower end of Mr Prices lande called the Wid Lande into plocke of William Nashes called the Hopmarsh.
> Wee doe finde the elm to be William Nashes.
> John Turbervile and George Hackfoote doe testifie that Thomas Dugmore his hedge is encroached on William Nashes ground.
> Edward Hackfoote doth testifie that when he sett the quick for William Nash in the Gobbett he left about a foote and a halfe for a ditch.

Public confirmation of ownership was extremely important in deciding not only who was responsible for maintenance and who could be fined for the lack thereof but also for the ownership of wood resources.

Although there is a gap in the records between around 1640 and 1660, there is little evidence from the manorial presentments to suggest that Canon Pyon residents were particularly argumentative or violent. Either they were simply fairly peaceable or, particularly after 1660, incidents of violence and felonies were no longer being dealt with through the manor courts. Only two of the surviving early 17th century presentments contain references to affray or bloodshed, though the lack of detail means we have no way of knowing the reason for the affrays:

- 15 October 1617: Presented - 'one affray betw[een] Richard Whetnall and [someone] unknown – in default the said Richard' (fine 2s.)
- 16 October 1619: Presented - 'that Simo[n] Bevan made an affray and drew blood on Hugh Yeomonds – in default the said Simon' (fine 2s. 6d.)[46]

The only other reference to violence is in an extract of fines dated 12 October 1630, in which James Blakeway was fined 3s. 4d. for 'affray and assault', but the presentment itself has not survived and again no other details are given.[47]

Of all the possible reasons for an inhabitant to be fined, the easiest was to simply not turn up for the court. Termed as 'default of suit of court', every presentment had a number of defaulters and the earlier 17th century ones sometimes recorded fines for a whole township (albeit some of these only consisted of a few households). In the 1665 presentment given at the start of this section, the individual fines were rated as 2d. for the poor and 4d. for others but conflicting evidence for varying fines make it hard to judge whether or not this was followed consistently. The earlier existing presentments (1617-1620) show that 2d. was the charge for everyone but in another presentment soon after, Richard Burchar and Richard Walton were fined 6d. and John Wootton 12d.[48] Much later, in 1667, only fines of 2d. (even for 'gentlemen') were given.[49]

Less common were the fines for the default of whole townships and the smallest of them were the most likely to do so. As with the fines for the non-use of bows, these were probably relative to the number of households. Few of the examples found give a value of the fine but in 1620, the combined townships of Easthope and Fulbridge were charged 7s. and again, in 1635, this time at the slightly less amount of 6s. 6d.[50] By 1660, presentments were no longer organised by townships and only individuals were fined for default of suit of court.

At the beginning of the 17th century, the courts were held at Canon Pyon and on a few occasions the manor house was given as the location (the assumption is that courts would have been held at The Court, now the site of Court Farm). By 1683 they were beginning to be held at the Canon Bakehouse (*Pistorium Canonicorum*) near the Cathedral in Hereford. Two of the court records in this year specifically mention the location, the April session being at the Canon Bakehouse and the October one at the manor house, but thereafter sessions were more often at the Bakehouse. The only exception found was on 12 October 1682, when it was noted that the court was held 'at the house of Charles Somerset, Esquire, within the manor at 2 o'clock in the afternoon'.[51] Somerset had said, in a court case of 1681, that he was living in the parish but in a house not belonging to the rectory so this does not enlighten us a great deal.[52]

The practical aspects of maintaining the land in the manor were the mainstay of the manorial courts whereas moral behaviour (or misbehaviour) of parishioners was dealt with by the church court and we shall consider this next.

THE CHURCH COURT

Just as the jurors or the homage were obliged to make presentments to the manor court, so the churchwardens produced presentments to be sent to the Cathedral Church in

Canon Pyon

Hereford. Although overseen by the vicar, this process relied heavily on the diligence of the churchwardens and their assistants, the sidesmen, whose duties had not changed since the Reformation. They themselves could be called up before the court for incomplete presentments or lack of care with the same.

CHURCHWARDENS AND SIDESMEN
Three main tasks faced those in this role:

1. to care for the church and churchyard and the ornaments, goods and money of the church
2. to maintain order in the church and churchyard
3. to discipline errant parishioners[53]

Churchwardens were responsible for all three of these but the sidesmen were only to assist with the second and third. As well as ensuring that the rector maintained the chancel,[54] the wardens must also 'maintain the bells, books, other ornaments and furniture and keep the churchyard properly enclosed with wall or fence'. Any faults were presented twice a year to the Ordinary at Hereford in response to a set of questions. With regards to discipline, the list of possible offences by parishioners (including the vicar) is a long one. Churchwardens must 'ensure that parishioners attend church on Sundays and Holy days' and report 'those who attend a church other than their parish church'. Also presented are 'schismatics and promoters of Popish and erroneous doctrine' and any who offend by 'adultery, whoredom, incest or drunkenness or by swearing, ribaldry, usury, and any other incleanness of wickedness of life'. The list continues with 'immorality, blasphemy, heresy, brawling in the church or churchyard and also fox-hunting on Sundays, tippling and card-playing instead of coming to church', sitting during the Creed or not kneeling during prayers and also leaving during the service.

Behaviour in church was of paramount importance for churchwardens to monitor. They 'should take care that people are properly seated' and do not walk about or stand idle during service. They could remove people who 'intrude into seats appropriated to other parishioners' or take off the hats of those who refused to do so.[55] Unfortunate misdemeanours recorded in 17th century presentments find their way to the present time. Thus, on the 6 February 1668, churchwardens Oliver and Rowland Gardner reported that Thomas Lewis was 'drunk and vomiting in the church in the time of divine service quarrelling in the churchyard and in words abusing many p[er]sons'.[56]

Indeed, a large number of the 'incidents' recorded in the 17th century Acts of Office volumes revolve around church life; not attending communion, regular absenteeism from services, working on the Sabbath or saints' days, even brawling or leaping about in the churchyard during service. But there were almost as many other, more personal cases, such as living 'incontinently' (with someone without being married, or sex outside of marriage), pregnancies outside of marriage, being married but living apart from the spouse, helping or harbouring unmarried pregnant women, and a myriad other 'offences'.

A VISIT TO THE CHURCH COURT

When the church court received such reports via the churchwardens' presentments, the offender would be called in to answer the charge. Summaries of the proceedings were recorded in the Act books mentioned above but often with little detail.

If the offender confessed and expressed regret, they may have been dismissed with an admonishment and the cost of the court fees. When George Scarlett, Anthony Kirwood and Richard Prees appeared in court in 1626 for 'leaping and jumping in the churchyard' at the time of the communion, they 'submitted' themselves to the *magister* (cleric with a degree, holding the court) and were lucky to be dismissed *gratis* (no costs) but with an admonishment.[57]

Their behaviour could merely have been high jinks but 'leaping' was classed as a sport or pastime, described by Alistair Dougall as 'an acrobatic sport involving springing from the ground or other standing place', turning somersaults 'or jumping through hoops'.[58] Although moralists had been trying to prevent such activities since the medieval times, the Church (in the main) merely discouraged them on Sundays if it lead to non-attendance at church or disruption of services.[59]

By the end of the 16th century, Puritans had endeavoured to make unlawful such revelries as church wakes and ales, May celebrations, dancing, leaping and games, particularly on Sundays but also on any other day. King James I, however, enjoyed many of these activities and sympathised with the people. He issued the Declaration of Sports, first in Lancashire in 1617 and then nationally in 1618, allowing recreations after divine service, including piping, dancing, archery, Morris dancing, May celebrations and also leaping and vaulting. The Declaration, also known as the Book of Sports, was to be read out in every parish church. Puritans despised the book, believing Sunday (or the Lord's Day) to be a day reserved for prayer, listening to preaching and visiting the sick. Many moderate Protestants and magistrates were also dismayed; ministers because they thought it encouraged absenteeism from church and magistrates because of the disorder and occasional violence which sometimes followed the recreations. Although King James was no lover of the Puritans, he did not enforce this declaration and thus avoided a political backlash.[60]

Not so for his son Charles I, who in 1633 re-published and enforced the Declaration (with a small addition involving allowing church wakes), causing division amongst churchmen, politicians and the public.[61] Puritans were horrified and those who were ministers created trouble for themselves by refusing to the read out the declaration in church, citing God's law and the sanctity of the Sabbath above the King's law. To these, even working on Sundays was (marginally) a lesser evil than playing games and sports. Some were content to allow the partaking of recreation so long as people attended church and did not disrupt services. Those who enjoyed traditional pastimes were happy that they were able to enjoy recreations after church services and attend wakes once more.[62] Historian Alexander Dougall puts forward strong arguments that the Book of Sports was a major contributory factor in the formation of the two sides which eventually descended into civil war.[63]

The court appearance of the three Canon Pyon leapers falls halfway between the two publications of the Book of Sports, at a time when Francis Godwin was the Bishop of Hereford. Visitation records appear to show that he supported recreation after church services, although other bishops did not.[64] The issue with this case seems to be that not only were they absent from church but that their antics were noisily disrupting the service. Scarlett had also been in trouble a few years earlier for shoeing a horse on the Sabbath, providing us with a hitherto unknown clue to his occupation but also an indication that he was unlikely to have held Puritan views.

A few years earlier in 1621, John Bishopp had been accused of being in the alehouse on Sunday 5 August at the time of evening prayer; he had denied the charge and was allowed to 'purge himself' by four others willing to swear for him. In the case of a person denying a charge, he or she could be purged of the accusation by finding a given number of parishioners who would swear to his or her innocence in a process called compurgation. If successful (that is, if there was no objection and the parishioners were 'respectable') the case would be dismissed. Bishopp must have had no luck finding anyone to vouch for him as he reappeared in court, confessed and submitted himself and he was consequently dismissed with an admonishment. Neither did the ale-sellers escape notice; Joanna Taylor and her daughter Catherine were charged for selling ale to Bishopp which they too denied and were allowed to find a compurgator, if done at once. When cited later to return to court, they did not appear and were excommunicated.[65]

Very often, in the case of absence from church, not taking communion or paying a church loan the offender could request to make amends and when this was done must return to court with a certificate signed by the vicar or churchwardens. We saw an example of this (in Chapter 1) when Edward Broughton was accused of not attending communion at Canon Pyon but returned with a certificate from the vicar of Kington.[66]

Cases involving sexual transgression of some sort nearly always resulted in a penance. Most common of these cases were the 'sex outside of marriage' kind or 'living incontinently' to use the contemporary term, which often resulted in a pregnancy. Both parties would be given a penance, a form of humiliation, usually in the local church in front of everyone who knew them. The offender stood bareheaded before the pulpit clad in a sheet, in some places with a paper writing fixed to the chest denoting the offence, in others carrying a white rod. After hearing an appropriate sermon, the offender must ask forgiveness from God and the congregation and promise not to sin again. In one such Canon Pyon case, Philip Clottworthin failed to purge himself of his accusation by six compurgators and was given three such days of penance: one in his own church, one at the Cathedral church and one at Holmer church.[67]

Occasionally, a case will reveal detail about parishioners which would be hard to find elsewhere. When William Mason was required to find six compurgators to swear his innocence, the six produced were named in the Act book as John Bowley, James Hill, John Gardiner, Richard Tailer, Richard Jones and George Beynam. However, four of these were objected to by Elizabeth Yeomans:

> … that the said John Bowley was and is tenant of the said John Mason [a name error or is this a relative?] and a daie labourer and that John Gardiner is the cosen German of the said Mason and a sollicitor for him in this cause and that Richard Tailer is a verie poore man and kept uppon the almes of the p[ar]ish and that Richard Jones is a single man and a poore servant unto Wm Knappe[68]

Collusion with employees and relatives is an obvious objection but a 'respectable' parishioner in the 17th century clearly did not include anyone in poverty. Further entries in the Act book include a description of Mason's adulterous behaviour for which he received hefty penances; one day at his own church, one at the Cathedral church and three times at a public place in the city of Hereford. He was required to return in two weeks with a certificate to prove completion of the penances but before three days were out, Mason petitioned for a commutation of his 'sentence' and it seems to have been replaced with a pecuniary one.[69]

Canon Pyon

Other Canon Pyon cases of this type of offence involved people who were married but living apart from each other, one couple who lived together before they married and then arranged to marry clandestinely, and married people accused of living with someone other than who they married.[70] In many of these and other types of cases, the alleged offenders simply did not turn up to the court when summoned and this would result in instant excommunication. Such a person would not be allowed in the church, take part in communion, or even communicate with other Christians. An excommunicate could go back to the court and request to be absolved if he or she was prepared to submit and possibly receive a penance. Sometimes, but not always, the excommunication would be revoked with just an admonition.

Another important task of the church courts was to deal with probate in the diocese. This might be simply to register with the court as the executor of a last will and testament and these entries can provide family details in the absence of parish registers. As an example, when Alice Emons died, her son Hugh registered as the executor at the court on 26 May 1612.[71] A person might also be summoned to court if it was believed he or she had insufficiently executed a will. When Thomas Berrington was called before the court about the will of James Berrington, probably his father, he claimed that James had left no goods, only his clothes.[72]

There is a little more evidence of violent behaviour in the records of the church court, compared with that of the manorial court but not significantly so. Anne, the wife of Richard Knappe was accused of 'beting abusing and [cur]sing Hughe Gardner her naturall father' in 1608.[73] The vicar Phillip Knapp had 'violent hands' laid upon him in 1611 by Edward Broughton and James Whetnoll. Then there was brawling in the churchyard, reported in 1626, between Oliver Gardner (who denied the charge) and widow Anne Knapp and her son John (the latter confessed to the charge).[74] These are interesting cases in that they may indicate long-standing aggravation between families. Phillip Knapp, the vicar, had a brother called Richard and a nephew John, so Anne Knappe may have been his sister-in-law. One of the churchwardens reporting the alleged abuse of Hughe Gardner was Edward Broughton and the court appearance was on the same day that the same churchwardens accused the vicar of not taking divine service every Sunday and other days. We have come across Broughton's clashes with the vicar before and it is not too great a step to consider extending Broughton's resentment with the vicar to that of his family.

Thus the church (or ecclesiastical) courts, dealing as they did with such personal matters, were understandably unpopular with parishioners of the time.

QUARTER SESSIONS AT HEREFORD

In the absence of records of the churchwardens' accounts for Canon Pyon in the 17th century, poorer parishioners can easily be under-represented in an account such as this. Sometimes references turn up in the civil court of the Quarter Sessions. We have already met the case of Richard Cowles who was to have a house built for him, by order of the sessions. The financial aspects of cases involving illegitimacy was often dealt with by this court. On 7 January 1667/8:

> ... it was ordered that the churchwardens and overseers of the poor of the parish of Canon Pyon doe take care for the p[re]sent relief and sustenance of Johane Williams who was greate with child of a bastard [an illegitimate child] ... but after her delivery the reputed father is to meynteyne the child and reymburse the s[ai]d ffines the charges of keeping the s[ai]d child in the meantime the s[ai]d Johan is to be [sent] to the house of correc[i]on ...[75]

Although time in gaol, or the house of correction in the above case, was often the punishment by this court, the magistrates may also have looked to prevent further wrong-doing by ordering the parish to provide an alternative life for him or her. This was evident in the case of Robert Powell, who had been caught stealing a cow from Mr. Kinnersley of Canon Pyon and had spent time in custody. At the sessions on 9 January 1672, he was ordered to be released and in no uncertain terms:

> This court doth order that Robert Powell who is fit and able to be an apprentice be bound by indenture unto some able p[er]son wthin the parish of Canon Pyon for seven years to follow the calling of husbandry. And the churchwardens and ov[er]seers of the poore of Canon Pyon aforesaid are hereby required that they take care to provide him the said Robert Powell such necesary apparell as lynen and wollen and all other things w[i]ch are fit and requisit for such a one in that employment and find out a p[er]son who is fit to be a M[aste]r for ye sd Robert and this they are required to do before the next Quarter Sessions or else they will be dealt with all as contemners of the order of this court.[76]

As an apprentice Powell was entitled to be fed and clothed but not given money, except perhaps by the benevolence of the master.

One shocking discovery in the Quarter Sessions order books is the accusation that poor children from Canon Pyon and neighbouring parishes may have been sent abroad. Just two years before the Powell case, in 1670:

> Uppon the complaint of Tho. Blythe of the p[ar]ish of Weobley that one John Seaborne sonne of Edw. Seaborne of the p[ar]ish of Canon Pyon d[e]vises a trade in inveigling and carrying away poore children and selling them for slaves into the Barbadas and in p[ar]ticular a child of the petic[i]oners. This court doth desire the Justices of the Peace in that allottm[en]t to send for the said John Seaborne and examine the truth of the premisses and if they soe cause to binde him over by recognizance with surety to appeare here to answer the same.[77]

Frustratingly, the court rolls for this date have not survived so the complaint remains an unproven accusation. There was an Edward Seaborne in Canon Pyon at this time as he appears in some manorial suit rolls and court records in the 1660s and he was buried at the parish church on 26 May 1671 but there are no manorial records naming a John Seaborne before or after this date. Currently, the only possible record of him is in a diocesan call book which lists John Seaborne as a chirurgeon for the parish of Canon Pyon in 1677 and 1680.[78]

Although we do not know what happened to Thomas Blythe's child, it is known that children were being 'kidnapped' and taken for labour in the American colonies. It is for this reason that Barbados administrators created a law in 1661 specifying that English children under 14 years of age could not be landed in Barbados without a legal document of consent from the parent or guardian. Those under 18 years of age who arrived without a contract or indenture could only serve a maximum of 7 years and would then be free to leave. Even those who went voluntarily but without a contract were given something called the 'custom of the country' which gave them some legal and social status as indentured servants and 'no resident European was ever considered a slave'.[79] Whilst acknowledging that many indentured servants also suffered incredibly harsh treatment at the hands of their masters, this status is in stark contrast to that of people taken from Africa; they never went voluntarily, served as slaves for life (and in the case of women for their children's lives) and had no legal or social rights until the 1830s. That people in rural 17th century Herefordshire were aware of Barbados and the possibility that children were being sent there at this date is, in itself, of interest and would merit further investigation.

COURTS OF EQUITY

Some disagreements were taken up at the national level in the courts of equity. These were courts based on what was regarded as morally right as opposed to the common law. People from all backgrounds could, and did, take up cases against fellow citizens and family members. Commonly known are the Court of Chancery and the Court of

Exchequer but when violence was claimed to be involved, a complainant often resorted to the Court of Star Chamber. It is in this court that Edward Broughton of Canon Pyon brought a case against James Berrington in 1610, in which he claimed (amongst other things) that his step-daughter was kidnapped by 'riotous' persons whilst he was away from home and his wife Isabell was ill.[80] Broughton's side of the story was dramatically told, with repetition of key phrases emphasising violence, and undoubtedly exaggerated to ensure sympathy for his cause.

CANON PYON'S LOVE STORY

In or about 1599, Edward Broughton married Isabell Willoughbie, the widow of Robert Willoughbie of Little Comberton in Worcestershire. Elinor Willoughbie was the daughter of Isabell and Robert Willoughbie and sole heir to Robert's sizeable estate. The Broughtons (with Elinor) leased and lived at 'the site and capital messuage in the manor of Canon Pyon. The defendant, James Berrington, leased and lived at Little Pyon with his son Thomas Berrington.

Broughton described Berrington as a 'man of small estate and dwelling near' to his own house at Canon Pyon and because Elinor was heir to an estate from her father, Berrington 'plotted and devised how to steal away the said Elinor Willoughbie and to marry her to his said son' without his and his wife's consent or 'good liking'. According to Broughton's deposition, on 30 of October 1610, the Berringtons:

> … ryottouslie routouslie and unlawfullie assembled unto them Lewys Gwyn James Durande William Munne John Wilkes Richard Nashe Hughe Edmonds Edward Edmonds Thomas Grene with dyvers other riottous and disordered p[er]sons unknown.

They assembled at Little Pyon and armed themselves 'with dyverse sorts of weapons as swords daggers fforest bills pikestaves and dyverse other sortes of weapons' and plotted in a 'riotous and routous warlike' manner. At 12 o'clock that same night, they marched to Broughton's house and there 'laye in ambushe about the said house and offered forciblie to breake and enter into the said house to the intent to effect theire said unlawfull purposes and designs' but they were disappointed, finding the house 'stronger than they expected'.

The 'riotous and disorderd' persons then tried to persuade the servants, 'both by threatenings and rewards,' to open the doors and bring Elinor to them but the servants refused and so the men withdrew and 'riotously and unlawfully' assembled at the house of the vicar Philip Knapp, it being by now about 3 or 4 o'clock in the morning. There they continued to plot to devise a better way to 'effect their said purpose'. By now the above 'riotous and disordered persons' also included William Trilloe, Philip Knapp the younger, Edward Sampson, clerk, Roger Nashe and others.

Broughton claimed that James Berrington, Thomas Berrington and Lewis Gwyne had decided to go early in the morning to the house and protest that they 'came only in kindness' to see Broughton's sick wife. Then, when admitted to the house, the others would be 'ready with their weapons and a horse' and with 'force and violence carrie her [Elinor] away'.

The house of the vicar Phillip Knappe was 'near adjoining the said [Broughton's] house' but when the Berringtons and Lewis Gwyn turned up at Broughton's house, it was locked and again the servants refused their entry 'doubting the said James Berringtons faire speeches' and believing he would 'unlawfully steal away the said Elinor' against their master's wishes. However, after vowing and protesting that he would not do such a thing, James Berrington allegedly persuaded the servants to let them in and then proceeded to take various goods 'of great value' and attempted to take Elinor. On finding their escape hampered by locked doors, they then 'commanded menaced and threatened' the servants to open the doors, which they refused to do. James Berrington 'then and there drewe out his dagger and did assaulte and grievouslie hurte and wounde' the servants, then took an axe and threatened to break down the doors and caused such a 'tumult and outcry' that Isabell, Broughton's wife, came down from her sick bed. She too was then allegedly attacked, struck down and 'lefte her then and there for deade'.

The other men then came from Philip Knapp's house, broke into the Broughtons' house, brought out Elinor and, having a horse ready, took her away and married her to the said Thomas Berrington 'without any lawful licence authority'. To add insult to injury, they also allegedly took 'divers goods writings plate jewells readie money fine linnen apparell and other things of great value'. Broughton appealed to the king and his court; that these unlawful misdemeanours were:

> ... repugnant and contrarie to the lawes and ordinances of this your maj[esties] realme of England and were p[er]petrated comitted and done since your majesties last free and general p[ar]don' and for restitution to be made for the great wrongs donne unto him.

Broughton finally requested that subpoenas be issued to the perpetrators, statements upon oath be taken and for punishment to be conferred on the wrong-doers.

Statements were indeed taken, from Elinor (now Elinor Berrington, aged 18, wife of Thomas of King's Pyon), the two vicars Phillip Knappe and Edward Sampson (the latter from King's Pyon), Richard Nashe (aged 40 of Hope), Lewis Gwinne (aged 70 of Canon Pyon), Hugh Emons (aged 30 of Canon Pyon), John Wilkes (ages 33 of Ivington), Edward Emons (aged 34 of Canon Pyon) and William Munne (aged 40 of Birley).

Elinor answered the interrogatory questions, as did the other witnesses, but she also made a longer deposition giving her side of the story and which throws a completely different light on the situation. She began by confirming that her mother was the widow of Robert Willoughbie of Little Comberton and did marry Broughton, whom she described as 'far in debt and of little or no worth means or ability at all (as she had often heard)'. Being Willoughbie's only daughter she was to inherit lands in Bourton on the Water, the reversions of the parsonage of 'Stowe on the Ould' and Little Comberton and also some land in the latter. She claimed that Broughton, by means of his marriage to her mother Isabell had 'gotten into his hands and custody' all these advowsons and lands, even though she had been made a ward of (the late) Queen Elizabeth. Her father had also the lease of the rectory and parsonage of Little Comberton which was to come to her, as well as two parts of his goods and chattels and a debt that her great uncle Harry Willoughbie owed, but her father died intestate.

Elinor was only five years old when her mother had married Broughton. Not only did he gain her property and the 'keeping and breeding' of her (the right to choose her husband) but Elinor accused him of 'defeating' her of all her legacies by procuring letters of administration in her mother's name for her father's estate. She spoke of a case against Broughton in the Court of Wards (she being His Majesty's ward) but Broughton was bringing his own law suits against her and Thomas Berrington 'to molest and trouble [her] and her said husband and to tire them out.... thereby to make them less able to prosecute their said suit in the Court of Wards'. Elinor claimed that her great uncle Harry Willoughbie, having obtained her wardship from Queen Elizabeth and the custody of her lands, did release them both to Elinor herself but Broughton had been collecting all the rents for himself.

Neither did he maintain her or allow 'breeding fitting for her estate and degree'. He would not consent to any meeting with potential suitors but instead endeavoured to match her with his younger brother John Broughton (who had no estate of his own and whom Elinor and her mother did not appear to like). This 'ill usage' by Broughton towards Elinor caused Isabell so much grief and sorrow that she 'fell into a languishing disease or consumption'. For some time, Isabell had wanted Elinor to marry Thomas Berrington, the only son of James Berrington and 'likely to have a good estate of inheritance after his father's decease', but Broughton did his level best to hinder them.

Canon Pyon

On 29 October 1609, when Broughton had gone to Little Comberton, Isabell sent her long-time servant Thomas Grene to request James Berrington to come to her to confer on the subject of marriage. He returned a message by his own servant Hugh Emons, agreeing with the proposal and she then sent Emons with some money to procure a marriage licence from the Ordinary at Hereford, which he did. The following morning, James Berrington went (with Lewys Gwynne but no weapons) to Broughton's house at Canon Pyon where James Storre, Broughton's servant, let them in and took them to Isabell's chamber where she 'lay sick in her bed' and where they talked for a while. Isabell then commanded Elinor to 'apparell herself' and go with James Berrington and be married to Thomas Berrington which she 'was very willing to do'. Storre, when he realised what was happening, sent for other servants of Broughton who 'began to take some exceptions'. Isabell got out of bed to pacify them but Storre and the others locked the doors, then 'began an assault and affray' on Berrington, wounding him and threatening Isabell. Elinor 'in time of which hurly burly tumult' used the opportunity to get out of the house.

Elinor went on to say that she was above seventeen years at the time and was 'now above eighteen years' of age and 'having the whole disposition of herself in marriage' did (with the consent of her mother) marry Thomas Berrington in the parish church of Hope under Dinmore.

It is somewhat ironic that Edward Broughton had accused James Berrington of plotting to marry his son to Elinor in order to gain an estate when it would appear that he himself had done exactly the same when marrying Isabell. There is another case in the Star Chamber records, dated 1603, against Broughton for the falsification of the probate of the will of Thomas Willoughby (Elinor's grandfather) regarding the tithes of Little Comberton and there may well be more cases of his unscrupulous dealings.[81] Unfortunately, the Orders and Decrees giving the decisions have been lost for the Court of Star Chamber so we do not know the outcome of any of these cases.

Elinor and Thomas' marriage at Hope under Dinmore cannot be verified in the parish register; as with Canon Pyon, the Hope registers for this date have not survived. In this case, Elinor's own remarkable account of events surely compensates for that lack. Why did they choose Dinmore and not Canon Pyon, Wellington or Kings Pyon? Although we cannot know for sure, the most likely reason was that Dinmore was the parish where Thomas's close relatives lived; there were Berington cousins at Winsley House on the lane between Westhope Hill and Dinmore.[82] It makes sense for the couple to have ridden up to Westhope, called in at Winsley and with family as escorts and witnesses, continued on to Dinmore church, a total distance of about 3 or 4 miles.

The match was well made as they remained together for many years. The Herald's Visitations of 1634 records them with their children James, William, John, Thomas, Mary, Jane and Katherin[e]. There is also a footnote in this record which indicates that Thomas's wife was known as Leah, which adds a personal touch to the family's history.[83]

In her statement, Elinor recorded that she did not take anything with her on her wedding day but her 'wearing apparel and 5s in her purse' but after her marriage, her mother sent her some things: 30s. as a gift, a chafing dish, a posnett, half a dozen saucers, a dozen trenchers, a trunk with cushions and samplers and other little boxes with silk, lace and thread, 'all which was her owne household stuff'. She also sent her a coffer in which were two rings (one a token and the other given her by her mother), three pairs of flax sheets, a dozen and a half of flaxen napkins and two flaxen table cloths, all marked with her name, together with some other apparel.

Marvellously rich in detail, the witness statements provide us with imagery of the event and also snippets of local and genealogical information. James Berrington's man, John Wilkes, said that his 'maister' had sent for him to come to the marriage of his son to Elinor Willoughbie and he then wished Wilkes to go with him to Canon Pyon. Whereby Wilkes, 'taking his horse in his hand and having his sword and dagger, went in the companie of his said maister and one Lewis Gwinne unto Canon Peawne aforesaid about the rysing of the sunne'. They went into the house of Philip Knapp the vicar where they found Hugh Emons, Edward Emons and Richard Nashe 'each one of them having a staff, and the said Thomas Berrington walking about the churchyard'. Edward Emons describes meeting the others at Little Pyon the evening before and all of them 'with staves, daggers [and him] a forest bill' went 'to Cannon Peawne along the churchwaye w[i]thin a stones throwe of the [Broughton] howse' (but only his brother Hugh went to the house that evening and was turned away by the servants).

Although it is not clear where the Broughtons lived, it is probable that it was at the house (or site of the house) known today as Court Farm which is within a 'stone's throw' of the church and 'near adjoining' the vicarage. It is also possible that there was an earlier building on the site of The Great House; the way from the direction of Little Pyon comes down the hill between the two. Another possibility is a lost building such as Baynham's House, a substantial property a little further down the lane from the church (in *c.* 1755), but this sits less easily with the tentative descriptions of the location.[84]

NOTES

1 For a useful explanation of these courts, see Stuart, Denis, *Manorial Records*, Phillimore & Co. Ltd, 1992, p.1.

2 HCA 4786.

3 HCA R1041.

4 Purveyances - royal right to buy provisions at below market rate, open to abuse by corrupt officials and finally abolished in 1660 (Tenures Abolition Act).

5 Constables duties and oath in: Dalton, Michael, *The Country Justice: containing the practice, duty and power of the justices of the peace, as well in as out of their sessions*, 1618, Chap 174, pp. 426-427 (reprint 1766) accessed on www.archive.org, October 2020.

6 HCA R1042.

7 HCA R1043.

8 Last four examples from HCA 4735.

9 HARC Q/SO/2 ff. 75A & 79A, 1677.

10 Dalton, *The Country Justice...*, Chap 28, p. 65.

11 HCA 4735.

12 HCA R1041, 1617-20.

13 Hardy, Robert & Strickland, Matthew, *The Great Warbow: From Hastings to the Mary Rose*, J.H. Haynes & Co Ltd, 2011.

14 HCA R1042, 1 April 1635.

15 Faraday, M. A. (ed), *Herefordshire Musters of 1539 and 1542*, published by lulu.com, 2012

16 Roth, Erik, *With a Bended Bow; Archery in Medieval and Renaissance Europe*, Spellmount, 2012, pp. 67, 121, 160.

17 HCA R1041.

18 Dalton, *The Country Justice...*, Chap 174, p. 427.

19 Roth, *With a Bended Bow...*, p.p. 163-164.

20 HARC BN81.

21 *Shorter Oxford English Dictionary*, 1973: Tranter – a person who buys up goods to sell

elsewhere; a pedlar, a hawker, formerly esp. one travelling by horse and cart. Originally also a retailer of ale. Trantery – the occupation of a tranter. See also Latham, *Revised Medieval Latin Word-List*, The British Academy, 1965; traventarius.

22 HCA 4735.

23 Campbell, Mildred, *The English Yeoman in the Tudor and Early Stuart Age*, Merlin Press Ltd, 1983, reproduced and printed in Great Britain by Whitstable Litho Ltd, Whitstable, Kent. (First published 1942 by Yale University Press), p. 187.

24 HCA R1041.

25 HCA R1043, presentment 11 April 1651.

26 HCA 4735, 26 Apr 1664, Mar 1665 & 18 Oct 1676.

27 *Ibid.*, presentment 16 October 1666.

28 HCA R1041.

29 Both examples in HCA 4735 (loose sheets).

30 HARC Canon Pyon parish register, MX312 (film).

31 Quotes from presentments 1660s to 1680s are from HCA 4735 (loose leaf documents).

32 Note - *Vannus* in the accusative case (singular) ought to be *vannum*, but all the examples are written *vannam*.

33 All three examples from HCA R1041.

34 Mechanisation of winnowing in England began in the early 18th century.

35 Britten, James, *Old Country and Farming Words: gleaned from agricultural books*, Trübner & Co., London, 1880. 'Ridder or rudder' is from *Dictionarium Rusticum* by J. Worlridge, 1681.

36 HCA 7001/1.

37 HCA 7001/2.

38 Cavill, Paul, *A New English Dictionary of English Field-Names*, English Place Name Society, 2018, p.109, an early example is Le Maynynge 1438.

39 Latham's Revised *Medieval Latin Word-List…*, has 'giva', or 'gyves', meaning prison, but with questionable provenance; it would be reasonable to assume a meaning similar to 'traps'. All examples in this paragraph are from HCA 4735.

40 *The Statutes at Large, from the first year of Edward the fourth to the end of the reign of Queen Elizabeth*, 2nd volume, London, 1763.

41 Dalton, *The Country Justice*...., Chap. 31, p.68.

42 HARC Q/SO/2 ff. 114A.

43 Dalton, *The Country Justice*...., Chap 31, p. 68.

44 HCA R1041.

45 HCA 4735.

46 HCA R1041.

47 HCA 4736 (and the only known occurrence of the surname Blakeway in the parish).

48 HCA R1042, f. 5, c. 1623-1630.

49 HCA 4736, 30 Sep 1667, extract of fines and amercements.

50 HCA R1042 and R1041.

51 HCA 4735.

52 TNA E112/412/184, Bedford v. Somerset.

53 Smith, Philip Vernon, *The Law of Churchwardens and Sidesmen in the 20th century*, London, 1903, pp. 6-12.

54 In Canon Pyon, this was the lessee of the manor.

55 Smith, *The Law of Churchwardens*..., pp. 6-12.

56 HCA 4591.

57 HCA 7002/1/3, 6 May 1626, f. 190r.

58 Dougall, Alistair, *The Devil's Book; Charles I, the Book of Sports and Puritanism in Tudor and Early Stuart England*, University of Exeter Press, 2011, (glossary p. xvi).

59 *Ibid.*, p. 12 and p. 19.

60 *Ibid.*, pp. 72-76 and p. 91.

61 *Ibid.*, p. 116.

62 *Ibid.*, Chapter 6.

63 *Ibid.*, pp. 160-164.

64 *Ibid.* p. 82.

'Our watch and ward have been duly kept': maintaining law and order

65 HCA 7002/1/3, 3 November 1621.

66 *Ibid.*, 1 Jul 1626, f. 191v.

67 *Ibid.*, 1 November 1620.

68 *Ibid.*, 9 May 1629, f. 319r.

69 *Ibid.*, 13 June 1629, f.320v.

70 HCA 7002/1/3 John & Margery Chambers 1629, HCA 7002/1/2 Francis & Alice Smallman 1620, HCA 7002/1/3 Hugh Yeomans & Margaret Jeffres1621, are a few examples.

71 HCA 7002/1/2, f. 199.

72 HCA 7002/1/3, 3 May 1629, f. 314v.

73 HCA 7002/1/2, 7 June 1608 f. 4.

74 HCA 7002/1/3, 23 September 1626, f. 203 v.

75 HARC Q/SO1, f. 87B.

76 HARC Q/SO/1, f. 205B, 1672.

77 HARC Q/SO/1, f. 171b, 1670.

78 HARC HD5/2/23, 1677 & 1680.

79 Handler, Jerome S., and Reilly, Matthew C., *Contesting "White Slavery" in the Carribbean: enslaved Africans and European indentured servants in seventeeth-century Barbados*, New West Indian Guide 91 (2017), pp. 30-55, accessed November 2021 from: https://brill.com/view/journals/nwig/91/1-2/article-p30_2.xml?language=en (my thanks to Guy Grannum for this article).

80 TNA STAC 8/68/23, Broughton v. Berrington.

81 TNA STAC 8/170/12, Handford v. Broughton

82 Will of William Berrington of Wynsley 1635 (his 'wellbeloved cousin Thomas Berington of Little Pewne gent to be my executor)'. Proved Hereford, Oct. 1636, 48/01/36. See also Berringtons of Stoke Lacey and Winsley in Siddons, Michael Powell (transcribed and edited by), *Visitation of Herefordshire* 1634, Harleian Society, London, 2002.

83 *Visitation of Herefordshire 1634…*, pp. 98-99.

84 Baynhams House - see Some Lost Houses in Chapter 2 (p. 51).

6

'Labourer, husbandman, yeoman, gent': more inhabitants of Canon Pyon in the 17th century

In this final chapter we will meet more occupants of the parish, their occupations and social standing in the parish and what can be discovered about the poorest amongst them.

SOCIAL HIERARCHY IN THE PARISH

The social hierarchy of families in the English countryside has been discussed by Mildred Campbell in *The English Yeoman*, beginning with the labourer, rising to husbandman, yeoman and then gentleman. For many, there was opportunity of upward movement through the social scale by endeavour, 'good' marriages and not least a little luck but the reverse could also occur. The practice of primogeniture (the eldest son inherits) meant that many younger sons of minor gentry became yeomen rather than gentlemen in their adult life. They often resided in leased properties deemed to be of a lower status than their parents and very often had careers in law or the church.[1]

In the case of Canon Pyon the lord of the manor was the Church, specifically the Dean and Chapter of Hereford Cathedral. The success of the lordship was reliant on each dean in turn and the competence of the steward he employed. Principal properties of the manor farm and court, the Derndale estate and Lawton's Hope (until the mid-17th century) were all leased and the rents used to provide the Petty Commons (in rents and corn) for the canons. Little Pyon's rents and profits were used to endow the prebend of Pyon Parva at the Cathedral. So although no doubt commanding respect due to personal status, even the person in the 'big house' was a tenant subject to the same rules of agronomy and behaviour according to the customs of the manor.

A lack of suit rolls or lists of tenants and inhabitants for the first half of the 16th century makes it difficult to assess any changes in the social dynamics of the manor during the century but a number of post-1660 records survive. A good example of one of the suit rolls (in that it gives the township for each inhabitant) is detailed below, although it must be stressed that it is unlikely to be complete:

3 April 1676 and 18 October 1676
A retorne of the names and inhabitants within the manor of Cannon Pion.[2]

The townshipe of Cannon Pion

Sr John Barnaby knt	Charles Somerset Esq[uire]
Bartholomew Walter	Griffith Jones
John Jones	Thomas Smith
Roger Chambers	Michael Whopper [Hooper]
Phillip Millard	Phillip Leeth
George Baynham ju[nior]	Thomas Jones sen[ior]
Richard Baynham	George Knapp
Thomas Steephenes	Richard Jones
John Stanton	Phillip Phillipes
ffrancis Willes	Richard Gayley
Arthur Taylor	John Jay
Thomas Bithell	Henry Mayos

Nupton and Collwall

Richard Burchar	Katherine Moune [Munn] wid[ow]
William Rogeres	

Eston ffoliat and Upper Dearndall

Edward Monnington	Oliver Gardnor
William Gardnor	George Baynham sen[ior]
Edward Reynolles	William Thomas

Lower Dearndall

John Kinersley gent	Katherine Jay wid[ow]
Rowland Gardnor	William Hornblow
George Thomas	Ralph Bolle [Bull]
John Simondes	Richard Witherston gent
William Went	

Canon Pyon

The townshipe of Smeathley and Lawtones Hope and Easthope

Ralfe Darnell Esq[uire]	Thomas Harris
Richard Benny	William Bulle

Westhope and fullbridge and Little Pion

Thomas Berington Esq[uire]	Wrainford Hill gent
Elinor Preece wid[ow]	James Preece gent
Elizabeth Yeomandes wid[ow]	Elizabeth Andrewes wid[ow]
John Holland	Henry Meredith gent
William Clarke	John Mason
Thomas Preece	William Knapp
Wiliam Nash	Thomas Seley sen[ior]
Thomas Seley jun[ior]	William Blucke
Alice Milles	John Turberville
William Plevey	James Plevey
Hugh Smallman	William Thomas
Thomas Meredith	George Phillipes
Thomas Smith	Jane Gayley wid[ow]
Edward Coney	George Pike
ffrances Gardnor	William Gayley
John Hordes	Joseph Wincely
William Wotton gent	Ann Moore spinster
William Williams	George Scarlett
Philip Celey	

Many of the surnames in this list will be very familiar to a researcher of pre-1800 Canon Pyon; the families of Baynham, Bythell, Bull, Gardner, Gayley, Jay, Leeth, Knapp, Nash, Plevey, Seley/Silly, Reignolds, Scarlett, Smallman, Turbervile and Yeomans appear regularly throughout the 17th century manorial records and some of them much earlier.

GENTLEMEN, ESQUIRE AND KNIGHT
Of the eighty-three names in the above list, seven of them have been given the status of gentlemen, three esquires and one knight. Generally considered above the rank of yeomen, gentlemen were those wealthy enough not to work and they may have had this status by inheritance or achievement. The esquire's medieval origins was as an assistant to a knight but by the 16th century esquires were often 'younger sons of noblemen'.[3]

Some of these people may have lived outside the manor but held copyhold lands within. The Berrington family had lived at Little Pyon for a number of generations. John Barnaby was married to Judith Vaughan, daughter of George Vaughan, whom we have met in the section on the manor leases and Charles Somerset was married to Judith's daughter Katherine. Both Barnaby and Somerset were associated with the manor and farm lease. Ralph Darnell/Darnall had purchased Lawton's Hope in 1647 and also leased some copyhold land. Richard Witherston had taken the lease for Dearndall earlier that year (1676) although he was described as 'of Burghill' so probably did not live in Canon Pyon and had an under-tenant in the property instead.[4] John Kinnersley was active in a manor court of April 1666; he was on the jury and an assessor in April 1673 so most likely did live in the parish.[5] Wrainford Hill had a daughter called Alice baptised at Canon Pyon church in 1675 and was a churchwarden in 1681 so also probably lived in the parish.

Of the other three – James Preece, Henry Meredith and William Wotton – it is not clear whether or not they lived in the parish. To this list of 'gentlemen' we should add Edward Monnington (on the list but status unspecified); he died intestate in Jan 1680/1 and his grant of administration describes him as a gentleman.[6] The Monnington family had been occupiers of Lawton's Hope and the Buttas in the 16th century and the family continued to live in Canon Pyon well into the following century.

YEOMEN

Yeoman status originally involved the holding of freehold land worth 40s. annually but there were wide variations on this; by the 17th century some could be freeholders, some copyholders or a mixture of both. Husbandmen, on the other hand, did not have freehold land originally. It was an occupational term rather than a status but a husbandman might be classed as a yeoman if he could prove that he had freehold land. Later, the land question became less of an issue but the husbandman continued to be associated with the rank below the yeoman.[7]

Many yeomen became relatively wealthy through good management of their lands and acquiring more acreage. The association with the soil and farming is without doubt paramount to the life of a yeoman although the wealthier ones would be able to pay labourers for extra help. Other occupations, particularly in towns (for example, mercers and clothiers), may have had a similar social status to yeomen but were nearly always known and titled by their occupation, rather than yeomen.

Fraternising did occur between yeomen and gentry, as did the occasional intermarriage and regular witnessing of each others documents and wills. This is evident

Canon Pyon

amongst the Canon Pyon yeomen, many of their 17th century wills being witnessed by the gentlemen and vice versa.

From the above list of tenants and inhabitants, those easily identified as yeomen families from their wills (which often provide the deceased's occupation or status) are: Baynham, Bithell/Bythell, Boole/Bull, Burchar, Celey/Silly, Gardner, Gayley, Knapp, Leeth/Leath, Munn, Reignolds/Reynolds, Simons, Steephens and Yeomans.

MILITIA ASSESSMENTS

Where it has not been possible to find written confirmation of 'yeomanry', it can be useful to compare information with a source such as the Herefordshire Militia Assessment of 1663. The post-reformation requirement for trained men who were able to mobilise quickly was to be funded by land-possessors in each county and the rating of individuals, though not without its difficulties, can offer an indication of the social distribution in a parish. 'Cottagers, tenants at will (with no security of tenure) and tenants paying a rack-rent' (rent equal to or nearly equal to the full annual value of the property) were not included as they had no income-generating land. The assessment could be based either on the annual value of the land, leasehold or copyhold, or on the personal wealth, whichever was the greater. They might therefore give us a tentative estimate of the relative wealth of the individuals who are listed (though some will have had land in other parishes).[8]

Those chosen to carry out the rating were 'the more substantial farmers who could have estimated adequately the incomes of others of their own class', though they may have found the finances of the gentry more difficult.[9] The raters for Canon Pyon in 1663 were Edward Monington, Richard Baynham and Thomas Syly. Although the Militia Assessments were taken thirteen years before the above list of inhabitants, many of the names appear on both. Of the yeomen already identified, the ratings in order of value are as follows (note there are some with more than one holding):

George Knapp	£20 and £3 and £25
Richard Burchar	£40 and £5
Philip Yeomans	£20 and £12 (spouse to Elizabeth Yeomandes)
Roul' Garner	£22 (Roland Gardner)
Richard Beynham	£13 and £6
Oliver Garner	£10 and £6 6s. 8d. (Gardner)
Thomas Syly	£13
Richard Gayley	£12

Thomas Stevens	£11
William Gayley	£8
Richard Syly	£6
Thomas Bythell	£2
William Booll	£2

A number of other people listed in the Assessment also appeared in the inhabitants list. They are as yet unidentified as yeomen and have ratings of under £10: John Mason £4 10s., George Scarlett £2 6s. 8d., Philip Syly £2, Arthur Taylor £1 6s., Griffith Jones £1, William Plene (probably Plevey) £1. There are also a number of families in the Assessments who do not appear on the 1676 inhabitants list at all but were in the parish at the time; the Turberviles, Ovens, Fletchers and Tylers (Henry Tyler, yeoman).[10]

HEARTH TAX RETURNS

The hearth tax returns of 1665 for Canon Pyon, just a couple of years after the militia assessment, contain many of the same names including the same three men as raters or 'chimney-men' as they were sometimes known. One shilling was payable by the house occupier for every hearth or stove in the house, twice a year at Michaelmas and Lady Day, with exemptions for those who were already exempt from church and poor rates. Those in houses worth less than 20s. rent per annum or without lands of the same value or without goods worth more than £10 were also exempt. By 1664 however, even those who had been exempt were liable if there were two or more hearths. There are limitations in these records too, relating to the compilation methods, accuracy and completeness but nevertheless they can provide additional information about social status of individuals.[11]

Curiously, John Barnaby and George Sayer (Sawyer) are both on the Canon Pyon hearth tax list for nine hearths, the highest in the assessment. Mostly likely it was John Barnaby and his wife Judith who were at the 'big house' as the Sawyers were living at Bullingham. Judith's daughter Katherine had married George Sawyer and was, by the custom of the manor, due to inherit the manor lease. Sawyer died at Bullingham that same year (1665) and he was buried in his native county of Berkshire. His wife Katherine Sawyer continued to live at Bullingham and is listed in the hearth tax assessment for that parish (as Katherine Sayer).[12]

Ralph Darnell lived at Lawton's Hope and he is listed in the assessment for eight hearths. Barnaby, Sawyer and Darnell were all designated as 'esquire'. Thomas Berrington is next at six hearths, described as 'gent' and he lived at Little Pyon.

Canon Pyon

The Canon Pyon yeomen previously identified were mostly in the 'one hearth' category, with a smaller number in the two or three hearth category. Some had 'stopped up' hearths; Richard Burchar, who lived at Nupton, had three of these. Whether or not this was a means of reducing the burden of the tax bill is difficult to say but it is likely that at least some of them were. It seems a little strange that the vicar Thomas Griffiths was taxed for only one hearth, particularly as there was probably a kitchen separate to the dwelling.[13]

The assessment of 1665 records one Richard Gayley (also a yeoman) as having three hearths but in 1672 this was disputed. In a letter to the Justices of the Peace, signed by churchwardens John Kinnersley and Thomas Steephens, it was explained that Gayley 'had his house surveyed severall times by officers Appointed for yt [that] purpose and also by ye Constables of the p[ar]ish and by the Constables retarnes for three fier herthes and no mor[e]'.[14] Gayley continued:

> Now soe it is that sum malitious person have informed of another fier herth w[i]ch is no such thinge in it: but is or it was in my Grandfathers time, mad[e] up wth stave worke by reason of a ffier that there hapned and licke to have burned downe the dwelling house had not god and good helpe p[re]vented.

In a further affidavit, Gayley declares that the offending hearth had been 'stopped up' for at least 20 years before 26 March 1662. This was witnessed as true by parishioners Arthur and William Taylor and both the Taylors and Gayley took 'the corporal oath' before Sir John Barneby, a Justice of the Peace of the county (and coincidentally a Canon Pyon resident, being married to Judith and living at the manor house).

As well as indicating some of the process involved in assessing for the hearth tax, and the interesting tale of the fire, this case tells us that the property had descended to him via his grandfather. Twenty years before this takes the history back to 1642 and the 1649 manorial survey lists a tenant Richard Gayley who had a messuage or tenement called Newbridge, one orchard and five acres of land 'by fealty suit of court and the yearly rent of 4s. 6d.'. Unfortunately, the younger Richard did not name his grandfather so the connection is not yet proved.

As an added bonus, the hearth tax returns give us an estimate of the number of houses in Canon Pyon around this time:

1664	80 houses
1665	78 houses
1671	100 houses
1673	97 houses

'Labourer, husbandman, yeomen, gent': more inhabitants

Even with the limitations of the estimations, this does indicate an increase in house building between 1664/5 and 1671. Much later, in 1801, there were still only 128 houses.[15]

OCCUPATIONS

Returning to the yeomen, we have seen from the manorial court records that many of the men in the early 17th century yeomen families were archers - Beynham, Knappe, Gardener, Leeth, Gayley, Yeomans – some of whom were fined for not continuing with archery practice.[16] The English yeomen had ancestors amongst the famous archers of the 14th and 15th centuries. Later, yeomen also regularly filled the parish offices of constable, churchwarden and overseer of the poor and they had long been regarded as a vital part of society.

Although the majority of families in 17th century Canon Pyon were involved in working on the land, there were other occupations. William Hornblow was a tanner, who leased a tan house and messuage in Derndale in 1683[17] (later leased to the Duggans and in the 18th century to the Jay family). Another tan yard existed by the brook in the 18th century - in the village near the bridge, on the site of the recent landscaping associated with the new housing. The surrounding field names - Mill Meadow, Mill Common Field - indicate that there was also a mill at this location before this date (no actual mill is marked on Isaac Taylor's map).

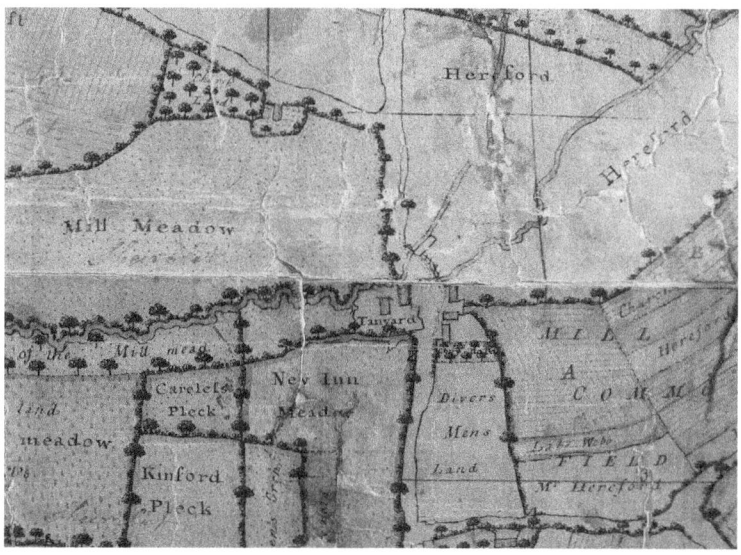

The tan yard (centre) by the brook c. 1755. The main road through the village runs north/south, the junction for the road to the church is at the top left of the image.
(HARC BN81)

Canon Pyon

In fact, there were probably three mills in Canon Pyon's manor in 1649, the first in the possession of Edward Monnington and held in free socage of the lord of the manor for the annual rent of 17s. 10d. and suit of court in 1649. The second had been held by Richard Bennett since April 1637 'in the right of his wife Joane, formerly the wife of James Beavan', along with a nook of customary land for the annual rent of 2s. 9d., a fine of 26s. 8d. and a 'licence to farm sett and rent'.[18] One of these may have been on the site of the later tannery. The third was the mill at Kinford which will we consider in the next section.

KINFORD: THE FAMILY AND THE MILL

The Kinford family name disappeared from Canon Pyon around the mid-17th century; the last known manorial references were to John Kinford and his sons William and James in the court records of *c.* 1635.[19] Between 1617 and 1619, John Kinford and Edward Kinford were sworn in to the homage (or jury) of the court and similarly for William Kinford in 1635.[20] John Kinforde was described in a glebe terrier of 1617 as 'one of the chiefest men of the parish' and must have been of relatively high status.[21]

There is no doubt that John Kinford and his sons lived at Kinford. They were the subject of a Chancery court case in 1638 wherein John Kinford was described as 'seised of a messuage known as Kinford in Canon Pyon, with a water corn mill, lands, tenements and heridataments of land, meadow, pasture and wood, of the yearly value of £50'.[22] The case was being brought by John's granddaughter Winifrid via a proctor or guardian named John Breynton, as she was a minor.

It was claimed that the premises had been part of a settlement on the marriage of Winifrid's parents, William Kinford (John's eldest son) and Katherine nee Breynton, daughter of John Breynton. The bill stated that John had made a deed of feoffment allowing his own use of the property until his decease and after this it was to descend to his son and daughter-in-law William and Katherine Kinford and then the male heirs of William. If there was no male heir, then any heir of his body (i.e. Winifrid) would inherit. If there had been no such heir, the next in line was to be William's brother James and his male heirs and if no such heirs to the 'right heirs' of William. There do not appear to have been any male heirs at all.

Part of the complaint was that certain persons had 'gotten into their hands custody and possession the said deed of feoffment' as well as other deeds and papers concerning the premises and were said to have '… wrongfully and unconsionably practified combined and confederated together to defeat and defraud [Winifrid] of the said premises and her said inheritance and title to the same'.

'Labourer, husbandman, yeomen, gent': more inhabitants

These 'persons', the defendants, were named as Katherine Kinford, widow (Winifrid's grandmother), Anne Kinford (Winifrid's aunt), John Mason and his wife Isabell, William Gregge, George Baynham and Susan Kinford, all of Canon Pyon; also John Leech and his wife Elizabeth of Lyde and Daniell Holder and his wife Joane of Hereford. They were accused of 'daily interrupting and disturbing her quiet use of the premises' and of committing 'waste spoils and distructions' in and upon the houses, buildings and woods, including felling timber trees.

The combined answer of the defendants is long and drawn out but full of detail of when deeds were drawn up and when each of the family members had died. John Kinford and his two sons had all died within the space of about a year, James only a couple of weeks after his father. John's wife Katherine (Winifrid's grandmother) and her daughter Anne confessed that they held the deeds and that they were advised to keep them in order to prove their right to the property. They claimed that a deed had been drawn up on 1 May 1637 in which John Kinford, Katherine Kinford and James Kinford (in that order) were to be seized of the messuage, land and corn mill.

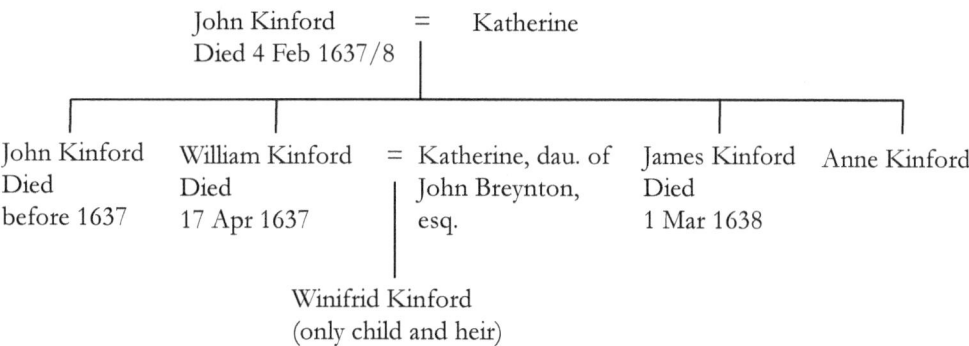

Being feoffees (a kind of trustee) was the only role of John Leech and Daniel Holder and they had no actual right to the premises. Nor were the defendants John Mason, William Gregge, George Baynham and Susan Kinford mentioned in the answer.

Katherine also stated that after Winifrid's parents and her own husband had died, she herself entered one moiety or half of the property and James the other, with the expectation that James would also enter the first moiety after her decease and that this was specified in a deed. When James died, Katherine claimed that he left a will, that there was a copy with her deeds and that it was proved at Hereford, leaving 'all his free lands and tenements' to Anne Kinford, his sister, for her natural life. After Anne's decease the premises were to go to John Leech, son of the defendant John Leech, and his heirs forever.[23]

James Kinford's will has not been found and the conclusion of the case is not known. It would most likely have centred on the production of the 'deeds, evidences and writings' and the acceptance or dismissal of these items. With the lack of male heirs, Katherine and Anne (and possibly Winifrid) may have been the last bearing the Kinford family name at Kinford.

Kinford farmhouse is a grade II listed building and has been described as 'probably 17th century with later alterations' but could be on the site of a much earlier building.[24] In 1418, the Dean and Chapter reduced the 30s. rent for a water mill in the lordship of Canon Pyon leased by Richard Kynford, heir of Richard Kynford the elder[25] and in 1451 a French millward by the name of Gillam Frenschmon was the servant of John Kyneford of Canon Pyon.[26] Although, we cannot say for sure that these Kynfords were at the location of the current Kinford property, the link between family and property is highly probable.

Did the family take the name from the property or was it the other way round? Initial research suggests the former as in 1320, the prior of nearby Wormsley Priory was one John *de* Kyneford but by the 1418 example above, the name appears to have lost the locatory 'de,' meaning 'of'.[27] The name itself is probably locatory in origin; either from *cyna ford*, a place where cattle crossed the watercourse, or possibly from *cyning's ford* meaning king's or royal ford, both from Old English.[28]

The earliest known visual representation of the area is on the *c.* 1755 map by Isaac Taylor which shows that the watercourse flowing from Little Pyon ran past Kinford house and the mill buildings on one side, whereas the brook which flowed through the village from the church passed the house on the other side and joined the 'mill brook' a little further on. The 'mill brook' appears to have run under the highway, though this is not very clear, whereas the second brook appears to have crossed the highway and could conceivably be the location of the original cattle ford. The map shows that the two watercourses are very different in nature, the mill brook being much straighter and therefore more able to provide the flow required to turn a wheel.

The image overleaf shows that the property was in the name of Mrs Hereford in *c.* 1755. Anne Hereford was the widow of Walwyn Hereford and in 1746 a lease was drawn up for part of the property to be leased to Mrs Anne Munn for nine years.[29] Mrs Munn was to have 'the farm commonly known as Kinford; two garretts over the hall and the kitchen and also the cellar in the capital messuage together with the wheat and corn mills belonging to the said farm'. Mrs Hereford was to retain:

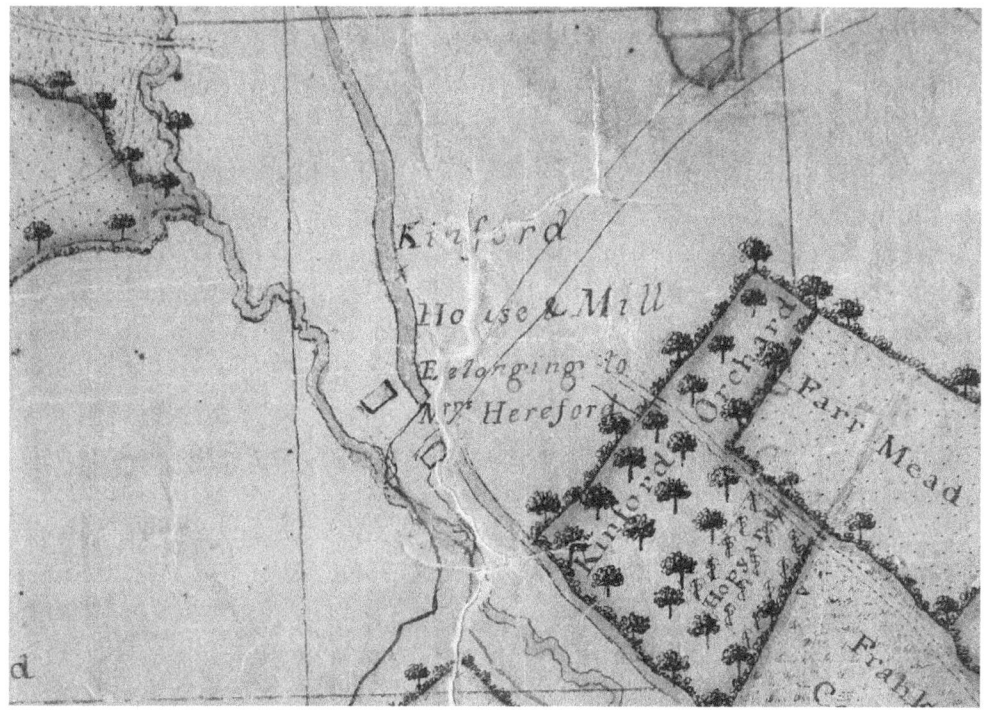

Kinford house and mill *c.* 1755 sandwiched between two watercourses. Ignoring the white line where the map is damaged, the 'highway' runs from the bottom centre of the image, around a sharp bend (still there today) and onwards towards Westhope. The house is on the left side of the highway and the mill building on the right (HARC BN81).

> … the said capital messuage (besides the garrett over the hall and the kitchen) the best stable now used with the capital messuage with the pigeon house and garden belonging to said capital messuage. Also timber, trees etc and also the room adjoining the best stable together with hayloft over best stable. Also liberty for Anne Hereford to put two hogsheads of liquor in the cellar. Also one pigscott with liberty for two pigs.

There were conditions to Mrs Munn's lease; she had certain farming tasks to do and free milling for Mrs Hereford. For her part, Mrs Hereford was 'to put in a new oven at the corn mill and a new millstone when required'. The deed is not signed and may not have been executed or may just be a copy. Combining the information from the lease and the map indicates that the mill cottage now existing had not yet been built (1746-1755).

By 1819, a cottage, corn mill, garden and orchard at this location were occupied by John Davies, with Herbert Yeomans occupying Kinford house.[30] Even in the 1880s, the

Canon Pyon

two watercourses continued to run, one by the house and under the road to the mill and the other across the road at the ford.[31]

THE MILL AT THE BUTTAS

Although in the parish of Kings Pyon, the Buttas (or Butthouse) is close to Canon Pyon church and there were connections with Canon Pyon vicar Jonathan Dryden and the Karver family of the Buttas. Whilst archival evidence is scant for Kinford in the 17th century and there is no description of the mill, for the Buttas there is a lucky survival. Detailed in a 'particular of the manor of Buttas and of the demeynes of that manor as nowe yt is', the mill was described as 'newly [re]edified in verie substanciall manor and furnished with new stones'. It was an 'overshott mill and driven by a brooke w[i]ch kumeth under the howse' (below the house) and was rented at £20 per year.[32]

The document is not dated and the catalogue has an estimate of 16th century but F. C. Morgan believed it to be related to a marriage of 1638 when the Buttas and other manors and lands were settled upon Richard Karver and Elinor, daughter of Richard Vaughan of Bredwardine. The whole of the Buttas property was available on a lease for a period of 'three lives', usually that of the husband, wife and eldest child or next heir.[33]

BLACKSMITHS

In common with most villages, there was at least one blacksmith's shop in Canon Pyon in the 17th century. A surrender of manorial land in May 1683 included 'half an acre in Upper Mill field near the smith's shop, shooting upon Mr Somersetts land on the north'. Three years before, in January 1680, about a quarter of an acre of land in Canon Pyon was surrendered by Thomas Bythell for the use of William Thomas, the smith, and his wife. It was described as arable land and was on the east side of the road leading 'from Hereford to Prestene'.[34] No smithy is mentioned in the surrender but William Thomas is the only named smith found (so far) in the 17th century.

A deed of June 1724 (which we have come across before, being lands belonging to the New Inn), includes references to smithies:

> Also a parcel of enclosed arable out of a field called The Upper Mill Field and planted containing ½ a quarter of an acre wherein a smith's shop is lately erected - built together with the said smith's shop.
> Also smith's shop and tenements etc belonging to it, in the last 23 yrs, lying in the parish of Canon Pyon and now in the possession of George Knapp and James Preece tenants or undertenants and heretofore several times bought and purchased and from several persons by Eward Adys in Canon Pyon…[35]

'Labourer, husbandman, yeomen, gent': more inhabitants

In modern terms 'lately' would imply not long ago but in old deeds it often meant many years ago and in this case, the smith's shop had been in existence since at least 1700/1701 and was quite possibly the same shop mentioned in 1683.

OTHER OCCUPATIONS

Occasionally the manor court records mentioned an occupation. A surrender of land in 1678 by labourer Thomas Dugmore and his wife Rebecka, to the use of William Plevey junior, glover (and his descendants), describes the land as 'one acre of arable cont 5 ridges in Upper Wood field, between lands of James Price of Hereford, mercer, on the east and west, shooting on the road from Westhope to Weobley on the south'.[36] A rare case of three occupations mentioned at once, this is the only reference found to a glover in the parish in this period.

Richard Burchar was a corvisor (shoemaker) when in May 1687 he surrendered some land in Canon Pyon for the use of Thomas Abraham of the New Inn, inn-holder, whom we have already met as a witness in the case of the Dean and Chapter against the vicar Thomas Bedford. There is one known record of a wheelwright in the parish - Richard Sealy who made his will on 20 July 1682.[37] Although his occupation is given as wheelwright, his inventory of goods is not particularly revealing; it included one cart and one pair of wheels worth £2 but no tools of trade.

Some occupations had to be licenced; clergy, schoolmasters, midwives and surgeons were all required to appear at the diocesan office, show their licences and pay a fee before they could practice their calling. These were recorded in the Diocesan Call Books and an example for 1680 shows that there were two chirurgeons (surgeons) for Canon Pyon - John Seaborn and Thomas Rogers.[38]

THE PARISH POOR

The earliest surviving volume of accounts by the overseers of the poor begins with records dating from 1780.[39] On the first pages of this volume, however, is a list of the churchwardens and overseers for every year between 1766 and 1803. Some of the surnames of these parish officers are also found, in other records, a hundred years earlier; Jay, Oven, Plevey, Turbervile, Eckley, Nash, Gardner, Munn and Yeomans are all present. There were only two names for each year which may mean that by the 1760s there was only one churchwarden and one overseer of the poor for each year. The offices also appear to be attached to certain properties or representing the townships of Nupton and Westhope and turns taken for annual office happened approximately every twelve years.

Canon Pyon

This contrasts with what has been discovered about the late 17th century parish whereby two churchwardens were chosen annually, one by the vicar and one by the parishioners, although nothing is known about the overseers of the poor.[40] By listing the churchwardens who signed the bishop's transcripts between 1662 and 1699, it can be seen that many of the names were from yeoman families and some are recognisable as inhabitants of Derndale (various Gardners, William Hornblow, Bartholomew Walter, John Duggan) and some from Westhope (Richard Sylly, William Plevey) – see Appendix 3. In these earlier records there is less of a pattern in terms of regularity of office-holding with some names only appearing once. This may support the theory that in the 17th century the churchwardens' role was not dependent on the tenancy of certain properties but it may also indicate greater mobility between properties.

There is a curious paragraph relating to the poor of Canon Pyon in the will of Humphrey Digges in 1681, in which he conveyed a certain mistrust in the system of benefitting the poor:

> … my grandmother Anne Knapp and aunt Katherine Gregg by their last wills did devise to the poore of the parish of Canon Pyon, £7 10s, both wills which I was executor and I have only paid the interest on this said sum, Now I doe give to the said poore 50s which will make up the sum of £10 which said sum is not to be disposed of to the com[m]on poor of the said parish nor such of them as are or shalbe in the poores Booke for then this Bequest would be only to ease the rich and not to help the poore but my will and meaning is that the Interest of this £10 bee only and truly paid to the Overseers of the Poore of the said parish a week before Christmas and a week before Easter by them to bee disposed of upon St Thomas day before Christmas and upon Good Friday yearly for ever to the poorer sort of the housekeepers of the said p[ar]ish in wheaten Bread. And I doe desire my executrix hereafter named to send a copy of this my Bequest to the Overseers of the poore of the parish of Canon Pyon within one moneth next after my Decease.[41]

Perhaps he thought that a money dole to the poor meant that the rich would feel less inclined to pay the poor rates and that providing bread would avoid this. Whatever the reason, the mention of a 'poores booke' is of interest. Did he mean the overseers' accounts or some other book (neither of which have survived)? Humphrey Digges lived at Bishopstone but had connections to Canon Pyon via his mother Joan (or Johan) Knapp and grandmother Anne Knappe.

In 1649 there were eight cottages on waste land at Westhope Hill.[42] Some of the cottages on the waste were built 'by order of Sessions according to the s[t]atute', probably for poor folk, as we found for Richard Cowles in a later Sessions of 1679.[43] A hundred years or so later, Canon Pyon had a 'parish house' as the accounts of *Mrs* Tunstall show in the overseers of the poor book from May 1777 - May 1778, when money was paid out for building materials 'for making an oven and other repairs at ye Parish House' and for thatching.[44] There is no clue as to the location of this house, nor is there any evidence for any earlier building.

A particularly informative record about the number of poorer inhabitants of the parish, albeit from a small snapshot in time, comes from the hearth tax returns, in particular two lists of parishioners who were certified exempt from the hearth tax for 1670 and 1672.[45] There is consistency across the two years, most of the 35 names in 1672 also being present on the earlier list of 43 names. All were certified as occupying property valued at less than 20s. per annum and having goods less than £10 and all those named on the 1672 list were noted as receiving alms - see Table 5, on the pages overleaf.

For some of the individuals on the list, nothing more is known, except perhaps a burial register entry (from the bishops' transcripts) which often labelled the deceased with the unfortunate term of 'pauper'. These were likely to be mainly elderly and infirm parishioners who, in the absence of any other pension system, would receive parish relief until they ended their days. Some of the others in the list have records of baptised children or appear in the manorial court records and were probably labourers, some maybe requiring help only seasonally. In the case of Simon Taylor and Richard Coole/Cole, who were occupying cottages on Thomas Jays hill without the statutory four acres, the fact that they were receiving alms builds the case that the cottages were probably built for labourers or for the poor.

A number of those on the list were also presented at the manor court for keeping goats. A presentment from October 1664 stipulated that:

> ... no person or persons whatsoever within the manor of Pewne shall from this day keep any goates as afore said unless they keep them on their owne landes' on pain of a fine of thirty shillings and eleven pence.[46]

Goats would have been allowed in certain fields and common ground for part of the year but had to be put away at other times, for example when winter wheat was sown. Those presented for not doing so probably did not have their own land to move them to.

In general, poor parishioners were usually given smaller fines than others; those who defaulted their suit of court (that is, did not turn up for their obligatory presence) were fined 2d. whereas others were fined 4d. (in a presentment of October 1665). There is, however, no record of the reduction of the 'goat fine' from 37s. 11d.[47]

Table 5

Hearth Tax exemptions 1670 and 1672 (TNA E179/19/509/47 and 48). Those in the 1670 list who were also in the 1672 document are marked Y. Spelling variants in 1672 are also recorded where found. All were noted as receiving alms in 1672. Biographical details, where found, are from a variety of manorial records, bishops transcripts, church court records, deeds and others.

1670	1672	Biographical notes
Mikell Whop[er] [Hooper]	Y	Married Anne Palmer November 1667, baptized children in 1668, 1672 and 1675. On a manorial suit roll for 1667 and for Canon Pyon township 1676 and 77.
Tho: Smyth	Y	Presented for keeping goats October 1666. Possibly buried 27 February 1681.
Rowland Ball		Married to Anne and baptized a child in 1688.
Henry Jones	Y	Buried 22 July 1681, described as a pauper.
Richard Jones	Y	Possibly at the manorial court in April 1665.
Thomas Palmer	Y	Buried 9 January 1676, described as a pauper.
Margarett Lewis		Buried 12 April 1671.
Nathaniel Gardner	Y	Presented for trantory in 1665-68, buried 4 August 1689.
Charles Williams	Y	Presented for the keeping of goats 1667. On suit roll for 1667 and also for Brockton and Derndall township in 1677. Wife Mary had admin of his estate. An inventory survives showing charges for his coffin etc, January 1684.
Simon Taylor	Y	In April 1666 and 1667, occupied a house without 4 acres of land upon Thomas Jays Hill near Dinmore (manorial court presentment).
Richard Coles (Coole in 1672)	Y	In April 1666, occupied a house without 4 acres of land upon Thomas Jays Hill near Dinmore (manorial court presentment). Presented for keeping of goats March 1665 (not on own land) and 1667.
Johan Bennett	Y	Buried 22 September 1694.
Thomas Griffitts (Griffithes in 1672)	Y	Possibly buried 24 February 1673, described as a pauper.
Olliver Browne	Y	Baptized children 1673 and 1676.
William Whetstone	Y	Possibly buried 7 May 1684.
George Whetston	Y	Baptized a child in 1671. Possibly the same man who was a witness in 1686/7 to the Little Pyon pew dispute.
Walter Cooper	Y	Possibly buried 4 March 1697.

1670	1672	Biographical notes
John Beavan	Y	Held an acre of copyhold land when he died in 1686.
Elizabeth Duppa, widow		Buried 13 April 1675, described as a pauper.
Elizabeth ffoxe, widow		John Fox buried 10 March 1670.
Richard Nicholls (Nicoles in 1672)	Y	Possibly buried 30 January 1691.
Anne Phillips		Possibly buried 27 April 1697.
Elizabeth Patshall (Pateshall in 1672)	Y	Elizabeth Patsall buried 8 July 1699, described as a widow and a pauper.
Margarett William, widow		Buried 14 November 1675, described as a pauper. Her death was presented at the manorial court April 1676.
Thomas Trilloe	Y	Probably lived at Derndale (Trillo's cottage).
Alice Pike	Y	Presented for not attending church in 1661. Occupied a cottage of the Somersetts about 1665.
Edward Hackford	Y	Married to Grace, baptized a child in February 1664. On 1667 suit roll. Grace buried April 1699, (widow, pauper). Name variant Hackfoot.
William Clark and Margaret Yeomans *		William Clark presented for keeping goats and trantory 1666 and 1667.
Phillip Leeth **		Possibly buried 20 November 1683.

1672 only		Biographical notes
Alice Powell		Presented for keeping goats 1665 and 1667.
James Williams		Possibly buried 28 August 1675, described as a pauper.

* William Clark and Margaret Yeomans had 'one house divided between them', each of which was under the value of 20s per annnum
** Phillip Leeth 'hath rented some land w[i]ch make him lyable to pay hearth mony w[i]ch before he was not'

Parishioners who were also in the 1670 exemption list but for whom no other information has been found are: Jane Meredith, Henry Davis, Ann Woode, Elizabeth Griffitts/Griffithes, John Coxe, William Griffitts/Griffithes, Thomas Taylor, Henry Hughes, Richard Parry, Philip Kirwood, Crispianus Williams and Margaret Griffitts.
Similarly for 1672: Elinor Ball (widow) and Ann Parry.

Canon Pyon

Another parishioner on the exemption list has left an unusual probate record. When Charles Williams died, his wife Mary had the administration of his estate (in January 1684/5). Charles was described as a labourer and an inventory of his goods survives.[48] Apart from his clothing, he left one young heifer, a horse, fifteen sheep, two small pigs, a small parcel of corn threshed, corn growing, a small iron pot, a posnet, a frying pan, one small flitch of bacon, three pounds of woollen yarn, bedding and other 'implements of household stuff', the whole being valued at £4 17s. We have no direct evidence that he was still in receipt of alms in 1684 but his goods amounted to less than the £10 qualification for exemption from the hearth tax. What is unusual about this inventory are the two lines below the inventory recording the charges of his final care and funeral costs:

Charges of funerall rites a coffing and s[h]rowd	0 12 0 [12 shillings]
and for one to look to him in time of his sickness	0 9 0 [9 shillings]

When comparing the above hearth tax exemptions of 1670 and 1672 with the list of inhabitants of 1676 (earlier in this chapter), it can be seen that only five of the thirty-five people listed as receiving alms in 1672 are present on the 1676 list. Even though some may have died by 1676 or no longer needed alms (and assuming that the numbers requiring parish relief remained fairly constant) this is a strong indicator that the poorer families were substantially under-represented in the 1676 list of inhabitants.

HEREFORDSHIRE'S 'OFFICIAL' TAKE ON THE POOR

Maintaining the poor was an expensive business and each parish was responsible only for those legally settled there; anyone else would be removed to their 'own' parish. Writing in 1634, Sergeant Hoskyns of Moorhampton, Herefordshire[49] set down his 'meanes to p[re]vent the charges of poore upon every parishe'. If a person requiring relief was born in the parish, his instruction was to:

> ... lett them be bound apprentices to eyther trade or husbandrye at eleven yeares of age to serve for fowre and twenty yeares for meate drinke and cloathes only and the worke of the latter tyme will give Recompense for the first ...[50]

Anyone refusing to take an apprentice were to be called in to the next court sessions (Quarter Sessions in Hereford) 'and there ordered by the discrec[io]n of the Bench'. If the person was not from the parish, Hoskyns continued:

> ... [they] may be sent backe if they be wanderers and Rogues by the next Justices of the peace before they be settled for a yeare to the place from where they came and if that be not found then to the next parishe where they passed unpunished.

Hoskyns also berated the jury and other officers for not presenting offenders of church absenteeism, drunkards, swearers, unlicensed alehouse keepers, and other offences, stating that:

> ... this Shire is wickedly and willfully neglected by our Jurors to the great displeasure of God wrong to the poore and charge to the parishes whoe this way might be easied [eased].

Although Hoskyns did not specifically mention that subsequent fines were used for the poor, the implication is such.

Forty years later, at Michaelmas 1673 (a year after the second hearth tax exemption list for Canon Pyon discussed above), the records of the Hereford Quarter Sessions note that there were a 'greate number of Vagrants that Travell this County unpunished...'. In spite of loans (levies) and taxes for the relief of the poor, 'theire numbers of poore doe dayley increase'.[51] It was written that:

> ... imploying and setting the poore on worke would bee a meanes not only of cutting of all excuses for wandring and of retrenchinge of the greate paym[en]t for the reliefe of the poore but alsoe of p[re]venting poverty by breeding up the younger sort whoe nowe wander or live idle in a course of Industry.

Neither did the parish officers taking care of the poor escape the notice of the court – in fact, they were blamed for the problem:

> ... observeinge that the gen[er]all neglect of inferior officers in not punishing vagabonds and vagrants and not setting on work theire poore according as by lawe is p[re]scribed to bee the main and p[re]incipal cause of the aforesaid inconveniences ...

The sessions continued by stating that from the next Easter, no adult in any parish in Herefordshire was to receive a weekly or monthly allowance unless 'utterly unable to work' and no child above seven years old unless infirm or sick. A levy or tax had to be raised in every parish after the feast of Easter in order to maintain those unable to work and to purchase 'a sufficient stocke of hemp fflax woll and other materials' for those poor who could work.

Each parish was to have a 'fit person' to be an overseer of the poor and manage the buying of the stock, deliver it to the poor, receive the manufactured goods back, pay the poor, sell the goods and keep accounts which were to be presented at the year end. An overseer who proved himself 'faithful and diligent' would receive 'twelve pence for every twenty shillings manefactured made and sold by him'. Such an officer would also be 'continued and named one of the Ov[er]seers of the poore for the next yeare and soe from yeare to yeare upon his rendring a good accompt [account] as aforesaid'. And this wasn't all; all fines 'forfeited by law' for the use of the parish poor were to be paid to the overseer, employed to the use of the poor and accounted for.

Twelve pence in the pound notwithstanding, this was a lot of work and responsibility for one person and one wonders how much this system was open to abuse. Almost forty years earlier, Sergeant Hoskyns had closed his missive on the treatment of the poor with the plea: 'God guide us all to the best for his s[er]vice and the good of the countrye and free us from confusion and disorder.'

BAYNHAM OF CANON PYON

In this section, we look at a surname long associated with the parish of Canon Pyon and how research into a particular branch of the family can reveal more about the parish.

Reaney and Wilson offer the origin of the surname Baynham as 'Welsh, ap Einion or ap Eynon', meaning 'son of Einion'.[52] The surname regularly appears in the parish in the 17th century, mostly in its later form, but a look back at earlier records (some from neighbouring parishes) illustrates the earlier form. A number of these records relate to property in Derndale and some of them are undoubtedly the same person, but with variations in the spelling (see Table 6 overleaf).

The earliest examples of the name were possibly patronymic in usage (son of Eynon) but by the mid-16th century, even though the 'ab/ap' is still present in some form, the surname would most likely be inherited. By around 1600, with the obvious exception of the 1631 example, the name was fairly well established as Baynham/Baynam/Beynam.

A connection between the earlier ap Eynons and Derndale can also be found in the name of a land holding. The 1649 survey of the manor has the following entry in the list of copyholders:

> Thomas Jay and Katherine his wife and Thomas their sonne hold by coppie of courte roll dated the one and twentyeth day of October in the nynth yeare of the raigne of King Charles [1633] three messuages and two yard land w[i]th thapputenances called Eynons Land lyeing in Brockton and Dernedall granted to the said Thomas and Katherine and Thomas and to the heires of the said

> Katherine by the yearly rent of xxviijs [£1 8s.] and three herriotts when they shall happen to become due and for the fine of eight pounds and eight shillings and the p[re]mises are clearly worth p[er] annu[m] xv li [£15]⁵³

A 'yardland' could be a varying amount of land, anything between 20 and 50 acres, so it would have been a fairly substantial holding and which had descended to the Jay family via Katherine according to the custom of the manor. Thomas and Katherine's marriage would have given us her surname and manorial surrenders and admissions would have given us her descent into the holding; unfortunately, both records are missing for this date. Eynons Land, however, is likely to be connected to the numerous leases to 'ap Eignons' and variants in the 16th century.

The Canon Pyon Baynhams appear to have hovered between the social status of husbandman and yeoman and certainly held customary land in the manor. In the absence of parish registers, other records may provide information about the family; in this case, a disagreement in 1609 tells us more.

A BAYNHAM FAMILY FEUD

George Baynham (hereafter George Baynham (R)), son of Anthony, was originally from Canon Pyon but in 1609 was living at Rocksavage in the county of Chester. He brought a case in the Star Chamber against another George Baynham (hereafter George Baynham (CP)), son of John, and possibly his cousin.⁵⁴

George Baynham (R) claimed that some pasture ground called the Knowles was customary land of the manor of Canon Pyon and that it was 'granted by the Dean & Chapter, about 30 yrs past' (*c.* 1579) to John Baynham, Anthony Baynham and George Baynham (R) and the heirs of Anthony. John Baynham was admitted and was to have the copyhold for the term of his life, then 'about 3 years past' (*c.* 1606), John Baynham died after which Anthony Baynham was lawfully seised of the premises. Sometime after (not specified but between 1606 and 1609), Anthony died and George Baynham (R) entered the premises and was lawfully seized, or so he claimed (see diagram on p. 172).

After this, George Baynham (CP), 'conspiring with Edward Broughton', a local gentleman, claimed the premises were freehold and were called Jbrooke and that they were his inheritance. The case thus revolved around the two Georges; which of the two rightfully owned the property and was the property called the Knowles or Jbrooke?

In the two years leading up to the case, there had been disturbances at Canon Pyon. Broughton had (allegedly) persuaded George Baynham (CP) about 5 April 1607 to make a lease of the premises for 21 years to Broughton and:

Year	Name	Details	Source
1426	John **ap Eynon**	Prior of Wormsley	Cookes 'History of Herefordshire..'
1438	John **ap Eynon**	Vicar of Weobley	Feoffment, TNA E40/8618
1482	John **ap Eynon**	Joint lessee of site and manor of Canon Pyon	HCA 3167
1539	John **ap Eygnon**	Billman of Canon Pyon	Faraday's 'Herefordshire Musters..'
1544	John **A Beynham**	Subsidy Tax assessed at £10 6s 8d	Faraday's 'Herefordshire Musters..'
1559	Thomas **Apeynon**	Dearndale lease, son of John	Lease for 29 years, HCA 4718/1
1559	Thomas **ap Eynon**	Husbandman of Canon Pyon	Bond, HCA 5223
1560/1	Thomas **Apenam**	Tenure of Derndale	Lease of Canon Pyon manor, HCA 4720/1
1563	Richard **Beynham**	Paid an heriot	View of Frankpledge, HCA 4735
1568	Richard **Beynhin** Thomas **Beynhin**	Copyholders	Terrier of demesne land in Canon Pyon, HCA 7001/1
1569	Thomas **A Beynham**	Tenure of Derndale	Lease of Canon Pyon manor, HCA 4720/2
1589	Thomas **A Beynham**	Tenure of Derndale	Lease of Canon Pyon manor, HCA 4720/4
1590	Ann **Abeynon** (dau. of Thomas)	Married William Smith, both tenants of Derndale	Lease for lives, HCA 4718/2
1609	George, Anthony & John **Baynham**	Tenure of Jbrooke	Star Chamber court case, STAC 8/76/4
1610	Elizabeth **Beynam**	Servant, received bequest in will of William Gardner	PCC Will, PROB 11/116/428
1623	George **Beynam**	The elder, yeoman of Canon Pyon	Quitclaim, HARC D4/13
1631	Thomas **ap Beighnam**	Tenure of Derndale	Lease for 1 year, HCA 4720/5
1635	George **Beynam**	Member of homage in manorial court roll	View of Frankpledge with Court Baron, HCA R1042
1658	George **Baynham**	The elder, of Canon Pyon	PCC Will, PROB 11/279/457

> ... on the 20th April did go with his wife Isabell, Thomas Greene, James Wheatnall and John Gregg and with force and armes did go to the premises and drive away the cattle that were depasturing there under the title of the sd Anthony Baynham'.

Soon after, on 1 of May the same people 'drewe away' sheep and cattle from the same premises. In June of that same year Anthony Baynham made a complaint in the High Court of Chancery, against George Baynham (CP) and Edward Broughton maintained the cause on George's behalf (this case has not been found).

Before long, Edward Vaughan of the Buttas became involved. He took up an 'action of trespasse' in the court of the Kings Bench against George Baynham (CP) for driving away 'eight beasts' of his out of the said premises. George alleged that the 'said copyhold' was freehold and Vaughan answered that it was freehold but belonging to the Dean & Chapter and that he had the command of the same to put his cattle on the premises, denying them to be the freehold of George Baynham (CP). This action lead to a trial in the Assizes at Hereford on the 18 July 'last past' (1608).

At this trial, Broughton maintained the cause against Edward Vaughan and 'reteyned Councell in the said cawse'. Broughton and George Baynham (CP) then procured one William Baineham and Thomas Uggan to swear that the pasture ground was the freehold of the said George Baynham (CP) and was known as Jbrooke. The jury decided that the ground *was* his freehold, which George Baynham (R) could not accept and requested subpoenas to be made to George Baynham (CP), Edward Broughton, Isabel his wife, Thomas Green, James Whetnoll, John Gregg and William Baingham.

This confusing story begins to unravel with the evidence of two surviving witness statements. William Baynham was examined on 11 February 1609 at Canon Pyon, by John Woolridge and John Greene. William was a husbandman, about 74 years of age and had known the parcel of land for 60 years. It had been called Knowles for the last 40 years and before that some of his elders had said it had been called Jbrooke. His remembrance was that it was freehold of the manor of Buttas, not copyhold or customary land of the manor of Canon Pyon. Neither had he ever heard John Baynham or John's father Richard Baynham say that the land was customary or copyhold.

John Baynham was William's father and he told him the land was called Jbrooke; it was known as this in the lifetime of Richard but in the lifetime of John it was known as Knowles. He also said that George Baynham (CP) had found a deed amongst his 'wrytinges' in which the land was called Jbrooke alias Knowles. Not only does William's

Opposite page: Table 6. Ap Eynon to Baynham; chronological changes in the locality

Canon Pyon

evidence give us three generations of his family but it indicates a possible change in property's name.

The second witness, Thomas Uggane [Wogan] of W[h]itbourne gent, aged about 75, recalled that he knew the land commonly called Knowles.⁵⁵ He had heard his father-in-law Walter Monnington (gent, deceased) and George Monnington (father of Walter and also deceased) say that the land was sometimes called Jbrooke and sometimes Knowles, though never that it was copyhold belonging to the manor of Canon Pyon. He also claimed to have seen a deed at the Assizes court shown by George Baynham (CP) mentioning land called Jbrooke alias Knowles.

There are no other witness statements with these documents and both George Baynham (CP) and Edward Broughton answer that they are not guilty of any of the charges made by George Baynham (R) and both accuse Edward Vaughan as being procured by him to help his case. These are the Baynham family relationships which can be determined from the case:

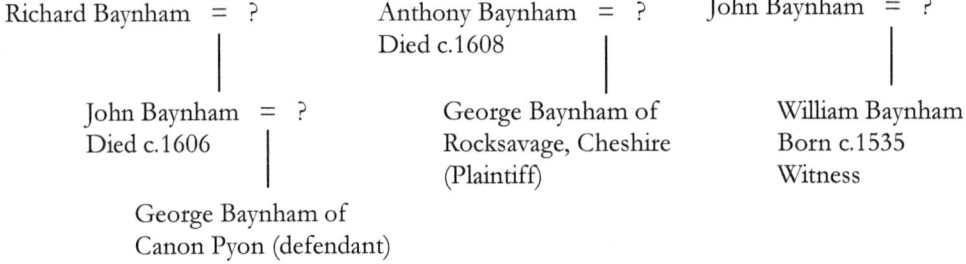

JBROOKE OR THE KNOWLES?

Can anything be discovered about the property? A fleeting reference to Jbrooke can be found in the 1568 terrier of customary lands, under the tenure of Edward Broughton:

> ... one p[ar]cell of land called Croggyshill cont[aining] by est[imation] xxxiiij acres nowe inclosed lying betwext the land of Thom[a]s Alton and Elizabeth P[ar]trige called Jbroke on the north p[ar]te and the glebe lands belonging to the vicarage of Canon Pewne aforesaid on the south p[ar]te and shoteth west unto the queen's highwaye leding from Canon Pewne to Kinges Pewne.⁵⁶

In the same 1568 terrier there is a reference to the Knowles in the tenure of Richard Beynham as 'one hill called the knoll inclosed by itself cont[aining] x [10] acres'; this is probably the Richard Baynham who was the grandfather of the defendant in the court case. No other information from this source is forthcoming but in a list of manorial fines dated 9 October 1563, Richard Beynham paid 13s. 4d. for a heriot for customary pasture land called 'le knowle' in Canon Pewne and £10 for the fine, an indication of the date when he first entered the land as tenant.[57] The entry is under the township of Nupton and Colwall, which is an area in Canon Pyon that is near to the Buttas and on the side of a hill.

It is therefore possible that Jbrooke may have been freehold land and the field/hill called Knowles was customary land; that they were separate but adjoining properties in 1563 and 1568 but became part of the same holding sometime later, thus causing the confusion.

It is likely that after this date a house was built as there are later references to a messuage. The property may have been known as Jbrooke alias Knowles for a while but the name Jbrooke seems to have been abandoned later. Thus in the 1649 survey, Richard Baineham, Elinor his wife and the heirs of Richard are recorded as having held one messuage and 10 acres of arable land and one parcel of the Knowles since 1641.[58] Later, at the manorial court of 23 April 1673, Richard and Elinor surrendered:

> ... one messuage with appurtenances and land called the Knowles containing by estimation ten acres of woodland and ten acres of arable land. For the use and behoof of the said Richard Bainham, sen, Richard Baynham jun, his son, and Elizabeth the wife of the said Richard the son and the heirs of the said Richard the son.[59]

They were to pay rent of 9s. 5d. per annum and a fine of 40s. to be admitted. Richard senior is likely to have been a son of one of the two sparring Georges.

It is also notable that the hillside was wooded by 1673. The next reference is from an interrogatory towards completing a glebe terrier in 1676 when the question was asked whether the tithe of a woodland ground called the Knowles near the Grange (then in the possession of Richard Baynham) belonged to the vicar. The answer was that 'the tithe of a woodland ground called ye Knowles above Butt[as] belongs to ye vicar'.[60]

The final reference is from a release of a messuage with lands called Knowles, dated 1732. This described the property as 'all that one customary messuage with the appurtenances and one parcel of land customary called the Knowles cont[aining] by estimac[i]on ten acres be it more or less'. Along with some other acreage, John and Catherine Baynham had borrowed £200 from Martha Johnson of Hereford in 1729 and the premises were the security against this loan - they were surrendered to Martha following the customs of the manor. In 1732 George Sawyer, at the request of the Baynhams, paid the loan with interest and Martha Johnson released and quitclaimed the premises to him, thus Knowles finally left the possession of the Baynhams.[61]

Canon Pyon

Jbrooke is a curious name; the spelling (in these few references) is always Jbrooke or Jbroke, never Jaybrooke so is unlikely to be a reference to the Jay family. There is also a possibility that the 'J' is an 'I'; a comparison of these letters in other parts of the document shows no difference. The place was probably on the lower hillside between Wormsley Grange and the Buttas, maybe extending down to the brook, whereas the Knowles was ten acres of the hillside itself. Isaac Taylor's *c*. 1755 map shows the wooded hillside labelled as 'Knowles Wood, copyhold and free'. By 1840, the hillside in that area was known as Baynhams Hill; it was still wooded by then (as it is now) but there is no sign of a building on either of the maps, making Jbrooke another of the lost houses of Canon Pyon.[62]

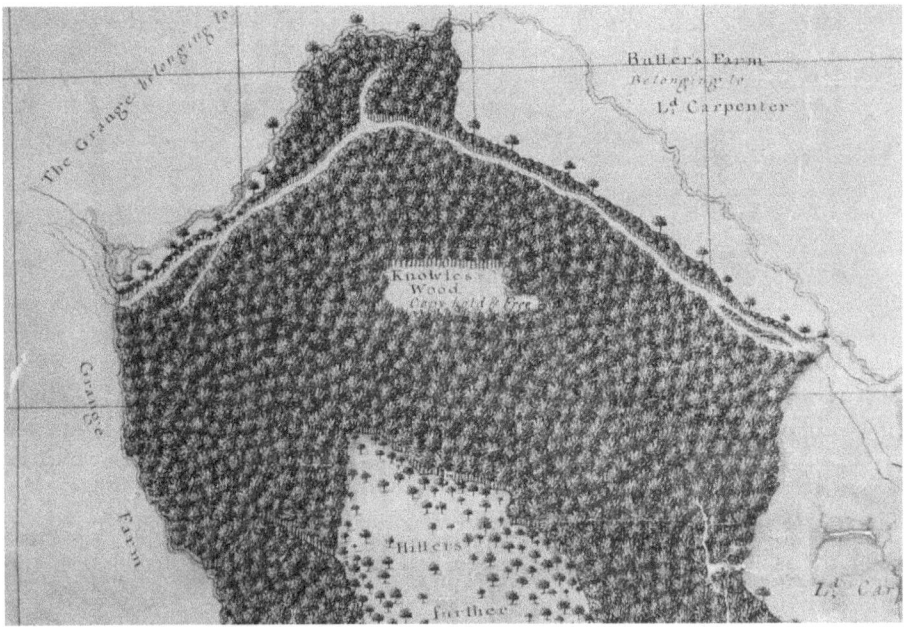

Knowles Wood, with Wormsley Grange land to the left of the image and Butter's Farm (Buttas) top right, from Isaac Taylors map of *c*. 1755 (HARC BN81)

NOTES

1 Campbell, Mildred, *The English Yeoman in the Tudor and Early Stuart Age*, Merlin Press Ltd, 1983, reproduced and printed in Great Britain by Whitstable Litho Ltd, Whitstable, Kent. (First published 1942 by Yale University Press), p. 27, 33-34.

2 HCA 4736, Suit Roll.

3 Waters, Colin, *A Dictionary of Old Trades, Titles and Occupations*, Countryside Books, 2nd ed., 2005, esquire and gentleman, pp. 109 & 130.

4 HCA 4718.

5 HCA 4735.

6 Hereford Deanery, 8 January 1680/1.

7 Campbell, *English Yeoman ...*, pp. 23-31.

8 Faraday, M. A., *Herefordshire Militia Assessments of 1663*, Royal Historical Society, London, 1972, pp. 1-5.

9 *Ibid.*, pp. 8-9.

10 *Ibid.*, pp. 74-75, with my notes in brackets.

11 Centre for Hearth Tax Research, University of Roehampton, London, https://www.roehampton.ac.uk/research-centres/centre-for-hearth-tax-research/the-hearth-tax/ (accessed September 2020).

12 Will of George Sawyer, TNA PROB/11/318/346, proved 31 October 1665. Hearth tax reference – see previous note (11).

13 Hamden, J, *Hearth Tax Assessment for Michaelmas 1665 for Herefordshire and Comparison with the Herefordshire Militia Assessments of 1663*, transcribed by J. Hamden, 1984, p. 45, residence notes mine, see chapter 3 on Thomas Griffiths for the kitchen.

14 TNA E179/119/509/49 and 50.

15 Hamden, *Hearth Tax Assessment for Michaelmas 1665...*

16 HCA R1041, manorial court record of October 1619.

17 HARC R28/11143.

18 Both mills noted in the 1649 manorial survey, HCA 7001/2 ff. 31-32. Free socage - rent paid in lieu of farm services to the lord of the manor. Licence to 'farm sett and lett' – may sub-let to an undertenant.

19 HCA R1042, surrender 13 April.

20 HCA R1041, HCA R1042.

21 HARC HD2/2/5.

22 TNA C3/407/17, Kinford v. Kinford 7 May 1638.

23 Further research may discover a family tie between James Kinford and the Leech family (perhaps a daughter or sister married one of the John Leeches); it might explain why Winifrid was excluded from the inheritance.

24 https://britishlistedbuildings.co.uk/101349794-kinford-farmhouse-canon-pyon#.X10FQGhKjIU accessed August 2020.

25 HCA 2480.

26 Englands Immigrants database - www.englandsimmigrants.com , original document TNA E179/117/62 m. 2 (tax assessment 19 July 1451), accessed August 2020.

27 Bannister, A. T., *The Prior of Austin Canons at Wormesley*, Woolhope Naturalists Field Club Papers, 1926.

28 Clark-Hall, J.R., *A Concise Anglo-Saxon Dictionary*, reprint by Wilder Publications, USA, 2011.

29 HARC AP39/26/1&2.

30 HARC AP39/379, Survey of the property of Thomas Carpenter Quick.

31 OS map, 1st ed., 25" to the mile, 1886.

32 HCA K15/6129/1.

33 Transactions of the Woolhope Club, *1946-8*, p. 242 - *The Manor of Buttas, Kings Pyon, 1638*, transcript by F C Morgan.

34 Both references from HCA 4734.

35 HARC Q/RD/7/19 & 20, Bargain and Sale, 25 June 1724.

36 HCA 4734.

37 Hereford Deanery, 9 October 1682.

38 HARC HD5/2/23, also in 1677.

39 HARC AP8/1.

40 HARC HD7/24/78, churchwardens' presentment 1686.

41 TNA PROB 11/368/466, proved 17 December 1681.

42 HCA 7001/2, p. 61.

43 HARC Q/SO/2 ff. 114A.

44 HARC AP8/1.

'Labourer, husbandman, yeomen, gent': more inhabitants

45 TNA E179/19/509/47 and 48.

46 HCA 4735.

47 *Ibid.*, manorial court presentments.

48 Hereford Deanery, 13 January 1684/5.

49 Probably John Hoskyns 1566-1638, Sergeant at Law from 1623, http://www.historyofparliamentonline.org/volume/1604-1629/member/hoskins-john-1566-1638 accessed April 2021.

50 HARC W52/2, manuscript of John Hoskyns. Note: he really does write 'to serve for fowre and twenty yeres'! Perhaps he meant until 24 yrs old.

51 Hereford Quarter Sessions, QO/SO/2, Michaelmas 25 Charles II [1673].

52 Reaney, P.H. & Wilson R. M., *A Dictionary of English Surnames*, Oxford University Press, 1995

53 HCA 7001/2, pp. 18-19.

54 TNA STAC 8/76/4, Baynham v. Baynham, 1609.

55 He signed the document as Thomas Wogan.

56 HCA 7001/1.

57 HCA 4735.

58 HCA 7001/2.

59 HCA 4735.

60 HARC HD2/2/6-8.

61 HARC R28/11212.

62 HARC BR39, Canon Pyon tithe map.

Afterword

By the 17th century, the manor of Canon Pyon had already been the property of the Cathedral Church in Hereford for over 600 years, conferring a remarkable long-term stability. As with the case of wardship and marriage, a custom that was shown to be in place since at least 1216, many of the manor's customs will have remained unchanged for a long time.

One of the biggest changes over this time was the steady enclosure of the large open fields, subtly changing the landscape and balance of crops and pasture and creating possibilities for more consolidated (though limited) land holdings for individuals. This may have contributed to the disappearance of the small townships of Easthope and Colwall and the renaming of Brockton and Eston Foliot to Lower and Upper Derndale. It could also be argued that the Civil War contributed to these changes; pre-war manorial court records list the townships but post-Restoration records do not. A few later suit rolls were maintained using the townships, as can be seen in the 1676 example, but their usage was certainly waning.

The Civil War and Interregnum caused disruption in the parish church, with vicars ejected and appointed according to the beliefs of whoever had the power to do so. The right of the lessee of the manor farm to present an incumbent seems to have vanished alongside the church officials during Parliamentary rule and the right reverted to the Dean once his position was re-established in 1660. However, apart from this period of uncertainty, Canon Pyon seems to have fared reasonably well spiritually, having no lengthy periods of absence of vicars. Whether or not parishioners were wholly satisfied with their spiritual guidance is debatable. There is certainly evidence of disagreements between tithe farmer and vicar, although this was more to do with worldly matters such as tithes. Any underlying divergence of opinion on spiritual matters is difficult to discern. Most parishioners attended the parish church but there were a few Quakers in the parish who would not have done so and also a few Roman Catholics, some of whom may have attended the parish church on occasion to avoid discovery or persecution.

Afterword

Wartime family loyalties were undoubtedly strained and people forced to choose sides, particularly servants of the richer folk or minor gentry. At least one family - the Berringtons of Little Pyon - left the parish for a while to live in Monmouth, causing them problems at a later date with rights to a family pew in the church. Groups of soldiers roamed the countryside for food and supplies and although the only evidence is an acerbic comment left by the vicar, the vicarage kitchen may have been ransacked at this time. It is difficult to gauge how much disruption there was to the manorial court proceedings during the Civil War and Interregnum due to the lack of survival of documents. At least three records survive from the 1650s (a surrender and admission, a view of frankpledge and a jury's presentment). The Parliamentarians would surely wish to continue to receive the rents and fines but little else has survived.

There are a few discernible pre- and post-war differences in the manorial court records which offer clues to the changing lifestyles of the inhabitants. Pre-war tenants were fined for not practising archery, for not hanging up the winnowing fan and occasionally for making an affray. Post-war tenants were fined for the butts being out of repair (but no mention of bows as before) and for keeping goats out too long. Some things did not change throughout both periods; tenants were required to cut hedges, maintain fences and scour ditches and were fined for not turning up at court, for trantory (selling ale outside of the market) and for erecting cottages without the statutory four acres.

It is often thought that the past was a lawless time but there were plenty of regulations to follow and rule-breakers found themselves brought before the manorial court, church court, Hereford Assizes or a national court. The church court in particular was unpopular, dealing as it did with moral and spiritual behaviour in a way that would confound us in our freedom of lifestyle choice today. Nevertheless, life in the manor continued in much the same vein as it had done for centuries, bound as it was to making a living from the land. So too did the families who lived here; many of the same surnames persisted from the beginning to end of the century and beyond, further testimony to the stability of the manor and parish.

In light of this, the social dynamics in the parish are unlikely to have undergone dramatic changes in the 17th century. Leases of the few larger properties remained in the hands of the same families and their descendants and although there was some opportunity for wealthier yeomen families to become sub-tenants of these properties, this was limited. Freehold properties with a dwelling seem to have been few and far between and also remained within the same families. Most other residences were cottages of modest proportions; this was an era when 'inmates' or lodgers were not only discouraged but were against the rules of the manor.

Canon Pyon

Sadly, only few properties remain which have obvious beginnings in the 17th century or earlier, though some will have these elements within them or in their foundations. Roads which were once dirt and broken stone are now surfaced, many husbandry ways have disappeared and the hilly ground in the parish is now wooded. Even so, the bones of the 17th century manor and parish are still recognisable in the 'townships' of Nupton, Fulbridge and Westhope and to some extent Canon Pyon, although the focus of this township has moved from the church area to that now known as New End.

As we have seen from 17th century documents, the name of the parish was often written as Cannon Pewne or simply Pewne or Peune (also recorded in the Domesday Book). A. D. Mills in *A Dictionary of English Place Names* proposes Pyon to be derived from Old English *pēona* (of the gnats) and *ēg* (island) thus meaning 'island of the gnats' (or other insects). It is not difficult to envisage marshy ground on the lower lying areas and it is probably no coincidence that the early townships, except Brockton and Derndale (and perhaps Fulbridge), were on higher ground. As a 1569 terrier shows, there were certainly fewer manorial tenants and they appear to have held more land in the common fields rather than in enclosed fields.

Today, the parish is still rural and largely agricultural although far fewer inhabitants now make their living from the land. Copyhold land was finally abolished in 1926 and manorial courts ceased to function but thankfully, many of their records are preserved in local archives.

Appendix 1

The customs of the manor of Canon Pyon
(from HCA 7001/2, survey of 1649)

Wee say that wee hold our coppiehold lands and tenements of the Lords of this mannor by coppie of Court Roll sibi et suis [for themselves and their heirs] and wee have an estate of inheritance in the same and our coppieholds doe discend to the heires according to the course of the com[m]on law except where there daughters or sisters hires [heirs] and there the eldest inherites the whole. And wee say that by our custome the widow of a coppieholder dieing siesed of any coppiehold lands or tenements within the mannor shall by the custome neither have dower or ffreebench in any of them except shee be named in the Coppie. And in case a Coppieholder die and leave his heire an infant, the neerest of kindred and the farthest from the land shall be the guardian of the infant during the minoritie according to the course of com[m]on (except the father in his life did appoint any other). And wee say that such guardian is to continue until such heire doe come to full age. And wee say that herriotts are due by coppieholders upon alienac[i]on and discent (vizt) the best beast or twenty six shillings and eight pence in lieu thereof at the ellec[i]on of the Lord and for want of a beast the best goods of such coppieholder and for other things such herriotts as are expressed in the severall coppies. And we say that our ffines are arbitrary but usually the Lords have not exceeded three years rent of the rent paid for the Coppiehold to wich the tenant was to be admitted. And the steward is to be a man indifferent to moderate the same and our Coppiehold rents and theise rents are due at Mich[alm]as only and are in the whole 24 li 0 s 4d ob [£24 0s 4½d]. And fowerteen hens due at the Purificac[i]on of the Virgin Mary and threescore and ten eggs and usually paid in by the Bayliffe to the Lords within ten dayes after all Saints and the henns and eggs at Candlemas, and for the Bayliffes default the Lord may enter upon his land or distreyne him or imprison him for it. And the said Bayliffe is to be chosen by the Homage and sworne at the Lords Courte after Mich[alm]as and the tenants usually pay their rents to the Lords Bayliffe and to no other. And wee say that Coppieholders may not make Leases of their Coppiehold lands or tenements for longer terme than a yeare and a day without Licence nor decay nor take downe any building nor sell any tymber from of their Coppiehold lands or tenements without Licence. And wee say that Coppieholders may fall any tymber from their Coppieholds for building or repaire of any building upon their Coppieholds and may take wood growing upon their Coppieholds, for hedgboote, heyboote, fireboote, ploughboote and carteboote, to be spent upon their Coppieholds and fell underwoods and vallett woods without Licence. And that the Lords may not enter upon any coppieholds to fall or cutt any timber or wood there unless they compound w[i]th us for soe doing. And wee say that all the Coppieholders of this mannor have right of com[m]on in all parts of the Lords wast and all com[m]onable places w[i]thin this mannor in respect of their sevrall Coppiehold lands as tenements as well as the ffreeholders. And wee say that the Lords of this mannor have w[i]thin this mannor a Courte Leete and a Court Baron to be kept as the Law directs, and waifs, estrays and felons goods and the Royaltie of the mannor And the Assize of bread and beere and all other things to the said Courtes belonging. And we say that all the inhabitants owe suite and service to the Courte Leete and all ffreeholders and coppieholders to the Courte Barron. And wee say that the Coppieholders may make surrenders of their Coppiehold lands and tenements w[i]thin this mannor out of courte into the hands of two tenants to be presented in Courte the next Court following or w[i]thin a year and a day. And wee say we know of no heriotts due or w[i]ch ought to be paid by ffreeholders in respect of any ffreehold messuages they shall dye seised of or make alienac[i]on of. And wee say that the inhabitants in Cannon Pion, Nupton, Collway, Westhope, Derndall als Eston ffolliott, Brocton als Derndall, Easthope, ffowlebridge, Smythley and Pyon does owe suite and service to the Courte Leete and divers freeholders and coppieholders there to the Court Baron. And we say that there are eight cottages built upon the Lords wast and some of them by order of Sessions according to the s[t]atute. And we say that there is only one wast within this manor called Westhope Hill conteyning about threescore acres where the com[m]oners may digg stones for their uses wthout Licence, and that there is a small brooke called Derndall Brooke wherin have benn taken some trowtes and eeles and wee suppose there are very few fish therein and the fishing therein belongeth to the Lords. And we say that the Lords of this mannor have the tyeths of the p[ar]ish of Cannon Pyon and the Advowson of the vicaridge and out of the same tyeths they are to repaire the Chauncell and to pay yearly to the vicar 32 bushells of wheat and forty two bushells of oats. And the Lords are to repair the com[m]on pound and to finde the jurie a dinner at everie courte.

Appendix 2

The tenures of Edward Broughton and George Vaughan

Part A. The manorial lands in the respective tenures of Edward Broughton and George Vaughan transcribed from a terrier *c.* 1568 (HCA7001/1). A later copy has some minor differences (HARC R28/11599).

The demaynes in the tenure of Edward Broughton by lease:
>The manor house wth two barnes and a gate house
>One close of pasture adjoining to the said house lying on the west side of the same house cont[eyning] by est[imacon] 3 acres
>Two poles and a little garden inclosed by itself cont[eyning] by est[imacon] 1 acre lying betwixt the said close of 3 acres on the north and a lesow or orchard parcell of the said demesnes called Swaynards Grene on the south
>One close cont[eyning] 1 acre called Dovehouse close lying betwixt Senct Mary lane est and the said manor house west

Swaynards Grene (pasture):
>One pasture or orchard called Swaynards Grene cont[eyning] four acres lying betwixt a broke there on the north west & a field called the West fyld on the south and est

The West Fylde (arable):
>The custom gobbett cont 20 acres lying betwixt the land of Walter Monyngton on the west and the copyhold of Thomas Beynham on the est
>Ten acres lying betwixt the land of Richard Silly on the west and the lands of Harry Geffreis on the est

A fylde called the Strode (arable and pasture):
>One croft of arable land cont[eyning] by est[imacon] 4 acres lying betwixt a close of 3 acres aforesaid parcell of the said demesnes on the est and a medow of John Kings on the west
>Seven acres of [arable] now enclosed lying betwixt Saint Mary Lane on the est and 3 acres parcell of the said demesnes wich 3 acres and the said 7 acres the said Edward Brocketon had now made a hedge on the west
>The said 4 acres lyeth betwixt the land of Harry Geffreis on the west and the

said 7 acres on the est

Fifteen acres parcel of Byrche Furlong lying betwixt the land of Richard Silly on the north and the land of Richard Beynham on the south & shooteth west upon the part meadow in the lordship of Kings Pewne (one parcel whereof win[d]ing to the said part medow is now enclosed and converted to pasture) containing by est[imacon] 4 acres

One croft of arable land now inclosed called Byrch Furlong cont[eyning] 15 acres lying betwixt the foresaid 15 acres on the south west and the queens high way est and Little Pewnes common [comen] north

Croggyshill (arable):
One parcel of land called Croggyshill cont[eyning] by est[imacon] 34 acres now enclosed lying betwixt the land of Thomas Alton and Elizabeth P[ar]trige called Jbroke on the north and the glebe lands belonging to the vicarage of Canon Pewne aforesaid on the south and shooteth west unto the queens highway leading from Canon Pewne to Kings Pewne.

The Bery Croft (arable):
One croft called Bery Croft cont[eyning] 20 acres lying betwixt the queens high way called Longe Lane on the north and certain medows parcel of the said demesnes called Howe Medowes on the south

Howe Medowes (medow and pasture):
The Howe medows [T]ompy Close and Long Lesow cont[eyning] 16 acres lying betwixt the said Bery croft on the north and Ashehil Fyld on the south

A ffyld called Ashe hill (arable):
Ten acres lying betwixt the land of Richard Beynh[a]m on the west and the lands of Walt[er] Monyngton Richard Beynh[a]m and John Appary on the est
Four acres lying betwixt the land of Richard Silly on the west and a lesowe of the said Richard and one acre parcel of the said demesnes on the est
The said one acre lying betwixt the said lesowe of the said Richard Silly on the north and the way leading through the said field on the south

The Ov[er] Mylfylde (arable):
Two acres lying betwixt the land of Richard Silly on the west and the land of Thomas Kynford on the est
One acre lying betwixt the land of Richard Sillie on the west and the lands of Harry Geffreis on the est
One acre lying betwixt the old broke on the west and the lands of Richard Beynh[a]m and others on the est

The Lower Myll Ffylde (arable):
Four acres lying betwixt the land of Thomas Kynford on the west and the land of John Apparry on the est
One gobet called the Ov[er] Custom Gobet cont[eyning] 6 acres lying betwixt the mill lane on the west and the land of John Apparry est
Three acres shooting north upon Woodcocke Medowe upon 2 acres parcel of the said demesnes
The said 2 acres lyeth betwixt the land of the said Thomas Kynford north and

diverse mens land on the south

Di (half) acre lying betwixt the land of John Parryes on the west & est and shooteth north upon Woodcocke Medow

One acre shooting eastward upon Rushemore & lyeth betwixt the land of Richard Silly on the north and the customary land of Walt[er] Monyngton on the south

Two acres called the Sonne Pitts lying betwixt a lesow called Frogge M[ar]rshe on the south and diverse mens lands on the north

Woods:

One valet called the Canon Vallet cont[eyning] by est[imacon] 20 acres lying betwixt Byrleis Comon [Birley's common] & Esthopes hill est & the Lye Vallet north and Ov[er] Woodfield south

The Redd hill:

Half an acre of vallet win[d]ing west to Byrles Comen [common]

Pewne hill:

One hill or wood called Pewne Hill containing by est[imacon] 15 acres lying betwixt Hafcomer on the south and est and the Old Field north and a parcel of the glebe land belonging to the vicarage north which the said Edward now by consent hath 'in sev[er]allta' but hath always before that agreement lay as waste and 'comen to the tenants of pewne'

Canon medowe:

One medowe called Canon Medowe lying near Lastons Bridge containing [blank] acres

George Vaughans copyhold in Pewne:

The mease

One mease croft called Saintt Mary Croft having no building on it cont[eyning] 4 acres lying betwixt the queens high way on the est and a field called the Strode on all other

A ffyld called the Strode (arable):

Seven acres shooting westward upon the part medowe and estward upon the free land of Richard Beynh[a]m

Eight acres lying betwixt a croft called P[ar]tridge Crofte north and the land of Harry Geffreis on the south (2 acres whereof shooteth north east upon Little Pewnes Comen)

One acre of pasture inclosed lying betwixt the land of Richard Beynh[a]m east and 2 acres parcel of the lords demesne west (pasture)

The Ov[er] Myllfyld (arable):

Two acres lying betwixt the land of Richard Beynh[a]m on the south and Thomas Kynfords land on the north

Two acres lying betwixt the Myll lane on the est & the copyhold of Richard Silly on the west

Half an acre shooting on the mylstreme est and west

Canon Pyon

The Cleylands (arable):
> Half an acre lying betwixt the land of Harry Geffreyes on the est and west sydes
> One acre at Bowecrofte betwixt the land of Richard Beynh[a]m on the west and the land of William Knapp on the est

The Old ffylde:
> Two acres lying betwixt Wynyards Wey on the west & the land of Richard Silly
> Three acres lying betwixt Kynfords knapp on the north and the high wey [l]eding to Longbrige from Pewne on the south
> Two acres lying betwixt Pewne Hill on the south and the said high wey on the north
> One acre called the Harpe Acre lying betwixt the said high wey on the south and & Croxhill on the north
> One acre lying betwixt the said high wey on the south and the vicar of Pewnes glebe lands on the north
> One croft containing 2 acres shooting westward upon a croft of Thomas Altons called Jbroke and estward upon William Knapp & Walt[er] Monyngtons land [William Knapp appears to be crossed out].

Seynct Mary Crofte (arable):
> One croft called Senct Mary Croft inclosed cont[eyning] 7 acres lying bet[wixt] the queens highway on the west & Haftecomer & parcel of the vicars glebe on the est

West ffylde (arable):
> One acre lying betwixt the queens highway leading from Pewne to Nupton on the est & the land of John Apparry on the west
> One acre called Olde Acre lying betwixt the land of John Apparry on the south and the land of Richard Abeynh[a]m on the north
> Half an acre in Howsmore lying betwixt the land of John Gregg on all parts

Ashill ffylde (arable):
> One acre di [and a half] lying at the pyteston betwixt the land of William Knapp on the est and the land of John Parry on the west
> Half an acre lying betwixt the church stye on the est and the land of William Knapp on the west
> One acre at Sichbroke [Sizebrook] shooting southward upon Sychbroke and northward upon the land of Harry Geffreyes
> Half an acre lying betwixt the said Sychbroke on the south and the custom land of Richard Silly on the north

Lydbarre ffylde (arable and meadow):
> One acre shooting northward upon Lydbarre Medow and lieth betwixt the land of John Gregg on both sides
> One other acre lying betwixt the land of John Gregg north and south
> One meadow called Lydbarre Medowe cont[eyning] 1 acre lying betwixt Lydbarre ffylde on the south and a moor of John Gregg on the north

Haftecomere (arable):
> Two acres in Haftecomber [slade] shooting north upon the queens high wey
> One acre di [and a half] lying betwixt the land of Harry Geffreyes on the west and est

Brodwat[er] (medow and pasture):
> Half an acre lying betwixt the copyhold of Georg[e] Vaughan belonging to Fulbrige on all parts
> One lesowe called Seynct Mary Grove cont[eyning] 4 acres lying betwixt the land of John Parry est and the land of Harry Geffreyes west
> Two acres lying in the Ov[er] Woodfyld in the township of Westhope betwixt the land of Hugh Edmonds on the est
> Three acres in Fulbrige Grene wherof a high waye is given out of it lat[e] parcel of George Vaughans copyhold in Pewne which William Gregg and Richard Silly holdeth by copy

Part B. The lands of George Vaughan at the time of his death in 1616, summarised from HCA 4257, the inspeximus of an award by the Court of Chancery.

Copyhold:
One messuage and one nook of land called Popes land in Fulbridge
One messuage and 1 yard land called Saint Marie in Fulbridge
One messuage and 1 ½ yards land, 22 acres of land and 10 acres of land in several places in Fulbridge
One meadow called Rose meadow in Fulbridge
Two acres of land in Fulbridge Green
One parcel of meadow or pasture called Rose hiron in Fulbridge
Two and ½ acres of six selions of land and 7 butts of land in a field called Clayland in Fulbridge
Other customary in Eston ffolyatt (purchased by Oliver Vaughan, his father)

Freehold land held of the Dean & Chapter by knight service:
One messuage and close adjoining called Vintners
Half of a messuage and 1 yard land in Bructon and Derndale
One messuage and 1 yard land in Nupton and in Colewall
Other diverse messuages, tenements and land in Canon Pyon manor (purchased by Oliver Vaughan from John Seaborne Esq and William Monington, gent).

Appendix 3

Canon Pyon churchwardens 1662-1699
(from HARC MX14, bishop's transcripts)

Year	Name	Name
1662-3	George Baynham	Thomas Sylley
1664-5	Edward Monnington	Thomas Jay
1667	William Plevey	
1668	Oliver Gardner	Roland Gardner
1669-71	John Jay	Thomas Jones
1673	Rowland Gardner	Thomas Steephens
1674	William Gardner	Hugh Jay
1675	John Jones	Hugh Meredith
1676-7	George Baynham	William Hornblow
1677-8	Henry Mayor	William Bluck
1678	John Turbervile	Bartholomew Walter
1679	Richard Sylly	
1681	Wraintfort Hill	William Rogers
1682	Thomas Abraham	Ralph Bull
1683	Thomas Joens	William Plevey
1684	Charles Andrews	William Gardner
1685	Hugh Smalman	John Joens
1686	Roland Gardner	Richard Steephenes
1688	George Baighnam	Ralph Bull
1689	William Yeamans	William Bluck

Year	Name	Name
1690	William Playdell	Thomas Abram
1691	John Duggan	William Thomas
1692	Joseph Evans	Henry Tyler
1693	Thomas Hill	John Gayly
1694	Hugh Jay	William Jones
1696	John Turbervile	William Scarlett
1697	Thomas Munne	Frances [sic] Smith
1699	George Knappe	Edward Reignolds

Pre-Civil War (with sources):
1605 Edward Jeffreyes and Edward Yeomans (HARC HD4/1/162, f. 8)
1608 Edward Broughton and John Kinford (HCA 7002/1/2, f. 3)
1611 Lewis Gwyn and Richard Daniell (HCA 7002/1/2, f. 138r)
1617 George Baynham and Francis Clarke (HD2/2/4 & 5)
1623 Simon Phillips, Richard Sillie, John Powell (HCA 7002/1/3)

Select chronology
(national events in italics)

1601	Oliver Vaughan dies and leaves manor lease to son George.
1601	Edward Broughton also has manor lease (different lands to Vaughan)
1601	Phillip Knapp is the vicar
1603	*Queen Elizabeth dies and James I comes to the throne*
1604	Canon laws of the Church of England are agreed, including the use of the Book of Common Prayer
1605	*Anti-Catholicism increases in the wake of the Gunpowder Plot and in Herefordshire's Whitsun Riots*
1606	*Oath of Allegiance requires Catholics to acknowledge the king's sovereignty over the Pope*
1608	Vicar Phillip Knapp is presented by the churchwardens for not taking some of services stipulated in the 1604 Canons
1608	The church is in need of tiling and the chancel paving
1609	The two George Baynhams are in disagreement over land in the parish
1610	Edward Broughton brings a case in Star Chamber against James Berrington for the alleged kidnap and marriage of his step-daughter to James' son
1611	Edward Broughton and 'his man Whetnoll' are presented for laying violent hands on vicar Phillip Knapp
1616	George Vaughan is dead, widow Katherine continues with manor lease
1617	*King James publishes his 'Declaration to his Subjects, Concerning Lawful Sports to be Used' (also known as the Book of Sports) but does not enforce it*
1617	Phillip Knapp compiles a terrier of the glebe lands (includes reference to sidesmen)
1621-4	Manorial inquiry and Chancery case to discover who has right of wardship and marriage (of Judith, dau. of George Vaughan) and what heriots are due after the death of George
1623-4	Edward Broughton is involved in court cases regarding his lease
1625	*King James dies and Charles I comes to the throne*
1627/8	Edward Broughton is no longer living at Canon Pyon
1628	Church court charges Phillip Knapp of refusing to marry a couple with a

Select Chronology

	licence, which he admits but claims he is not at fault
1630s	*Laudianism at its highest point and with the support of King Charles promotes the return of icons and images and other pre-reformation practices*
1631	Robert Lochard signs one-year lease for the manor
1633	The Dean & Chapter complains to the Council of Wales and the Marches about bailiff Thomas Berrington of Little Pyon
1633	*Charles I republishes the Book of Sports and enforces it*
1638	Chancery court case between Winifred Kinford and Katherine Kinford regarding the inheritance of Kinford and the mill
1639	Vicar Phillip Knapp dies and is buried in the chancel of the church
c. **1639**	Jonathan Dryden becomes the new vicar at Canon Pyon
1640	*Archbishop Laud is arrested by Parliament and iconoclasm begins in earnest*
1642	*Start of Civil War; puritanism increases in significance, growth of 'liberty of conscience'*
1642	*Committee for Plundered Ministers is created*
1642	Robert Harley's 'puritan survey' of the ministry in Herefordshire
1644	Royalist forces roam the countryside for food, shelter and horse fodder
1645	Herefordshire Clubmen forms and in July the Scottish army lays siege to Hereford, leading to more raiding. In December, Hereford is taken by the Parliamentarian army
1645	*Archbishop Laud is executed (his trial did not start until 1644)*
1645	*The Directory for Public Worship replaces the Book of Common Prayer*
1645	A new army is raised; 2000 men to be recruited in Herefordshire
1646	Vicar Jonathan Dryden claims (via an order for plundered ministers) £50 from the rent corn (recorded in the 1649 survey)
1646	John Aubrey's memory of Edward Broughton (written 1680s)
c. **1647**	Vicar Dryden leaves the parish (at St Giles, Camberwell by 1650); his daughter and son-in-law Karver go too
1649	*Charles I is executed (January) and the Interregnum begins (or Commonwealth)*
1649	The Parliamentarians compile a survey of Canon Pyon manor (July) and other church properties
c. **1650**	Thomas Griffithes, vicar of Kings Pyon, may now be vicar at Canon Pyon
1650	William Lochard is dead, widow Judith continues with the manor lease
c. **1651**	Thomas Bedford may be in place of Thomas Griffithes as vicar
1653	Jonathan Dryden dies in Camberwell (November)
1653	*Oliver Cromwell becomes Lord Protector (December)*
1653	*Secular marriages are now allowed and banns are to be read in the market-place*

Canon Pyon

c. **1654**	Judith (nee Vaughan) marries John Barneby
1654	Katherine Baskervile marries George Sawyer at London
1658	*Oliver Cromwell dies and is succeeded by his son Richard who resigns after a few months*
1660	The monarchy is restored and Charles II comes to the throne
1660	The Act for confirming and restoring of ministers is introduced
1660	Thomas Griffithes is presented to the living of Canon Pyon church and blames Cromwell and others for the state of the vicarage kitchen.
1660	The churchwardens report want of a Book of Common Prayer and surplice (both to be used again)
1662	*The Act of Uniformity is passed leading to renewed persecution of non-conformists*
1660s	Judith Barneby, Lochard family members and others are presented by the churchwardens as Roman Catholics
1665	George Sawyer dies at Bullingham but is buried in his native Berkshire
c. **1666**	Katherine Sawyer marries Charles Somersett between now and 1668
1670	(also 1672) Hearth Tax exemption certificates give names of those in the parish receiving alms
1672	Vicar Thomas Griffithes dies and is buried at Canon Pyon
1672	Daniel Wycherley is to be the new vicar but becomes prebendary of Hinton and Rector of Whitney
1672	Richard Gayley disputes his hearth tax demand
1673	*The Test Act is passed; anyone in public office has to swear an oath for Royal supremacy and also against transubstantiation*
1673	Thomas Bedford becomes the vicar for Canon Pyon
1676	Constable William Gardner is called before the Quarter Sessions for 'neglect of duty'
1677	Church court case between vicar Thomas Bedford and George Karver of the Butthouse about unpaid tithes
1678	Judith Barneby is buried at Canon Pyon
1678	Thomas Bedford fears he is in danger and believes he is suspended from office
1680	Rainford Hill and Charles Somersett are named in the Papist Oath Rolls
1680s	First documentary evidence of Quakers in the parish
1681	Court case involving tithes between vicar Thomas Bedford and Charles Somerset
1681	Church court case between the churchwardens and Charles Somersett for non-payment of his church 'loan'

Select Chronology

1681	The will of Humphrey Digges conveys mistrust in the poor relief system of the parish
1683/4	First document found recording a tannery at Derndale (well established)
1685	*Charles II dies and his brother James II comes to the throne*
1686	The Dean & Chapter begins a disciplinary case against Thomas Bedford
1687	Church court case about the Little Pyon pew at the church
1687	*The Declaration of Indulgence is passed, allowing freedom of worship*
1687	Dissenters and Roman Catholics no longer presented by churchwardens
1687	Thomas Gwillim, curate, tears up the Royal edict before the congregation
1688	Vicar Thomas Bedford dies and is buried at Canon Pyon (February)
1688	Herbert Hooke is presented to the living at Canon Pyon in June
1688	*Catholic James II goes into exile (November) and is deposed by protestant William of Orange and his wife Mary on the invitation of Parliament*
1689	*The Declaration of Rights; includes a clause disallowing the monarch to marry a Roman Catholic*
1696	Vicar Herbert Hooke marries Penelope Stallard at Eardisland
1707	Court case between the Hookes and the Hills; Herbert Hooke dies.

Select Bibliography

Aylmer Gerald and Tiller, John (eds.), *Hereford Cathedral: A History*, Hambledon Continuum, 2000

Baker, Geoff, *Reading and Politics in early modern England: The mental world of a seventeenth-century Catholic gentleman*, Manchester University Press, 2010

Bannister, A.T., *The Cathedral Church of Hereford, It's History and Constitution*, SPCK, London, 1924.

Bannister, A. T., *The Prior of Austin Canons at Wormesley*, Woolhope Naturalists Field Club Papers, 1926

Barrow, J. S. (ed), *Fasti Ecclesiae Anglicanae 1066-1300: Volume 8*, Hereford, London, 2002

Blanch, William Hartnett, *History of the Parish of Camberwell*, 1875, Re-print, ed. Michael Wood, FamLoc Books, 2015

Bristow, Joy, *The Local Historians Glossary of Words and Terms*, Countryside Books, 2001

Campbell, Mildred, *The English Yeoman in the Tudor and Early Stuart Age*, Merlin Press Ltd, 1983, reproduced and printed in Great Britain by Whitstable Litho Ltd, Whitstable, Kent. (First published 1942 by Yale University Press)

Cavill, Paul, *A New English Dictionary of English Field-Names*, English Place Name Society, 2018

Cooke, Henry William, *Collections towards the History and Antiquities of the County of Hereford, in continuation of Duncumb's History*, London, 1886 (the Hundred of Grimsworth)

Cressy, David, *Birth, Marriage and Death: Ritual, Religion, and the life-cycle in Tudor and Stuart England*, Oxford University Press, 1999

Di Palma, Vittoria, *Wasteland: a History*, Yale University Press, 2014

Dougall, Alistair, *The Devil's Book: Charles I, the Book of Sports and Puritanism in Tudor and Early Stuart England*, University of Exeter Press, 2011

Faraday, M. A., *Herefordshire Militia Assessments of 1663*, Royal Historical Society, London, 1972

Select Bibliography

Faraday, M. A (ed.)., *Herefordshire Taxes in the Reign of Henry VIII*, Woolhope Naturalists' Field Club, Herefordshire, 2005

Hardy, Robert & Strickland, Matthew, *The Great Warbow: From Hastings to the Mary Rose*, J.H. Haynes & Co Ltd, 2011

Mills, A. D., *A Dictionary of English Place Names* (2nd edition), Oxford University Press, 1998

Moore, Susan T., *Tracing your ancestors through the Equity Courts*, Pen & Sword, 2017

O'Day, Rosemary, *The English Clergy; the Emergence and Consolidation of a Profession, 1558-1642*, Leicester University Press, 1979

Parker, Keith, *Radnorshire from Civil War to Restoration*, Logaston Press, 2000

Perkins, Diane, *The English Civil War; a people's history*, Harper Perennial, 2007

Reaney, P.H. & Wilson R. M., *A Dictionary of English Surnames*, Oxford University Press, 1995

Rizzo, Betty, *Swift's Favourite Cousin 'poor Pat Rolt' and other relations*, News and Queries (Journal), Oxford University Press, Dec 1983

Roth, Erik, *With a Bended Bow; Archery in Medieval and Renaissance Europe*, Spellmount, 2012

Ross, David, *Royalist, But ... Herefordshire in the English Civil War, 1640-51*, Logaston Press, 2012

Schofield, John, *Cromwell to Cromwell: Reformation to Civil War*, The History Press, 2009

Siddons, Michael Powell (transcribed and edited by), *Visitation of Herefordshire 1634*, Harleian Society, London, 2002

Smith, Philip Vernon, *The Law of Churchwardens and Sidesmen in the 20th century*, London, 1903

Spraggon, Julie, *Puritan Iconoclasm during the English Civil War*, The Boydell Press, 2003

Spurr, John, *English Puritanism 1603-1689*, Macmillan Press Ltd, 1998

Spurr, John, *The Post-Reformation; Religion, Politics and Society in Britain 1603-1714*, Pearson/Longman, 2006

Stuart, Denis, *Manorial Records*, Phillimore & Co. Ltd, 1992

Tarver, Anne, *Church Court Records: An introduction for family and local historians*, Phillimore, 1995

Waters, Colin, *A Dictionary of Old Trades, Titles and Occupations*, Countryside Books, 2nd ed., 2005

Watts, Michael, *The Dissenters: From the Reformation to the French Revolution*, Oxford University Press, 1978 (reprinted 1999)

Canon Pyon

PRINTED WORKS ACCESSED ONLINE (WITH IMAGES OF THE ORIGINAL PUBLICATION)

Besse, J. A., *A collection of the Sufferings of the People called Quakers*, London, 1753 (Vol 1)
https://openlibrary.org/works/OL2882067W/Collection_of_the_sufferings_of_the_people_called_Quakers

Britten, James, *Old Country and Farming Words: gleaned from agricultural books*, Trübner & Co., London, 1880
https://archive.org/details/oldcountryandfa00britgoog/page/n111/mode/2up

Brogden, Wendy Elizabeth, *Catholicism, community and identity in late Tudor and early Stuart Herefordshire*, 2018 (thesis, University of Birmingham)
https://etheses.bham.ac.uk/id/eprint/8483/5/Brogden18PhD.pdf
(note – also available in printed form in the Hereford Archives and Record Centre's library)

Clark, Andrew, *Brief Lives, chiefly of Contemporaries, set down by John Aubrey between the years 1669 & 1696*, edited from the Author's manuscript, Clarendon Press, 1898
https://archive.org/details/brieflives01clargoog

Dalton, Michael, *The Country Justice*, first published 1618, (1746 version, with additions)
https://archive.org/details/countryjusticeco00dalt/page/n5/mode/2up

Hamden, J, *Hearth Tax Assessment for Michaelmas 1665 for Herefordshire and Comparison with the Herefordshire Militia Assessments of 1663*, transcribed by J. Hamden, 1984
https://www.woolhopeclub.org.uk/people/1665-hearth-tax

Hibbard, Caroline M., *Early Stuart Catholicism: Revisions and Re-Revisions*, originally from the Journal of Modern History 52, p.p. 1-34, University of Chicago Press, March 1980
https://hdl.handle.net/2142/811 (Illinois Digital Environment for Access to Learning and Scholarship)

Ruffhead, Owen, *The Statutes at Large, from the first year of Edward the fourth to the end of the reign of Queen Elizabeth*, 2nd volume, London, 1763
https://archive.org/details/statutesatlargef01grea

Spring, Bernard, Thesis: *The Administration and its Personnel under the Protectorate of Oliver Cromwell, 1653-1658* by Bernard Spring, B. A., University of British Columbia, 1966
https://open.library.ubc.ca/cIRcle/collections/ubctheses/831/items/1.0104532

OTHER ONLINE SOURCES

Alumni Oxiensis: Oxford University Alumni, 1500-1886: www.ancestry.com

Clergy of the Church of England Database: https://theclergydatabase.org.uk/

British Civil War Project: http://bcw-project.org/

Select Bibliography

Canon laws 1604: https://www.anglican.net/doctrines/1604-canon-law/

Genealogy sites: www.ancestry.co.uk and www.findmypast.co.uk

Historic currency conversion: www.nationalarchives.gov.uk/currency-converter

Information on soap ashes: https://www.british-history.ac.uk/no-series/traded-goods-dictionary/1550-1820/soap-ashes-soy

Inner Temple Admissions Database: www.innertemplearchives.org.uk
Institute for Name Studies:
https://www.nottingham.ac.uk/research/groups/ins/resources/kepn.aspx]

Manorial Documents Register: https://discovery.nationalarchives.gov.uk/manor-search
Parliamentary history (including biographies of M.P.s): www.historyofparliamentonline.org

Index

(Introduction, Afterword and Select Chronology not indexed)

A Baynham/Apenam/ap Eynon (see also Baynham) 168-170
    Ann 170
    John 11, 36, 170
    Richard 186
    Thomas 8, 11, 36, 170
Abraham, Thomas (inn-holder) 50, 105, 107, 161 (of New Inn), 188-189 (churchwarden)
Acts (and Oaths)
    Confirming and Restoring Ministers (Act for) 95
    Constable's Oath 120
    Declaration of Indulgence 74, 109
    Declaration of Rights/Bill of Rights 109
    Declaration of Sports (Book of Sports) 133-134
    Erection of Cottages Act 128
    Oath of Allegiance and Supremacy 66, 73, 82, 110
    Test Act 73, 99
    Toleration Act 95
    Uniformity, Act of 97
Addis/Adys
    Edmund/Edward (of Lyde Arundel, gent) 47-50
agriculture 25-29, 118, 127, 145(n) (winnowing)
Alderne
    Daniel 90
    Edward (Doctor) 90
    Thomas (Captain) 90-91
Allensmore 82
Alton, Thomas 172, 184, 186
Andrews
    Charles 48, 188 (churchwarden)
    Elizabeth 150

ap Griffith, Gwillim 51
apprentices 137, 166
appropriation 29(n), 58
Aquablanca, Bishop (Peter of Aigueblanche) 4, 58
assault 83, 106, 130, 136, 140
Aubrey, John 15-16

Baily, Richard 35
Ball
    Elinor (widow) 165
    Rowland 164
Barbados 138
Barneby/Barnaby
    family 35
    John 22, 24, 35, 44 (Sir), 97, 149, 151, 153, 154
    Judith (Mrs) 71, 72, 153
Barrow/e
    Katherine 23-24
    James 23-24
    Richard 23-24
Baskervile
    Frances 19-20, 24
    Katherine 20-22, 24
    Walter 19-20, 23-24, 71
Bayneham/Baynham/Beynam (see also A Baynham/Apenam) 168-174
    Anthony 169-172
    Catherine 106-107, 173
    Elinor 173
    Elizabeth 170
    family (yeomen) 152, 155
    George 4 (junior), 51, 52, 84 (churchwarden), 105 (yeoman), 120, 121 (constable), 123, 124 (junior), 135, 149 (senior and junior), 169-173

(including of Rocksavage, co.
  Cheshire), 173, 188-189
  (churchwarden)
 house of 51, 143
 John 124, 169-173
 Richard 4, 123, 149, 152, 170-173, 184-186
 Thomas 170, 183
 William (husbandman) 171
Beavan/Bevan
 Henry 41
 John 164
 James 41, 156
 Simon 130
Bedford
 Benjamin 95
 Deborah 95, 105-107
 James 108
 Thomas (vicar) 50, 60-63, 65, 69, 72-73, 92, 94-95, 96, 98, 99-109, 111, 161
 William (minister of Monkland) 105, 108, 116(n)
 William (vicar of Eardisland) 108
Bennett/Benney
 Joan (Johane) 41, 156, 164
 Lawrencia 41
 Richard 41, 64, 129-130, 150, 156
Benney/Benny - see Bennett
Benson, George (Dean) 99, 101
Berrington
 Bishopston (of) 71
 coat of arms 44-45
 Eleanor 37, 139-143 (nee Willoughbie)
 family 86, 151
 James 37, 70-71, 82-83, 136, 139-143
 Jane 143
 John 143
 Katherine 13, 24, 71, 143
 Mary 43-44, 143
 Mr 99
 Thomas (gent) 7, 20, 24, 36-37, 42-44, 83, 119, 124, 136, 139-143, 150, 153
 William 143
 Winsley (of) 71, 143
Besse, J. A. 66
Best, John Dr 14-15
Birch, Colonel 90
Bircher/Burchar
 family (yeomen) 152

Richard 121, 131, 149, 152, 154, 161
  (corvisor)
 William (husbandman) 105, 107-108
Birley/Bearley 5
 common 10, 40, 185
Bishopp, John 134
Bithell/Bythell
 family (yeomen) 152
 Thomas 149, 153, 160
blacksmiths 160-161
 shop 48-49, 160
Blakeway, James 130
Bluck/Bluke, William 65, 121, 129, 150, 188
  (churchwarden)
Blunt, Thomas 36
Blythe, Thomas (of Weobley) 138
Book of Common Prayer 65, 82, 93, 97
Botchett, William (miller of Eaton Bishop) 44
Bourton on the Water 141
Bowley, John 135
Boyle, Ann 13
Breynton, John 156
Brick House - see Little Pyon
Bridges
 Bodenham 94
 Dorothy 92, 94
 John (Sir) 90
 Thomas (gent of Morcott) 94
Bridstow 16, 109
Brodford (Mrs) 74
Broughton
 Edward 8-12, 14-15, 19, 26, 59, 62, 81, 82-83, 135, 136, 139-143, 169, 172, 183-185, 189 (churchwarden)
 Elizabeth 16
 Ellynor/Elianor (widow) 12, 14
 of Knighton and Bitterley 16
 Isabell (formerly Willoughbie) 139-143, 171
 John 141
 William 12
Browne, Olliver 164
Broxash hundred 88
Bull/Bolle/Boole
 family (yeomen) 152
 Ralph 110, 149, 188 (churchwarden)
 Richard 66
 William 41, 150, 153
Bullingham (Lower/Nether) 23-24, 153

Burghill/Burghfields 5, 151
Burghill, Robert 14-15
Burton, Thomas (gent) 26
Buttas/Butthouse 39, 62, 89, 102, 126, 151, 160 (mill), 171, 173, 174

Calvinism 82
Campbell, Mildred (author) 148
Canon Pyon church 45, 53, 63
   advowson of 7, 59, 79, 102
   attendance certificates 73
   chancel maintenance 7, 12, 64, 132
   churchwardens (including presentments) 64, 66, 71, 74, 82, 88, 95-96, 97, 98, 100, 103, 108, 110, 128, 132, 161
   churchyard 63-64 (including rent), 132
   communion at Easter 16
   custom 65
   Easter offerings 62, 66, 99-100
   glebe land 58-60, 186
   glebe terrier 42, 84, 96, 156, 173
   hats, removal in church 66, 68-69, 132
   loans (lewnes) 64-65, 66, 75(n)
   Little Pyon chapel 44
   ornaments (bells, books, surplice) 64-65, 132
   pews/seats 43-46
   repairs 65, 82, 86
   St Michael's chapel 44
   sidesmen 132
   vicar (generally) 7, 9, 11, 16, 19, 42, 60-61 (vicar's corn), 63-64, 71, 80-81, 110
   vicarage (see also Old Vicarage) 51-52, 63 (repairs), 84 (description), 86, 96-97 (kitchen), 98, 100-103, 109 (repairs), 126

Canon Pyon manor
   archery - see butts
   assize of bread and beer 6, 125 (ale)
   bailiff 6, 53, 81, 119
   boundary/boundaries 4-5, 129-130
   bridges 122, 127
   brooks (and watercourses) 125-126, 127, 158, 185 (mill stream)
   buckings 125
   butts (including archery) 53, 122-124
   constables 119-122, 154
   copyhold tenancies 5-6, 11
   copyhold tenants 4, 13, 18, 25

corn rents 8
court (including presentments) 6, 9, 11, 19, 25, 26, 52, 53, 72, 118-131
court rolls 51
crow net 53, 122
custom/s 4-7, 10, 12, 16-19, 40, 42, 43, 53, 62, 119, 181-182
demesne lands 59, 75(n) - see also terrier
dung 9, 11, 19
enclosed land/severals 61-62
engrossing 125
estate of inheritance 5
farm and site 8, 11, 12
fences, gates and hedges 6, 11, 25, 122, 123, 127
fish 182
forestalling 125
freebench 5
freehold tenants 6, 18
goats 72, 122, 163
hare traps 128
heriots 6, 16, 18, 40, 129, 169, 173
highways 53, 122
homage 6
house/farmhouse 15, 21, 22, 131
inmates (lodgers) 129
leases 8-25, 35, 58, 61, 71, 80, 103, 143, 151
licence to 'farm sett and lett' 175(n)
open (common) fields 25-29
pigs/swine 7, 30(n)
ploughing services 7, 53
rectory (also parsonage) 22, 58-59, 61
regrading/regrating 125
rents and fines/pains 6, 26, 41, 42, 45, 50, 59, 119, 122-128, 132, 154, 156, 163, 169, 173
rights of common 6
rights of way 128
scolds and evesdroppers 122
statutary four acres 128
steward 118
stocks 53, 122
suit of court/suit rolls 72, 97, 122, 131, 148-150
terrier of demesne lands 11, 13, 127-128
survey 4, 11, 19, 20, 36, 37, 41, 42, 59-60, 94, 96, 128, 154
tithable produce 60-61, 80

tithe farmer/lay rector 58-60, 63, 64
tithes (including modus payments 7, 8, 42, 58-63, 65, 66, 84, 95, 97, 102-103, 106
trantory/trauntory 122, 124, 144-145(n)
waifs and strays 6
washing clothes 125
waste land 6, 9, 11, 15, 128, 162
wells 125-126
winnowing fan/basket 127-128
wood/s 6, 9, 10, 11, 12, 15, 30(n)
woodwardship 9, 11
canons (1604) 82
Carpenter, George (constable) 121
Cathedral Church of Hereford 4, 45, 49, 63, 92, 96, 131, 132, 135
    canon bakehouse 9, 14, 131
    canons non-resident 9
    canons residentiary 4, 8
    Dean and Chapter 4, 7-19, 24, 36, 53, 58-59, 79, 97, 102-103, 119, 148, 158, 161, 169
    ecclesiastical court (church/Consistory court) 16, 19, 20, 43, 60, 64, 84-87, 100-108, 116(n), 131-136 (including sports, compurgation, penances, excommunication, probate)
    prebend 98
Ceely/Ceelye/Celye/Selley/Silly/Sylly
    Anne 44
    Catharine/Katherine (widow) 7, 44, 46
    Elizabeth 127
    family (yeomen) 152
    Hannah 126
    Mrs (Scilly) 43
    Philip 4, 7, 126 (apothecary of Leominster), 150, 153
    Richard 44, 46, 53, 120, 123, 127, 153, 161 (wheelwright), 162, 183-187, 188-189 (churchwarden)
    Thomas (constable) 121, 123, 126, 128, 150 (senior and junior), 152, 188 (churchwarden)
    William 127
census returns 46-47
Chamberlain, Master Justice 18
Chambers
    Anthony 45
    Roger 149

Charles I 4, 84, 85 (personal rule), 87, 90, 93, 94, 112(n) (personal rule), 134
Charles II 69, 73, 95
church court - see Cathedral Church of Hereford, ecclesiastical court
Civil Wars 44, 70, 71, 79, 88-90, 92, 94
Clark/e
    Francis (churchwarden) 84, 189
    William 66, 150, 164
Clergy of the Church of England database 92, 94, 95
Clotworthie/Clottworthin, Phillip 16, 135
Clubmen, Herefordshire 88
Cole/Coole (see also Cowles), Richard 128-129, 163-164
Coleys Yate 5
Coleman Street, London 91
Collyer, --- 66
Colville, John 43-45, 49
Colwall (Canon Pyon) 39, 42, 124, 149, 173, 187
Committee for Plundered Ministers 89, 91, 113(n)
Coney, Edward 150
Consistory court - see Cathedral Church of Hereford, ecclesiastical court
Cook/e, William 35, 123
Cooper, Walter 66, 163
Cope, Simon 121
Council of Wales and the Marches 119
Court
    of Chancery 14, 17, 23, 94, 156, 171, 110, 113(n)
    of Chivalry, High 87
    of Equity 17, 118
    of Exchequer 61, 102, 138
    of King's Bench 171
    of Star Chamber 139, 169
    of Wards 141
Court, The/Court Farm 27, 59, 65, 131, 138, 143
Cowles (see also Coole), Richard 128, 137, 162
Cox/e
    Anne 40
    John 121 (senior, constable), 165
    Richard 27, 40-41 (clothier of Ledbury)
Croft, Herbert (Dean) 95
Cromwell
    Oliver 95, 96

Richard 95
Crown House/Crown Inn
　house 46
　inn 27, 50

Daniell, Richard (churchwarden) 189
Darnal/Darnell, Ralph (esquire) 23, 40-41, 150, 151, 153
Dauncer, Peter (of Moreton on Lugg) 24
David, John (constable) 68
Davies/Davis
　Alice 105, 107-108
　Henry 165
　John 159
　Thomas 124
Derndale/Derndall 7, 8, 11, 27, 34-39, 47, 49, 62, 148, 151, 155, 162, 170
　Brockton 34-39, 123, 124, 168, 187
　brook 7
　Eston Folyatt 34-39, 123, 149, 187
　Eynons Land 168
　house and lands 37
　lease 36, 55(n)
　Lower 34, 36-39, 149
　Upper 27, 34-35, 39, 149
Di Palma, Vittoria (author) 9
Dictionary of English Place Names 39
Diggs/es
　Dina 40
　Humphrey (of Bishopston) 162
　John 40-41
Dinmore 128
Directory of Public Worship 93, 97
dissent/ers (see also recusants) 65-66, 74, 79, 90-91 (Independents), 94 (non-conformity), 97, 100, 110
Dougall, Alistair (author) 133
Dovers Croft 21
Drew (alias Dunn, of Weobley), John 68
Dryden
　Constance 91
　Frances 91
　Henry 91
　John (poet) 87
　Jonathan (junior) 89, 92
　Jonathan (vicar) 86, 87-92, 99, 111, 160
　Martha 89-90
　Mary 91
　Robert 91

Duggan 155
　Anne 38
　John 38, 162, 189 (churchwarden)
　Richard 38
Dugmore
　Rebecca 161
　Thomas 97-98, 129-130, 161 (labourer)
Dunn (alias Drew, of Weobley), John 68
Duppa, Elizabeth (widow) 165
Durande, James 139

Eardisland 110
Easthope/Esthope 40-41, 129, 131, 150
　Hill 10, 40, 185
Eaton Bishop 44
Eckley 161
　Ann 106-107
　Roland 64, 106-108
Edmonds/Emons
　Alice 136
　Edward 139, 143
　Hugh 136, 139-143, 187
Edwards, Richard (constable)121
Eedes, Francis 4
Elizabeth I 123, 141
Evans (Eavans)
　Joseph 189 (churchwarden)
　Morgan (Justice) 68

field (and hill) names (but see seperate entry for Pyon Hill) 13
　Ashil/Ashehill Field 28, 184, 186
　Badnedge coppice 5
　Barn Meadow
　Bar'sby Croft 37
　Berge Moore 37
　Bery Croft 184
　Blanches Acres 48
　Bowcroft 124, 186
　Broad Meadow 37
　Brodwater 187
　Byrche Furlong 184
　Canon Meadow 185
　Canvas, The 48
　Cinders/Sinders 28
　Claylands/Cleylands, Fulbridge 26, 48, 186-187
　Coal Pits Orchard 39
　Common Hill alias Hareleather 60

Coxhill 48 (including woods)
Croggyshill 172, 184
Croxhill 186
Derndall Field 5
Dovehouse Close 183
French Meadow 37
Frogg Marshe 185
Fulbridge/Foulbridge Green 48, 187
Gobbett 130
Half Comer/Haftecomer 11, 28, 48, 127-128, 185-187
Hareleather - see Common Hill
Harpe Acre 186
Harrill Hill 37
Hassell Field 26, 48
Hewing Grove 35
High Moores 37
Hogmarsh/Hopmarsh 129-130
Hopwards 65
Horfell Field 37
Housemore/Howsmore 20, 186
Howe Meadows 184
In Meeting House Field 69-70
Kynfords Knapp 186
Little Moore 37
Little Pyon Field 46
Little Pyons Common 184-185
Long Fryday 48
Long Leasow 184
Lords Close 51
Lower Coal Pitts 39
Lower Severals 62
Lower Wood Field 28
Lydbarre Field 186
Lydbarre Meadow 186
Marsh, The 37
Mill Common Field 155
Mill Fields (Upper and Lower) 28, 37, 48, 160, 184-185
Mill Meadow 155
Moores, The 65
New Enclosure 48
New Inn fields 49
New Inn Meadow 48
New Meadow 48
New Tyndings, The 37
Old Field 11, 27, 28, 127-128, 185-186
One Acre Field 20, 27, 28, 70
Over Custom Gobbett 184
Over/Upper Woodfield 10, 26, 28, 161, 185, 187
Oxe Leasow 48
Park Field 26
Partridge Croft 185
Perry Tree Plock 48
Pope Close 20
Popes Land, Fulbridge 187
Priests Close 50
Redd Hill 185
Rose Hiron, Fulbridge 187
Rose Meadow, Fulbridge 187
Round Hawthorn 20
Rushemore 185
Rye/Rie Field 27, 28, 48, 51
St Marie, Fulbridge 187
St Mary Croft 185-186
St Mary Grove 186
Safron Close 84
Seven Ridges 26
Sonne Pitts
Strowde/Stroud/Strooode 5, 20, 28, 183, 185
Swaynards Green 183
Thatchie land 5
Tompy Close 184
Turnors Land 51
Upper Severals 62
Vuthills 37
Wall Green 37
West Field 28, 183, 186
Westhopes field 7, 125
Woodcocke Meadow 185
Widlands, 125, 130
Yew Tree Gobbett 48
fire 68, 154
Fletcher 153
    Elizabeth 34
    John 41
Foliot family 39
Forfeited Estates Commission 49
Fortie/Fortrie - see Vaut tree/Votrey
Foxe, Elizabeth 165
free socage 175(n)
French pox 107
Frenschmon, Gillam 158
Fulbridge/Foulbridge 14, 17, 27, 40-41, 65, 125, 128, 131, 150, 187
funeral costs 166

Gailey/Gayley 83
　family (yeomen) 152, 155
　Jane (widow) 150
　John (churchwarden) 189
　land/farm 48-49
　Nathaniel 124
　Richard 4, 50, 53, 84, 121 (constable),
　　123, 125, 130, 149, 152, 154
　　(yeoman)
　William 123, 130, 150, 153
gaol/house of correction 137
Gardener/Gardner/Gardiner
　Andrew 124
　family 152, 155, 161, 162
　Frances 150
　John 34, 135
　George 55(n)
　Henry 55(n)
　Hughe 136
　Margerie 85
　Nathaniel 164
　Oliver 4, 34, 53, 123, 132 (churchwarden),
　　136, 149, 188 (churchwarden)
　Phillip 124
　Roland/Roland 35, 38, 121 (constable),
　　123, 129-130, 132 (churchwarden),
　　152, 188 (churchwarden)
　Thomas 123, 149
　William 34, 121 (constable), 123, 129-130,
　　149, 170, 188 (churchwarden)
gate (gatt) house 13, 22
George, Thomas 60
Glorious Revolution 109
Gloucester Cathedral 109
Godiva 4
Godwin, Francis (Bishop of Hereford) 87, 134
Goodman, William 123
Goodwin, Master John 91
Great House, The (Home Farm) 21, 22, 27,
　　51, 59, 143
Great House Cottage 51
Green/Grene
　John 119, 171
　Thomas 139, 142, 171
Gregg/e
　John 171, 186
　Katherine 162
　William 123, 124, 157, 187

Griffithes/Griffiths
　Benjamin (gent) 97
　Dorothy 97
　Elizabeth 165
　Lewes 94
　Mr (vicar of Kings Pyon) 88
　Margaret 165
　Sylvanus
　Thomas 164
　Thomas (vicar) 64, 69, 92-94, 95-98, 111,
　　154
　William 128, 165
Grimsworth hundred 15, 46, 55(n), 88
Gunpowder Plot 82
Gwillim, William (curate) 108-109
Gwyn, Lewis 139, 141, 143, 189
　(churchwarden)

Hackfoote/Hackford
　Edward 130, 165
　George 130
Hackney parish 91
Hall, Mrs (of the Grange) 74
Harcourt, Elizabeth 41
Harley, Sir Robert (Kt) 15, 88, 90-91
Harris
　John (Mr) 50
　Thomas 150
hearth tax 21, 23, 72-73, 97, 153-155, 163-166
Hentland 95
Heralds' Visitations 45, 145
Hereford 90
　Governor of 96
　Justice of the Peace 120
　Anne (Mrs) 158
　Mr 56(n)
　market house 87
　Walwyn 158
Herring, Ann 50, 103-107
Heywood manor, Berkshire 23
Hibbard, Caroline (author) 71
highways/lanes 47
　Longe lane 184
　Mill lane 185
　St Mary lane 183
　Winyards Wey 186
Hill/e
　Alice 151
　James 135

Katherine 110, 113(n)
Miles 4, 88, 96
Thomas 110, 113(n)
Wrangford/Rainford (and variants) 41, 73-74, 150-151, 188 (churchwarden)
Thomas 189 (churchwarden)
Hinton prebend 98
Holder
    Daniel 85, 157 (of Hereford)
    Joane 157
Holkins, Thomas 51
Holland, John 150
Holmer church 135
Home Farm - see Great House, The
Hooke
    Christopher (vicar of Bridstow) 109
    Herbert (vicar) 109-111
    Mary (nee Westfaling) 109
Hooper (Whooper), Michael 149, 164
Hope under Dinmore 5, 142 (church)
Hordes, John 150
Hornblow, William (tanner) 37, 149, 155, 162, 188 (churchwarden)
Hoskyns, Sergeant (of Moorhampton) 166-168
houses (number of) 154
Hughes/Hughs
    Abraham 68
    Henry 165
    John (of Landegley, co. Radnor) 68
husbandmen 151

iconoclasm 87-88
illegitimacy 85, 106, 121, 135, 137
impropriation 29(n), 58
Inner Temple, London 13, 22, 23, 24
Institute of Place Name Studies 39
Interregnum 79, 92
    marriage 22-23

James I 82, 84, 133-134
    seal of 17
James II 109
Jay
    family 155, 161, 174
    Hugh 8, 188-189 (churchwarden)
    John 149, 188 (churchwarden)
    Katherine (widow) 149, 168
    Thomas, 4, 7, 38, 121 (constable), 128, 163, 168, 188 (churchwarden)
Jbrooke/Jbroke (alias The Knowles) 169-174, 186
Jeffries/Jeffreys/Geffreis
    Edward (churchwarden) 189
    Harry 183-187
    Margaret 20
    Simon 86, 124
Johnson, Martha (of Hereford) 173
Jones/Joens
    Griffith 121, 123, 149, 153
    Henry 164
    John 149, 188 (churchwarden)
    Mary 126
    Richard (yeoman) 44, 86 (parish clark), 135, 149, 164
    Thomas (yeoman) 43, 123, 129-130, 149 (senior), 188 (churchwarden)
    William 126, 189 (churchwarden)
Jesuit college (Cwm) 71

Karver
    Elinor (nee Vaughan) 160
    George 102
    Richard 160
    William 89
Kinford/Kynford/Kineford/Kinard 8, 27, 48, 56(n), 70, 85, 156-160
    Anne 157-158
    Edward 156-157
    farm 47, 50
    house 158-160
    James 156-158
    Joan 85
    John 53, 82, 84, 120, 156-157, 158, 189
    Katherine (nee Breynton) 156-158
    mill 27, 47, 50, 156-160
    Richard 158
    Susan 157
    Thomas 184-185
    William 156-157
    Winifrid 156-158
King, John 183
Kings Pyon 5, 67, 92-93 (parish register), 94, 160, 184
Kington 16, 135
Kinnersley 137 (Mr)
    John (churchwarden) 98, 129-130 (gent), 149 (gent), 151, 154 (churchwarden)

Canon Pyon

Kirwood
    Anthony 133
    Phillipe 52, 165
Knapp/e/Napp
    Anne 86, 136, 162
    Edward 85, 127
    Elizabeth 40
    family (yeomen) 152, 155
    George 47-50, 51, 110, 149, 152, 189 (churchwarden)
    Henry 40-41, 51, 81, 121, 124, 129
    house 51
    Joan (Johan) 162
    John 51, 136
    Phillip 124, 140
    Phillip (vicar) 59, 61, 80-86, 111, 136, 139, 140, 143
    Richard 51, 85, 136
    William 7, 40 (Cnapp), 44, 51, 81, 86 (yeoman), 89, 129, 135, 150, 186
Knowles, The (alias Jbrooke) 169-174

Lamb, William (Justice) 68
Lastons Bridge 185
Laudianism/Archbishop Laud 82, 84, 85, 87, 92, 93
Lawton's Hope 23, 27, 41-42, 68-69, 70, 148, 150, 151, 153
Leath/Leeth
    Ann 106
    family (yeomen) 152, 155
    George 124
    Phillip 149, 165
Leech
    Elizabeth 157-158
    John (of Lyde) 157-158
Lewis
    Margaret 164
    Thomas 132
Little Comberton, Worcestershire 141
Little Pyon/Pyon Parva (including Brick House) 5, 20, 24, 27, 36, 42-46, 45 (Pionia Stephani), 70, 71, 86, 109 (prebend), 119, 139, 143, 150, 151, 153, 158
    common 184-185

Lochard
    Anthony (Mr) 71
    Bridget (Mrs) 71
    Francis 26, 74
    Judith 21-22
    Katherine 17
    Robert 16, 18, 19-20, 71, 124 (gent)
    William 20-21, 24, 71
Longbridge 186
lost houses 51-52

Mason
    Benjamin 96
    Isabell 157
    John 7, 123, 129-130, 150, 153, 157
    Rebecca 97-98
    Richard 123
    William 120, 135
Massey, Colonel 16
Maynard, John 91
Mayor, Henry 188 (churchwarden)
Mayos, Henry 149
Meeting House, The 70
Meredith
    Henry (gent) 150-151
    Hugh 188 (churchwarden)
    Katherine 110, 113(n)
    Thomas 150
Militia Assessments 72, 97, 152-153
Millard
    Elizabeth 121
    Phillip 149
Milles Alice 150
mills 156-160, 175(n)
Monmouth/shire 44, 70, 96
Monnington/Monington
    Edward 4, 123, 149, 151, 152, 156, 188
    George 172
    John 123
    Walter (gent) 172, 183-186
    William (gent) 187
Monno (see also Munn/e), John 4
Moor/Moore
    Ann (spinster) 150
    Moor's house 51
Moravian with Protestant Episcopal Church, Leominster 70
Mordiford 90
Morgan, F.C. (author) 160
Morvan, Richard (constable) 121, 123
Munn/e

Anne (Mrs) 158
Aspasia 38
family 152, 161
John Mr, 7
Katherine (widow) 149
Thomas (churchwarden) 189
William (of Birley) 139, 141

Nags Head, The 46-47, 49
Nash 161
    Frances 71-72
    Ralfe/Ralph 71-72, 128
    Richard (of Hope) 139, 141, 143
    Roger 140
    Walter 4, 72, 121, 123
    William 129-130, 150
Navy, The 90
New End 46-47
New Inn, The 26, 46-50, 49, 160
New Model Army 96
Newbridge 154
Newgate market, London
Nicoles/Nicholls
    Richard 165
    William 80
Nicholetts, Richard 4
Norton (Canon) 11, 18
Nupton 27, 39, 47, 123, 124, 154, 161, 173, 186, 187
    farm 62
    lane 62

oaths - see Acts
occupations 46-47, 155-161
O'Day, Rosemary 60
Old Croft 129-130
Old Crown, the - see Crown House/Crown Inn
Old Vicarage, The (see also Canon Pyon church, vicarage) 59
Oven
    family 68, 74, 153, 161
    Hester 66
    James 67
    Jane 67
    Joanne 67
    John 66, 67 (husbandman), 68
    Joseph 47, 67
    Mary 67

    Sarah 68
    widow 66
    William 67
Oxford University colleges
    Brasenose 108
    Jesus 109

Palmer, Thomas 164
Parke/s, The 5, 26
Parliament/arians 4, 87, 90, 92, 96
Parliamentary Committee 15, 70
Parry
    Ann 165
    John 184-187 (including Appary)
    Richard 165
parsonage - see Canon Pyon manor, rectory
Partridge 20
    Elizabeth 172, 184
Pateshall/Patshall, Elizabeth 165
Patrick, Ernest 70
Pember, Francis (esquire) 42
Pembridge 22
    Byletts, The 16, 20, 71
Phillips
    Ann 165
    John (yeoman) 38, 121 (constable), 123
    George 100, 150
    Oliver 124
    Phillip 100
    Simon (churchwarden) 189
Pike
    Alice (widow) 71-72, 165
    family 73
    George 150
    John 71
    Thomas 72, 74
Pionia Stephani - see Little Pyon
Playdell, William (churchwarden) 189
Pleavey/Plevai/Plevy 161
    Henry 72-73
    James 150
    John 70
    Sarah 72-74
    William 123, 150, 153, 161 (glover), 162, 188 (churchwarden)
Poole, Richard (of Barrs Court, Hereford, gent) 47
poor, the 72-73, 86, 100, 128, 131, 135, 137, 161-168

poor (continued)
    overseers 128, 161-162, 168
    parish house 163
pound, the 7, 52-54
Powell
    Alice 165
    John (churchwarden) 189
    Rachell 68
    Robert 137
prebendaries/prebends 45
predestination 66, 82, 84
Preece/Prees
    Elinor (widow) 150
    James 48, 150-151 (gent)
    Richard 133
    Thomas 150
Preston (on Wye) 11, 18
Price/Prise
    Elizabeth (widow) 7
    James (Mr) 129-130, 161 (mercer of Hereford)
    Mary 27
    Oliver 27
Pritchard
    James (servant) 124
    William 20, 124
Probart, Walter 66
Protectorate, the 95
Puritan/s 16, 66, 85, 88, 91, 93, 96, 133-134
purveyances 144(n)
Pyfinch, William 37-38
Pyon Close 49
Pyon/Pewne Hill 11, 21, 27, 127, 185
Pyon Parva/Piona Parva - see Little Pyon

Quakers (Society of Friends) 65-70, 79
    Almeley Meeting 67, 68
    Canon Pyon Meeting 68
    Leominster Meeting 67
quarrying 46
Quarter Sessions 73-74, 121, 137-138, 162, 166-168
Quick, Thomas Carpenter 56(n)

Raglan Castle 70-71
Raulins/Rawlins, Thomas 96
rector - see Canon Pyon manor, tithe farmer/lay rector
recusants (see also dissent/ers) 49, 70-73, 77(n), 82, 95 (recusancy laws), 120
Red Castle 27
republican rule 4
Reynolds/Reynolls/Reighnolds
    Edward 149, 189 (churchwarden)
    family (yeomen) 152
    Griffith (Hereford Registrar) 99
Rich, Joseph 68
rid/riddering 26, 127
Rizzo, Betty 89
Rogers
    Thomas (chirurgeon) 161
    William 149, 188 (churchwarden)
    Wroth 96
Roman Catholicism 70-74, 82, 99, 110
Ross, Ann 74
Rowe 91
    Dorothie 90
    Owen 90, 114(n)
Royalists 88-90
Rupert, Prince 88

St Andrew's church, Holborn 22, 24
St Clement Danes' church, London 24
St Giles' church, Camberwell, Surrey 89, 91
St Helen's church, Bishopsgate, London 90
St John's church, Hereford 87
St Owen's church, Hereford 87
St Stephen's church, Coleman Street, London 91
St Weonards 95
Sampson
    Edward (vicar of Kings Pyon) 83, 140
    Harry 123
Sawyer
    Anthony 19, 21, 25, 56(n), 63
    Edmond 23
    George 22-25, 97, 153, 173
    Katherine 25, 153
    Herbert 23
Scarlet/Scarlett 48
    George 4, 121 (constable), 123, 133-134, 150, 153
    John (sidesman) 84, 124
    William (churchwarden) 189
Scottish army 88
Seaborne
    Edward 138
    John 138, 161 (chirurgeon), 187 (esquire)

Shire Glatt 27, 51-52
Sibley, Joseph 91
sidesmen 84
Silly/Syllye - see Ceely/Ceelye/Celye
Simmonds - see Symonds
Sizebrook (Sichbrook) 27, 46-47, 186
Smallman, Hugh 40, 44 (husbandman), 130, 150, 188 (churchwarden)
Smethley/Smithley 41-42, 150
Smirley - see Smethley
Smith/Smyth
    Ann 36
    Franc[i]s (churchwarden) 189
    Thomas 149, 150, 164
    William 36, 170
soap ashes 16, 31(n)
social hierarchy 148-155
Society of Friends - see Quakers
Somerset/t
    Catherine/Katherine 24, 35, 72, 103, 151
    Charles (esquire) 8, 24, 35, 60-62, 65, 71, 72, 74, 102, 131, 149, 151, 160 (Mr)
    Elizabeth 74
    family 70
    Henry 24-25
    Mary 74
Sontley, Hugh (vicar of Kings Pyon) 93
Spurstowe, William 91
Stallard
    John 110
    Penelope 110
Stanton, John 149
Staunton, William 123
Stephens/Steephens/Stevens
    family (yeomen) 152
    Richard (churchwarden) 188
    Thomas 4, 7, 27, 98 (churchwarden), 149, 153, 154 (churchwarden), 188 (churchwarden)
Storre, James (servant) 142
Stowe on the Wold 141
stray animals 53
Stretford hundred 88
Stretfords bridge 5
Swift
    Jonathan (author) 87
    Thomas (vicar of Goodrich) 87, 90 (Dr, rector of Bridstow)

Symonds/Simonds/Simons
    family (yeomen) 152
    John (constable) 121, 123, 149
    Roger 123

tan house/yard 37-38, 155
Taylor
    Arthur 122, 149, 153, 154
    Catherine 134
    Daniell 16
    Isaac (map of) 10, 13, 21, 25, 28, 34, 36, 39, 40, 46, 48, 49, 51, 53, 59, 63, 70, 124, 126, 143, 155, 158-159, 174
    Joanna 134
    Richard 135
    Simon 128, 163-164
    Thomas 165
    William 154
taxation certificate 15
Thomas
    George 149
    William 149, 150, 160 (smith), 188 (churchwarden)
Tichborne, Robert (Alderman) 23
Tomkins, James (of Monnington on Wye) 20
Towne, William (chief constable) 106
townships 34-42, 55(n), 120, 123, 131, 149, 161
transubstantiation 73, 99
Trillo/Trylloe
    Frances 38
    Thomas 38, 165
    William 38, 121 (constable), 140
Trumper, William 128
Tucker, Charles 38
Tunstal
    John 47
    Mrs 163
Tupsley 90
Turbervile, John 68-69, 129-130, 150, 153 (family), 161 (family), 188-189 (churchwarden)
Tyler, Henry (yeoman) 153, 189 (churchwarden)

Uggan (Wogan), Thomas (of Whitbourne) 171-172

vagrants 167

Vaughan
    Edward 171
    George 8, 11-13, 16-21, 24, 26, 59, 61-62, 71, 107, 151, 185-187
    Hugh 13
    Judith 16, 19-20, 24, 71, 151
    Katherine 16, 20
    Martha 87
    Oliver 13, 19-20, 80, 187
    Richard (of Bredwardine) 160
    William 13
Vaut tree/Votrey (also Fortie/Fortrie) 51-52, 126-127
Venmore, William 8
vicarage - see Canon Pyon Church, also Old Vicarage
Vintners (freehold) 187

Walter
    Bartholomew (churchwarden) 72, 162, 188 (churchwarden)
    Margaret 106-107
Walton, Richard 131
Walwyn, Thomas (gent) 47
wardship 16-19 (custom), 141
Waring, Rev. Richard 55(n)
Watery Lane 52, 127
Watts, Michael 74
Weaver/Wever
    Joanne 125
    Thomas (master) 91
    Richard (Mr) 7
Wellington 5
Welsh brook 39
Wenland, Mary (of Warham) 47
Went, William 149
Westhope 7, 27, 46, 47, 70, 123, 124, 125-126, 130, 150, 161-162, 187
    Common 10, 40
    Hill 5, 6, 40, 142, 162
Whetnall/Whetnoll
    James 52, 83, 124, 136, 171
    Richard 124, 130
Whetstone
    George 43 (husbandman of Wellington), 46, 164
    William 164
White Waltham, Berkshire 23
Whitlock, Justice 15

Whitney (on Wye) 87, 90, 91, 99
    Sir Robert, kt 87
Whitsun Riots 82
Wiles/Willes
    Francis 149
    Katherine 26
Wilkes, John (of Ivington) 139, 141, 143
William (of Orange) and Mary 109-110
Williams
    Charles 164, 166
    Crispianus 165
    James 165
    Johane/Joan 137
    Margaret (widow) 165
    Mary 166
    William 150
Willoughbie/Willoughby
    Eleanor 36, 83, 139-143
    Henry 141
    Isabel 12, 139-140
    Robert 139-141
    Thomas 142
wills (probate)
    Alderne, Thomas 90
    Barrowe, James 23
    Bedford, William 108
    Berrington, Thomas 42
    Bridges, Thomas 94
    Broughton, Edward 12
    Digges, Humphrey 162
    Dryden, Jonathan 89
    Fletcher, John 41
    Gardner, William 170
    Griffithes, Lewes 94
    Griffithes, Thomas (inventory) 97-98
    Hooke, Herbert 110
    Karver, William 89
    Knapp, Phillip 85
    Knapp, William 86
    Lochard, William 22
    Oven, William 67
    Sawyer, George 24
    Sealy, Richard 161
    Vaughan, George 12
    Vaughan, Oliver 13, 80
    Williams, Charles (inventory) 166
Wincely, Joseph 150
Winsley House 142
Winstanley, Gerrard (Diggers) 7

Witherston, Richard (gent) 37, 149
Withington Parva (prebend) 87, 91
Wogan - see Uggan
Wolrich/e
    Edward (of Dinmore) 12
    John (servant) 124, 171 (Woolridge)
Woode, Ann 165
Woodhouse, Francis (of Mordiford, gent) 47
woodland names
    Canon Vallett 10, 11, 40, 185
    Lye Vallett 10, 185
Woolhope 11, 18
Wormsley 5, 19, 126, 158 (Priory), 170
    Grange 5, 20, 173, 174
Wootton/Wotton
    Edward 123
    John (senior and junior) 131
    Thomas (sidesman) 84
    William (gent) 150-151
Wulviva 4
Wycherley, Daniel (vicar) 98-99, 111

Yapp, William 70
Yeomans/Yeomonds
    Edward 4, 7, 120, 189 (churchwarden)
    Elizabeth (widow) 97, 135, 150, 152
    family (yeomen) 152, 155, 161
    Herbert 159
    Hughe 16, 85, 130
    Margaret 165
    Phillip 97, 121, 123, 124, 128, 152
    William 65, 188 (churchwarden)
yeomen 151-152, 155

www.ingramcontent.com/pod-product-compliance
Lightning Source LLC
Chambersburg PA
CBHW060420010526
44118CB00017B/2294